SO-AIV-438

1844

JZ 5584 .U6 C8 1965

Curti, Merle Eugene, 1897-
The American peace crusade, 1815-1860.

18844

DATE DUE

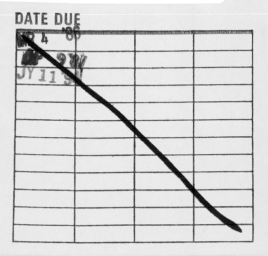

The American peace crusade, 1815-1860
JX1961.U6C8 1965   18844

Curti, Merle Eugene
          VRJC/WRIGHT LIBRARY

THE AMERICAN PEACE CRUSADE

CRUSADE

1815-1860

WILLIAM LADD

The American Peace Crusade
Crusade
1815-1860

By MERLE EUGENE CURTI

OCTAGON BOOKS

A DIVISION OF FARRAR, STRAUS AND GIROUX

New York   1973

Copyright 1929, by Duke University Press

Reprinted 1965
by special arrangement with Duke University Press

Second Octagon printing 1973

OCTAGON BOOKS
A DIVISION OF FARRAR, STRAUS & GIROUX, INC.
19 Union Square West
New York, N. Y. 10003

LIBRARY OF CONGRESS CATALOG CARD NUMBER 65-16769
ISBN 0-374-91976-3

Printed in U.S.A. by
NOBLE OFFSET PRINTERS, INC.
New York, N.Y. 10003

TO

My Father and Mother

JOHN EUGENE CURTI
ALICE HUNT CURTI

PREFACE

THIS STUDY was originally a doctoral thesis presented to the Department of History at Harvard University. My original intention was to confine the work to the early organized peace movement in America. This was a virtually unworked field, rich in manuscript and printed sources. However, since the work of peace organizations, even in those early years, became increasingly international in scope, it was found inadvisable to limit the study of their activities to the United States. Indeed, at least one American pioneer of peace was more closely identified with the European peace movement than with the American. The activities of this early period may be thought of as essentially crusading in character, so ardent was the zeal not only for making converts at home but for winning Europe to the faith. Hence the emphasis throughout is on the coöperation between American and European friends of peace.

While in England and France the peace movement was broader than the peace societies, including particularly the collateral work of the Free Traders and the Socialists, the movement in America was more closely confined to the labors of the formally organized peace societies. Some communistic societies, it is true, did at least lip service to peace sentiment, and some of the abolitionists adopted, for a time, a non-resistance position. It is also true that, despite our fondness for military presidents, there was considerable latent opposition to militarism. I have not tried to evaluate or analyze this unorganized sentiment against war.

It is my plan to continue the study to the present time, and to emphasize more strongly the European aspects of the later movement. Since the peace movement became much more extensive in this later period I hope to correlate it with economic, social, and cultural forces working towards internationalism, and to gauge the influence of pacifists and internationalists in breaking down the American tradition of isolation and in effecting a more widespread peace consciousness.

I wish to thank those who have aided me in this work. To Professor Arthur M. Schlesinger of Harvard University, at whose suggestion the work was begun, I am greatly indebted for valuable criticisms and for unfailing encouragement. My wife, Dr. Margaret Wooster Curti, copied important manuscripts, made invaluable suggestions, and greatly aided in the preparation of the book. Mr. Earl Cruikshank generously let me read his Master's thesis on the early history of the peace movement, prepared at the University of Kansas. I am indebted to Professor G. P. Gooch and to Professor C. K. Webster for suggestions made during conversations. My colleagues, Professor Harold Underwood Faulkner, Dr. Jean Wilson, Mr. Granville Hicks, and Miss Ruth Agnew read the manuscript and made many helpful suggestions. I am also indebted for criticism to Mrs. Lucia Ames Mead, Dr. James Brown Scott, and Professor James T. Shotwell who also read the manuscript.

I wish to express my appreciation to the authorities and staffs of the libraries of Smith College, Amherst College, Harvard College, the American Antiquarian Society, the Western Reserve Historical Society, and especially to Miss Greta Brown of the Library of the Institute of New Britain, Connecticut, and to Mr. Worthington C. Ford of the Massachusetts Historical Society. Dr. Arthur Deerin Call, secretary of the American Peace Society, generously put at my disposal the manuscript collections of the Society, and Mrs. Mabel Call, librarian of the Society, extended to me many courtesies. The portrait of Dr. George C. Beckwith is taken from a cut in the possession of the American Peace Society.

Finally, I am deeply grateful to the Duke University Press for making possible the publication of this book. I especially appreciate the kindness and helpfulness of Professor William K. Boyd, under whose editorship the book is brought out.

M. E. C.

CONTENTS

THE AMERICAN PEACE CRUSADE

CRUSADE

1815-1860

I

ORGANIZATION FOR PEACE, 1815-1816

THE HISTORIAN is interested in the recorded dreams of the past because they reflect the needs of the dreamers, and also because they sometimes point ahead to future realization. What men most feel the need of, that they are apt finally to obtain in some way. If what they lack cannot be actually experienced, they may continue to dream of it, and in their dreaming they may find some compensation. Plato, distressed by the "charming disorder" of the government of his day, found refuge in the contemplation of beauty and dreamed his ideal state. The slave has dreamed of rest and freedom. Peoples oppressed by harsh rulers dream of liberty. Men weary of struggle and of war dream of peace. Even in ancient times these dreams of peace were written down. The vision of the time when swords shall be beaten into ploughshares and spears into pruning hooks has remained since Biblical times vividly in the minds of lovers of humanity.

Dreams alone, however, will not permanently satisfy a continuing need. A characteristic of waking dreams which continue to possess the imaginations of men is that they are likely to stimulate the dreamers to action. Men do not rest content with the world as it is. Constantly they seek to change it. Slowly it changes. These changes often represent plans, dreams if you will, which after centuries become realities.

The dream of peace has thus gradually taken shape in various definite projects for realizing peace. As early as the beginning of the fourteenth century Dante advocated a world empire for ending war, and a young Norman lawyer, Pierre Dubois, recommended a permanent tribunal of arbitration. The Christian humanists, especially Erasmus, condemned war and considered the advantages of peace and means of securing it. The seventeenth century had its Sully, its Eméric Crucé, its Grotius, and its William Penn with their plans for a federation of Europe and for the development of an international law of peace.

After the disastrous wars ending in 1713 the Abbé de Saint-Pierre elaborated his *Projet pour rendre la paix perpétuelle en Europe*. The eighteenth century also saw no little pacifist activity on the part of American as well as British Friends.[1] Moreover, with the development in that century of its peculiar philosophy of enlightenment and progress, and with the growth of economic realism, new voices, those of Kant, Rousseau, Thomas Paine and Thomas Jefferson, and of Jeremy Bentham, Dean Tucker, Turgot, Krause and Franklin,[2] diagnosed the causes of war and suggested means for its prevention.

Important as was the work of these persons for the development of pacifist thought, it remained for humbler men to take the first practical steps toward educating their fellows in the doctrine of peace. It is a remarkable fact that in 1815 peace societies were actually formed in several different parts of the world without definite knowledge of each other's existence. This can hardly be accounted for as a coincidence, but can be understood as a natural result of conditions prevailing at the time.

In 1815 probably not a single American remembered a time when the western world had enjoyed any very long respite from war. Patriarchs recalled the colonial wars, many remembered the struggle for American Independence, and all but the very youngest knew the unparalleled contests growing out of the French Revolution and the rise of Napoleon, struggles to which their own War of 1812, then just ending, bore an immediate relation. The world in 1815 had particular reason to be weary of war, and the prevalent war weariness expressed itself naturally in projects for perpetual peace, just as had weariness from earlier cycles of war. The seventeenth and eighteenth century projects for peace had not achieved any tangible result other than adding

---

[1] Margaret E. Hirst, *The Quakers in Peace and War*, London, 1923, *passim*.

[2] For a brief summary of the more important of these early peace projects see James Brown Scott's *Introduction* to his edition of William Ladd's *Essay on a Congress of Nations*, New York, 1914, pp. iii-xlv. See also Edwin Mead's *Washington, Jefferson and Franklin on War*, Boston, 1913, and Christian L. Lange, *Histoire de la doctrine pacifique*, Paris, 1927, chaps. ii, v, ix, xii.

to the body of pacifist literature, though they were now, in 1815, to bear withered fruit in the Holy Alliance. But the weariness from war found another and a new expression. Kings and czars might have their Holy Alliance, but the lesson from the French Revolution's appeal to the people was not lost. The reaction against war now found, for the first time, outlets other than doctrinaire projects for leagues of nations with which monarchs amused themselves. About the year 1815 there began an organized popular peace movement designed to appeal to public opinion.

What with the existence of arguments indicting war in the abstract and the increasing hardships of maintaining the struggle against Napoleon, it is not strange that in England there were Anglican clergymen, as well as Dissenters and Friends, bold enough to print their pacifist convictions during the thick of battle. In October, 1813, a Presbyterian minister, the Reverend David Bogue, had gone so far as to advocate the formation of a society to combat war. Such a society, he maintained, could within ten years' time so diffuse peace principles through every rank in the community that the people of Britain could not easily be prevailed on to engage in war.[3] This suggestion, indeed, may have had no relation at all to the fact that in June, 1814, a meeting was held at the house of a London Quaker, William Allen, "to consider of a new Society to spread tracts, etc., against war." But this circumstance, and the appearance of a letter dated April, 1815, in the *Philanthropist,* suggesting the formation of a peace society,[4] shows clearly enough that foes of war in England were considering the formation of societies for popularizing peace doctrines at the very time when a remarkable tract from

[3] David Bogue, D.D., *On Universal Peace, Extracts from a Discourse delivered in October, 1813,* reprinted by the Peace Association of Friends in America, New Vienna, Ohio, 1869, p. 22. Bogue's sermon was included in the peace tracts of the London Peace Society, of which organization he became a member when it was formed.

[4] Hirst, *The Quakers in Peace and War,* p. 243; *The Philanthropist,* no. 15, p. 275, cited in *Friend of Peace,* vol. i, no. 9, p. 15.

New England arrived, in the late spring of 1815, proposing that very thing.

New England was likely soil for such a proposal. Here no mean amount of peace literature had been brought out by the Quakers during the War of 1812[5] and political and economic opposition to "Mr. Madison's War" had led the Federalists to make the most of sentimental and moral arguments against war as an institution. This they did with considerable gusto in pacific addresses to their Washington Benevolent Societies.[6] In this atmosphere it was quite in place for Deacon Baalis Bullard of Uxbridge, Massachusetts, to petition the legislature for exemption from military service on account of conscientious scruples and for the Reverend John I. Wells of Hartford, Connecticut, to come out in the printed word as well as in the pulpit against this pernicious war, and indeed, all war, as utterly unchristian. Nor were they alone, for Dr. Nathaniel Bowditch almost had to give up his studies, so intently did he ponder on the evil results of war, and the Reverend Otis Thompson did not mince words in decrying its patently wicked character.[7]

If these gentlemen did little more than voice their sentiments, two other New Englanders were not content to stop short of organizing their fellows into formal societies for spreading the gospel of peace. The first one to realize this design was a pious Connecticut merchant then living in New York, David Low Dodge. It was a personal experience which first led him to reflect on the relation of the Scriptures to the doctrine of self-defence. At

---

[5] Clarkson's *Portraiture of Quakerism*, New Bedford, 1814; I. Scott, *War Inconsistent with the Doctrine and Example of Jesus Christ*, New Bedford, 1813, are examples.

[6] Jacob Catlin, *The Horrors of War*, Stockbridge, 1813; F. W. Holland, Ms. *History of the American Peace Cause*, Boston Public Library, vol. i, p. 6.

[7] *Advocate of Peace*, vol. xii, November and December, 1857, p. 382; *Memoir of Dr. Nathaniel Bowditch* in *Common School Journal*, vol. ii, November 2, 1840, p. 349; John I. Wells, *An Essay on War, Showing that the Spirit of War existing in the Rational Mind is ever Inimical to the Spirit of the Gospel*, New York, 1812; Otis Thompson, *Prayer for Peace*, Providence, 1812.

what seemed the point of death Dodge regretted that he had not testified publicly in regard to his growing conviction that every kind of carnal warfare was, from the Scriptural point of view, unlawful. The very next year, in 1809, he printed a peace pamphlet, *The Mediator's Kingdom Not of This World*. This anonymous tract was the first non-Quaker publication in America expressly and exclusively devoted to the cause of peace. Its argument, which took the extreme non-resistant position, was largely drawn from the Sermon on the Mount. Within ten days the edition of a thousand copies was exhausted, and presently a spirited reply challenged Dodge's reasoning and conclusions. He saw fit to answer, and from 1809 until 1815 spent much of his time, strength, and money in propagating pacific doctrines, converting, after a four year struggle, one of the four eminent divines with whom he contended. As early as 1810 some twenty of his friends met at his New York house to discuss the cause of peace. Again, two years later, there was talk about forming a peace society, but nothing was done. It was feared that the likelihood of a war with England would make people regard such an organization as a political gesture.

Since Dodge had in some respects modified his own position, he was asked to prepare a fuller view of the subject, and early in 1815 he published a small volume of a hundred and thirty pages entitled *War Inconsistent with the Religion of Jesus Christ*. This systematic little treatise opened with a direct reference to the suffering involved in the Napoleonic wars and then went on to indict war as inhuman, unwise, and criminal. It oppresses the poor, hardens the human heart, and spreads terror and distress. It squanders foolishly vast sums of gold. By appealing to history Dodge attempted to refute the notion that preparation for war is necessary to prevent it. Indeed, the idea of defense, he insisted, was the source of most of the wars that had desolated the world, and any pretended distinction between offensive and defensive war is merely quibbling. War, he declared, destroys the liberties of men and often brings humanity under an atrocious despotism like that of Napoleon. The soldier is but a slave. There follows in the wake of battle dissipation, idleness and a whole train of evils, not the least important of which is the desecration of the Sabbath. If the religion of Christ forbids the return of evil for evil, then war plainly violates that religion. Cast in a strong theological mold, this essay is marked by force, moral earnestness, logic, a hatred of inhumanity, and by keen penetration and an inspiring tone. Essentially humanitarian and religious, it also condemns war on economic grounds because property is destroyed, individuals are reduced to beggary and nations are impoverished. Napoleon's seizures had seriously pinched the firm of which Dodge was a member, and perhaps these mercantile losses had stimulated him to think on the economic implications of war and peace, as well as on their religious and humanitarian aspects.[8]

When the Connecticut merchant returned to New York early in 1815, after a few years' absence, he met with friends of peace to discuss the organization of a society, and in August, 1815, they finally formed the New York Peace Society, "probably the first one that was ever formed in the world for that specific object."[9] The articles of association were of the strictest kind, condemning all carnal warfare, whether offensive or defensive, as being "wholly opposed to the example of Christ." Of the thirty-odd men who thus banded themselves together and chose Dodge as their president, several were "respectable clergymen." Indeed, it was stipulated that new members must be unanimously approved and that they must be members in good standing of evangelical churches. Within two years the society had increased

---

[8] *Autobiography of David L. Dodge*, in *Memorial of David L. Dodge*, Boston, 1854, pp. 89 ff. For an excellent sketch of Dodge's life see Edwin D. Mead's edition of Dodge's *War Inconsistent with the Religion of Jesus Christ*, Boston, 1905, pp. vii-xxiv.

[9] Dodge, *Autobiography*, p. 99.

to sixty members. It began its propaganda for peace by printing tracts which were inclosed in boxes packed with Dodge's merchandise.[10]

While this pious New England merchant deserves the honor of having formed the first peace society, and that without the knowledge that anyone outside its circle had ever recommended such a procedure, another New Englander, the Reverend Noah Worcester of Brighton, Massachusetts, only four months later inaugurated the Massachusetts Peace Society, which in importance was to outdo the New York organization. As a child Worcester had listened to Quaker testimony against war, and a neighboring Baptist minister, educated among Friends, had upheld their views in his presence. Though Worcester felt later that he had in no way been influenced by this experience, these Quaker principles may well have made their impression on his young mind. It is true that they did not keep him from taking part in the battle of Bunker Hill and from serving in the Revolutionary army as a "fife-major." Near the close of the war the minister of the New Hampshire town where he had settled put in his hands a little book in which the principles of war were examined in respect to their agreement or disagreement with the tenets of the Gospel. As a result Worcester's ideas on the whole subject became "dark, perplexed, and confused." After he had become minister of the town he felt, when praying with the military company, that the business of war was horrible and that it was thoroughly opposed to his own feelings as a Christian. It needed only the War of 1812 to complete the revolution in his attitude. To him the War was the result of domestic party contests and he did not doubt that the evils of Britain's spoliations and impressment of sailors were exaggerated. On the day appointed by President Madison for national fasting, this New England parson delivered a sermon on the pacific conduct of

[10] Dodge to Ladd, March 12, 1838, in *Advocate of Peace*, vol. ii, no. 4, September, 1838, pp. 92-94.

Abraham and Lot and ventured to pray that the lives of soldiers on both sides might be spared.[11]

Having meantime removed to Brighton, Worcester resolved in the year 1814 to inquire in an article whether the custom of war was not the result of a popular delusion. But instead of an article he wrote the *Solemn Review of the Custom of War,* an epoch-making classic in the history of peace literature. Mild and candid in spirit, this little book's impressive earnestness, sincerity, peculiar concentration, and heroic firmness largely account for the fact that after a hundred years it is still powerful and convincing in its appeal. Its great originality at the time lay in the fact that it was the first treatise on peace to point out to Christians a course of joint action against war; namely, the forming of peace societies. Another constructive aspect of the *Solemn Review* was that it presented with fine logic the feasibility of a confederacy of nations with a high court of equity for the settlement of national controversies. Compliance with the decisions of such a court could, it was argued, through the education of the public by peace societies, be made a point of national honor. Though such a court would not insure absolute justice, still such an appeal would be, as in the case of an individual who appealed to a civil court, "more honorable, more safe, and more certain, as well as more benevolent, than an attempt to obtain redress by pistol or sword."[12] Although many before Worcester had raised their voices against war, and shown its unchristian, its unhumanitarian, and its extravagant character, and although many had devised schemes for courts and confederacies of nations, none had taken care to give his voice the power of increase and perpetuity by binding together, in such a society as Worcester recommended and presently formed, a company of believers who would carry on the challenge in the years thereafter.

[11] S. E. Coues, Ms. *Peace Album,* testimony of John Pierce, November 4, 1844, and of Charles Brooks, October 30, 1844; Henry Ware's *Memoirs of the Rev. Noah Worcester,* Boston, 1844, pp. 60 ff.; Noah Worcester, *Abraham and Lot,* Concord, New Hampshire, 1812.

[12] Noah Worcester, *Solemn Review of the Custom of War,* p. 11.

Yet in his purpose of effecting organization for peace Noah Worcester met grave obstacles. Although Dodge's tract, *War Inconsistent with the Religion of Jesus Christ,* had been written, it had not yet been published. Even in Federalist New England Worcester could not find a publisher willing to risk such a book as his while the country was still at war with England. Although he was desperately poor, he determined to take half the risk for its printing. No Boston book dealer could foresee that in fifteen months from the date of its first appearance, Christmas Day, 1814, it would pass through five editions, and that by 1846 it would be reprinted in the United States alone more than a dozen times.[13]

Although Worcester was presently publishing peace tracts for children and editing a peace periodical, the *Friend of Peace,* the steps which he took to carry out his own precepts in the *Solemn Review* were of more immediate importance. Largely through his zeal the Massachusetts Peace Society was organized on December 28, 1815. The constitution, signed on that day, established a society aiming to promote the cause of peace "by exhibiting with all clearness and distinctness the pacific nature of the gospel, and by turning the attention of the community to the nature, spirit, causes, and effects of war." As to the question of whether the Scriptures prohibited war in all cases, the Society took sufficiently broad ground to include "the friends of peace who differ on this as well as on other subjects." The Society undertook to encourage the formation of similar societies "in this country and in foreign countries" by the dispersion of tracts, by correspondence, and by "other suitable means."[14] Here was a peace society less doctrinaire and more catholic than that sponsored by Dodge a few months earlier in New York. But Dodge was not entirely pleased, for it seemed to him that Worcester was giving too much time to those who believed that the Scriptures justified defensive war. This conviction kept him from ever

---

[13] *Christian Examiner,* vol. xxiii, January, 1838, p. 364.

[14] *Friend of Peace,* vol. i, no. 4, pp. 37 ff.

coöperating very actively with the Massachusetts society,[15] and it was clear that, from the very first, contention was bound to center around the question of how far peace doctrines should be carried.

Worcester, left more or less in the lurch by Dodge, found in the Reverend William Ellery Channing, one of the twenty-two gentlemen who signed the constitution of the Massachusetts Peace Society, a stout and valuable friend. As early as 1798, when Channing was a tutor in a Virginia family, he had attacked war as a horrible institution. Time deepened his convictions and on April 5, 1810, a day of public fast, Channing in a sermon regretted the effect of European wars on the arts of life, commerce, and agriculture. Unable to justify the Second War with Great Britain because it appeared that we had not sought redress for grievances in a truly pacific spirit, he openly criticized it as dangerous to our morals, commerce, religion and "our dearest rights." It was natural for such a man to lend support to Worcester in the organization of a society to labor for peace.[16]

Three weeks before the Massachusetts Peace Society was formed in Channing's study, a similar organization sprang up in Warren County, Ohio, a state which presumably had been as enthusiastic about the War of 1812 as Massachusetts was reluctant. The first letter of its corresponding secretary to Noah Worcester related a few bare facts. "Having seen the *Solemn Review of the Custom of War* and impressed with the horrors, the devastations, the grief, misery and woe, a number of citizens of Warren County, of different religious denominations, formed themselves into a society without having any knowledge at that time that any similar society existed on earth."[17] In a very short time came the report that the Warren County Peace Society had grown to more than a hundred members, including "some re-

[15] Dodge, *Autobiography*, pp. 89 ff., and 101 ff.

[16] William H. Channing, *Memoir of William Ellery Channing, with extracts from his correspondence and manuscripts* (3 vols., Boston, 1848), vol. i, p. 90, pp. 328-329, 338; vol. ii, pp. 103 ff., 109-110.

[17] *Friend of Peace*, vol. i, no. 10, p. 34.

spectable clergy and statesmen." The peace movement in Ohio was presently organized into four branches and the circulation of peace literature begun. Clearly the war spirit in the West was not so universal as has commonly been thought. The fact that the community of Shakers in Warren County was the headquarters of that sect in the West, and that the corresponding secretary of the Ohio Peace Society was a Quaker,[18] suggests that those religious bodies played a more important part in starting the movement in Ohio than their fellows in New York and Massachusetts played in those states. Certainly the spontaneous way in which the peace movement broke out in Ohio, without knowledge of what was being done in Boston and New York, seems to indicate that it was in part an expression of a rather widespread reaction against the War of 1812, and, indirectly, the wars of Napoleon.

Turning back to England, one finds more support for this inference. When Noah Worcester's *Solemn Review* reached England in the late spring of 1815, suggesting the formation of peace societies, something had already been done towards that end. Indeed, Worcester, in addressing his communication to Wilberforce, was unaware of the coincidence that a few months before the formation of the Massachusetts Peace Society an Englishman, William Pitt Scargill, had sent a letter to William Ellery Channing along with his essay on *The Impolicy of War*. This letter, dated June 1, 1815, gave notice that projects were afoot in England for the formation of a peace society and urged similar exertions in Boston. There can be no doubt that in both England and America foes of war were independently thinking about organizations to work for peace and were also taking steps to stir up similar activity on the other side of the ocean. "This remarkable coincidence of events, impressions, and efforts," wrote Noah Worcester, "may afford ground of hope, that God

[18] *Ibid.*, no. 11, p. 16; Josiah Morrow, *The History of Warren County Ohio*, Chicago, 1882, pp. 1065-1066.

is engaged in the cause for the abolition of war, and that the exertions of the friends of peace will not be in vain."[19]

Although an attempt was made in London to form a peace society in June, 1814, only three persons attended the meeting called, and organization was not actually achieved until June, 1816. It is clear from a report of the committee that "the information which had been received of the establishment of a peace society in Massachusetts had a considerable effect on the proceedings of this day, and whilst it increased the ardour of those who were foremost in promoting the measure, it served to encourage others who were more dubious of the benefits likely to accrue." Thus if English pacifists were not indebted to the *Solemn Review* for the idea of forming a peace society, they were admittedly spurred on to take such action by the example of what had been done in Boston. Even before the London society was fully organized, the committee decided to print a thousand copies of the *Solemn Review*. On the other hand, the founders of the cause in Boston were doubtless encouraged by their knowledge of plans for the formation of an English peace society. "With joy have we learned," declared the new Massachusetts Peace Society, "that Peace Societies have been proposed, if not already established on the other side of the Atlantic."[20]

The new organization in London chose for its name the Society for the Promotion of Permanent and Universal Peace, but it was more often called the Peace Society. Although the chief promoters among the ten men who formed the group were Friends, there were also Churchmen and Dissenters. None was more widely known than the antislave-trade agitator, Thomas Clarkson. The object of the society was "to print and circulate tracts, and to diffuse information tending to show that *War* is

---

[19] *Friend of Peace*, vol. i, no. 2, p. 36; *Christian Examiner*, vol. xxiii, January, 1838, p. 367; F. W. Holland, Ms. *History of the American Peace Cause*, vol. i, p. 7.

[20] *Herald of Peace*, vol. i, January, 1819, p. 2; vol. iv, pt. 2, July, August and September, 1828, pp. 411 ff.

inconsistent with the spirit of Christianity, and the true interests of mankind, and to point out the means best calculated to maintain permanent and universal peace, upon the basis of Christian principles."[21] The organization, like that which Worcester was instrumental in forming, looked forward to activities "unlimited by local attachment, extending to the whole human race." The business of the society was to be conducted by a committee elected annually. That the London Peace Society may have been consciously modelled after the one in Massachusetts is suggested by an interesting statement on the first page of the first number of its periodical, the *Herald of Peace*. "The formation of Peace Societies in the metropolis and in various parts of Britain, after the model of those in America where they originated, may be considered as an effect produced by one of the many causes which in our day appear to be rendered operative in promoting the general amelioration of humanity."[22]

It is significant that the movement for international peace began at practically the same time in England and in America, and that English friends of peace took heart from the fact that a society had actually been formed in Massachusetts, and were thereby encouraged to complete the action they had long been considering. And it is a point equally worthy of note that from the very beginning of the movement for international peace, its champions, free from a narrowly patriotic desire for leadership, showed genuine international-mindedness in their efforts to stimulate and to coöperate with opponents of war in other countries. Because similar efforts were made in England and America, such international coöperation between the peace men of these countries was from the first a reality.

A problem quite as interesting as that of determining the degree of American influence on the origins of the British peace movement is that of measuring and explaining the relative parts

---

[21] *Ibid.*, vol. i, January, 1819, p. 23.
[22] Foreword, *Herald of Peace*, vol. i, January, 1819.

played by American and by British Friends. Quakers may have taken a leading part in bringing about the Ohio Peace Society, but no mention is made in any contemporary document of their participation in forming either the New York or the Massachusetts societies. On the other hand, such Friends as William Allen and Joseph T. Price seem to have been foremost in accomplishing the London organization. Three years after its inception, Joseph Sturge, a prominent Quaker industrialist and philanthropist in Birmingham, formed an auxiliary in that city and henceforth labored with unstinted zeal in the cause of peace. Jonathan Dymond, a prominent Quaker, founded an auxiliary peace society in Exeter in 1825, and by his writings contributed vigor and influence to the English peace movement. Although individual Quakers in America were at times to contribute funds to the peace societies, their support, save in Ohio and in Rhode Island, was never very active, and their periodicals seldom gave more than brief accounts of the peace societies. In England, however, the Friends continued to favor the London Society.

This contrast may be explained by a number of considerations. The American Friends were beset during this period with discussions of doctrine and church organization, and these differences presently led to "secessions." Many Quakers were also migrating to the West.[23] As an organization, the Society of Friends has seldom taken the lead in any reform or social movement, but a few Friends, acting as individuals, have done the work for which the society has received credit. It was only after something had been accomplished by John Woolman and Elizabeth Fry that these leaders received the endorsement of the Meetings. Quakerism in a very peculiar way arose from individual activity, and its emphasis on individualism and quietism perhaps in large part explains its failure, as a body, to coöperate vigorously with other organizations for social reform.[24]

[23] Hirst, *The Quakers in Peace and War*, p. 244.

[24] For these suggestions the writer is indebted to Mr. Wilbur K. Thomas, secretary of the American Friends Service Committee. Miss Hirst, in a letter to the

As individuals the Friends in England had more reason to work actively for peace than the Quakers in America. While the War of 1812 had been no great thorn in the flesh of American Quakers, the Napoleonic struggle had grievously troubled British Friends. In 1814 and again in 1815 it was reported at the London Yearly Meeting that ten young Quakers were in prison for refusal to do military service.[25]

Still another possible explanation of the greater activity of English Friends is the fact that their Yearly Meeting took place in London, the center of philanthropic movements. In America, on the other hand, there was no common Yearly Meeting similar to that in London; and Philadelphia, the most important single center of Quaker activity, was far removed from the peace labors of Dodge and Worcester. Dodge, moreover, had a peculiar prejudice against the Quakers. Furthermore, although the New York Society had turned its face against all war, whether offensive or defensive, the Massachusetts group had taken a more catholic position, a position which later seemed to the editor of a Quaker journal, *The Friend,* something like a half-way covenant.[26] The resolutions of the London Society, on the other hand, declared against all war. Those who could not go the entire way of condemning it as "inconsistent with Christianity and the true interests of mankind" were urged to form their own societies to work along with the more thorough-going London organization.[27] This stand may well have encouraged the English Friends to feel that the Peace Society virtually made the Quaker position its own.

Thus within the short space of three years the world saw a remarkable development in active and practical organization against war—a development so spontaneous, so rapid, and so

author, maintains that in England, at least, peace activity, both in word and deed, was one of the most characteristic *corporate* activities of the Society.

[25] Hirst, *The Quakers in Peace and War,* p. 44.
[26] *Cf. post.,* p. 49.
[27] *Herald of Peace,* vol. ii, October, 1821, pp. 289-390.

widespread as to change such a pessimist as the Reverend Samuel Whelpley of Newark, New Jersey, into an ardent worker for peace. Whelpley was so inspired by the new movement as to be ready to entertain a belief that the Millennium was at last under way.[28] As a rebound from moral despair, such extravagant optimism, in those days of still lingering faith in the possibility of almost unlimited social progress, was only natural.

This optimism was apparently not, however, the prevailing mood among the early leaders, only a few of whom were daring enough to cherish a genuine hope for peace in their day. The first report of the New York Peace Society well represents the moderate position taken by the leaders of the movement: "The Committee indulge no extravagant and fanciful expectations of a sudden and perfect attainment of the object of the society. The rooted prejudices and violent passions which support a barbarous custom can be supplanted and subdued only by the gradual influence of the proper means and agencies."[29] Such an attitude is by no means visionary, and indicates that in general the early organizers of the peace movement were in no sense impractical fanatics. They were men of sober vision who realized, dimly at that time to be sure, but intelligently, that the fight for peace would be a long struggle, waged against tremendous obstacles. Such men were Dodge in New York, Price in London, and a little later William Ladd, of Maine—all practical idealists who saw that bricks could not be made out of straw and that if peace ideals were to prevail, there would have to be definite organization, hard work, and careful planning for the future.

The peace movement represented, as we have seen, a specific protest against the horrors, the waste, the weariness of the long war period. It was an antiwar reaction related to the religious

---

[28] Cf. Samuel Whelpley, The Fall of Wicked Nations, sermon at Newark, New Jersey, September 9, 1813, and the same author's Letters Addressed to Caleb Strong, Esquire, New York, 1816, pp. 122-123.

[29] Report of the New York Peace Society, at the anniversary, December 25, 1818, New York, 1818, pp. 6-7.

and economic forces in the thought and experience of the time. But it cannot be understood merely as a reaction against war. The movement was, in fact, part of a general humanitarian development which had its origin, long before these wars, in the development of eighteenth-century idealistic doctrines. This humanitarian trend was checked somewhat during the long period of turmoil, but remained a vital one. Now, with the upheaval at an end, there was opportunity for its expression. General disgust with the train of social woes which came with the wars found outlet and direction in the large number of organizations designed to combat those evils.

In America another influence tending to encourage philanthropic organization was the liberal reaction in New England against the older deterministic Calvinism. Faith in the ability of man to better his world was growing. Intemperance was one of the first evils to be attacked; in 1813 the Massachusetts Society for the Suppression of Intemperance was formed. In 1814 the New England Tract Society began its work of spreading the Gospel. In 1814, also, Thomas H. Gallaudet, at Hartford, began a movement to found a school for deaf mutes. In the same year the American Colonization Society was founded in the interest of the Negro. Three years later the McLean Asylum for the Insane was established. In 1825 the Prison Discipline Society united in one organization previous efforts to better conditions in prisons. These were only a few of the many organizations to improve the world.[30]

In England the crying need for reform called out a whole crop of humanitarian societies. There were the British and Foreign Bible Society (1808), the Royal Society for the Prevention of Cruelty to Animals (1824) and the Society for the Promotion of Useful Knowledge (1825). By 1816 Elizabeth Fry was visiting systematically the prisoners of Newgate, and by that year two

---

[30] Emerson Davis, *The Half Century, with Introduction by Mark Hopkins,* Boston, 1851, *passim.*

thousand persons annually were inspecting Robert Owen's New Lanark Institutions.[31]

In France, where eighteenth century humanitarian theory was so prominent, there was apparently less practical outcome in organization. At least one philanthropic society, however, embracing many reforms in its scope, did become prominent. This was the Société de la Morale Chrétienne, founded in 1821 to work for prison reform, peace, the abolition of the slave trade, and a number of other reforms.[32]

Organization for peace in America, then, represented more than a special reaction against war. It is to be understood as only one expression of a larger philanthropic enthusiasm for perfecting man and society, an enthusiasm rooted deep in prevalent social theory, and manifesting itself spontaneously, as it were, in societies in France and England as well as in the United States. It remains to be seen how the peace movement worked out an organization, and what were its accomplishments.

[31] H. D. Traill and J. S. Mann, editors, *Social History of England*, London, 1904, vol. vi, pp. 305, 838.

[32] *Journal de la Société de la Morale Chrétienne*, tome i (1822-1823), *passim*.

II

THE COÖPERATION OF LOCAL SOCIETIES, 1815-1828

From 1815 to 1828 American peace sentiment was marked by its local character, since the peace societies, spontaneously formed in widely separated communities, maintained independent existences. But soon they began to exchange letters with one another, and gradually something like a unified action in the interest of peace developed. Until the formation of the American Peace Society in 1828, however, the story is largely the story of local, independent organizations. Of these the Massachusetts Peace Society was by far the most important.

Although largely religious in origin, the Massachusetts Peace Society included among its members many laymen. President John Thornton Kirkland of Harvard College and some of the professors of that institution were among its early members. Noah Worcester wrote to the editor of the British *Herald of Peace* in 1819 that the Society included "many justices of the peace and members of the State Legislature, several who have occupied seats in Congress, several respectable judges in our courts, amongst whom is the chief justice of the Supreme Court of this state. We also have two of our former governors. Our president has been lieutenant governor during the whole of his presidency."[1] Of the non-clerical members none was destined to play for so long as important a rôle as Joshua P. Blanchard, a Boston merchant, who, because of his "Quaker" principles, refused to serve in the militia and had opposed the War of 1812. From the time he attended his first meeting of the Massachusetts Peace Society on January 11, 1816, until his death in 1868, he was one of the most devoted and loyal workers in the American movement. The contribution to the cause of such a humble layman as Blanchard proved far more important than that of many more distinguished men. Worcester felt, none the less, the

[1] *Herald of Peace*, vol. i, January, 1819, p. 5.

necessity of securing the support of political leaders, and, if possible, of listing them as members of the Massachusetts Peace Society. To this end he corresponded with John Adams, John Jay, and Thomas Jefferson. Adams refused to have anything to do with the new organization on the ground that if its principles were acted upon "the human flock would soon be fleeced or butchered by one or a few." With his interest in arbitration it was natural for John Jay to approve the Society in so far as its object was "to expose the guilt and evils of unjust and unnecessary war," and he was ready to admit that there were few wars which were manifestly necessary and just.[2] Jefferson was even willing to accept enrollment as an honorary member. Despairing of the abolition of war, still he hoped that its evils might be lessened, and he felt that no means should be neglected "which may add weight to the better scale."[3]

Despite the efforts to enlist lay members, the personnel of the Massachusetts Peace Society was in large part religious. The chief worker during this entire period was the secretary of the Society, the Reverend Noah Worcester. So great was his devotion that he often lived on bread and water and made his own shoes in order to put his meager earnings as a preacher into the work he had so much at heart.[4] As far as one can estimate, from one third to one fourth of the original members of the Society were clergymen, although this proportion appears to have decreased to some ten per cent within a very few years. A convention of Congregational ministers in Boston, in May, 1816, listened to the Reverend William Ellery Channing's thought-provoking address on war and recommended that all its members join the Massachusetts Peace Society and influence their people to follow the example.[5]

[2] *Friend of Peace*, vol. i, no. 4, p. 24; no. 11, pp. 29 ff.

[3] *Ibid.*, no. 4, pp. 21-22; *Thomas Jefferson Papers*, in the Library of Congress, Worcester to Jefferson, October 10, 1815, vol. 205; October 31, 1816, vol. 208; October 22, 1817, vol. 211.

[4] F. W. Holland, Ms. *History of the American Peace Cause*, vol. i, p. 13.

[5] *Friend of Peace*, vol. i, no. 5, pp. 31-32; *The Works of William Ellery Channing*, Boston, 1886, pp. 642-652.

Although the orthodox and Unitarian sects adhered most freely to the Massachusetts Peace Society, the net was spread for others. Baptists came, and at least one Catholic layman. Worcester sounded the trumpet to the Masons, whose lodges, he contended, might become peace societies without adding a jot or tittle to their principles. With more reason to expect response, he bowed his knee to the Quakers. A few individual Friends circulated the literature of the Peace Society, and others made possible a wider distribution of the *Friend of Peace*. But apparently few affiliated themselves with the peace societies, and there is no mention of any one of the thousand-odd Quaker congregations in the country taking counsel on ways and means to aid the organized movement against war.[6]

If the Quakers responded less actively than peace advocates had reason to expect, women on the whole proved more ready to listen. As early as 1818 the editor of the *Friend of Peace,* Noah Worcester, appealed to the supposed feminine virtues of gentleness, peacefulness, and dislike of cruelty. "By thirty years of faithful and united exertion on the part of the females of Christendom," he argued, "war might lose all its fascinating charms, and be regarded by the next generation with more abhorrence than the people of today look back on the gladiatorial combats of Rome, the papal crusade, or the flames of martyrdom." Since women formed their own societies for other benevolent purposes, they were urged to unite for the great object of promoting and preserving peace. That membership of women in the Massachusetts Peace Society itself was exceptional may be inferred from the fact that only one feminine name appears in the list of the one hundred and twenty-five new members admitted to the organization in 1818. As early as 1821, however, the Andover branch of the Massachusetts Peace Society reported twenty-one "females," and by 1826 the Portsmouth branch included eighteen

---

[6] *Friend of Peace,* vol. iii, no. 8, p. 241; vol. i, no. 8, pp. 1-7; no. 2, p. 44; vol. ii, no. 1, p. 36; vol. iv, no. 13, p. 412.

men and seventeen women.[7] It is interesting to note that almost immediately after the organization of the peace movement women were invited to affiliate themselves in groups with men and that to some extent, at least, they took advantage of the opportunity, although at that time women did not generally participate on equal terms in philanthropic organizations.

As for the growth of the Massachusetts Peace Society, lack of complete data makes anything like a full statement impossible. It seems fairly certain, however, that the real growth in numbers came between 1815 and 1820, when the original twenty-two members increased to 633, exclusive of members of branch societies. The annual report of the Society for 1823 frankly confessed that interest was falling off and that members were not paying their annual subscriptions. Lists of members and statements of the total membership were omitted from the annual reports from this time on. In 1825 the *Friend of Peace* tried to explain the decline in interest by pointing out that in the years immediately following the organization of the Society memory of the War of 1812 was still fresh, whereas with the passing of time the evils of the struggle were forgotten. It is also not unlikely that part of the subsequent decline in the membership of the parent body resulted from the increase in the number of branch societies. Wherever ten members could be found to unite, a branch organization was encouraged. Each branch received in the form of literature the equivalent of the sum paid into the treasury of the central organization. By December, 1818, six branches had been formed, numbering from twelve to seventy-three members each. In all, fifteen such units were organized, bringing up the total membership of the Massachusetts Peace Society, at its crest, to a figure approximating a thousand.[8]

It would be hard to estimate how much real strength these

[7] *Ibid.,* vol. i, no. 12, pp. 24 ff.; vol. iii, no. 3, p. 95; vol. iv, no. 9, p. 287; vol. iii, no. 10, p. 319.

[8] Annual Reports of the Massachusetts Peace Society in the *Friend of Peace,* vols. i-iv, *passim.*

branches brought to the movement. They sometimes printed the addresses made at their meetings. The members, however, were bound together by such loose ties that their zeal easily waned, and the annual dues of a dollar a member often came in tardily, if at all. One of the peace workers felt that the branch society "was no better than an unwieldy raft, making slight headway, often half-submerged, and a little perilous."[9] Yet perilous and hard to keep afloat as they undoubtedly were, these small craft must in the early days have succeeded at least in conveying news of the little known movement to places here and there.

The work of the Massachusetts Peace Society was, of course, conditioned by its resources. Although many of its members were men of wealth, contributions at the annual meetings frequently failed to reach the hundred dollar mark. By 1822 the Society was in debt because of the delinquency of members in paying their annual dollar, and this indebtedness increased. Considering these financial handicaps, the record of the Society's publications is a commendable one. During the first year it distributed 4,820 copies of one or another kind of peace publication. By 1820 the high-water mark was reached with the circulation of 18,940 tracts and copies of the *Friend of Peace*. By 1826, however, the Society put out only 10,327 units of propaganda, and this figure was not improved during the remainder of its separate career.[10]

Of this propaganda the most important item, in quality as well as in quantity, was Noah Worcester's quarterly journal, the *Friend of Peace,* which was published from 1815 to 1828. Worcester's own pen and purse largely maintained this, the first periodical in the world devoted exclusively to peace. Although it found relatively few readers, the fourth number went through seven editions.[11] The arguments Worcester used in his periodical

[9] F. W. Holland, Ms. *History of the American Peace Cause,* vol. i, p. 8.
[10] *Friend of Peace,* vol. ii, no. 8, p. 39; vol. i, no. 7, pp. 30 ff.; vol. iii, no. 8, p. 210; no. 11, p. 337; vol. iv, no. 2, pp. 81 ff.; no. 4, p. 209; *Christian Disciple,* vol. iii, p. 78, p. 473.
[11] Holland, Ms. *History of the American Peace Cause,* vol. ii, p. 41.

were largely religious and philanthropic, moral and political, and to a less extent, economic.

Apart from the publication of the *Friend of Peace* and the circulation of Worcester's *Solemn Review,* the outstanding project of the Massachusetts Peace Society was a statistical inquiry into the character of the war machine. Reports summarized statistics from various sources on the standing armies of the chief European states and the comparative expense of their maintenance. The report of the investigating committee estimated that between 1800 and 1817 some 5,060,000 lives had been sacrificed through war in Europe alone. There then followed an amazing calculation of the total number of lives lost through war since the earth was created, 5,800 years before! On the basis of relative increases in population the report concluded that "the enormous amount of 3,346,000,000 of human beings have been sacrificed on the earth to the idol of war." The committee's report then modestly regretted that it had been unable to get more accurate and specific facts. The second report compared the expenditures for military purposes in a given period with those for the support of the civil branches of governments, religion, literary, and charitable institutions. Great Britain and the United States together, the report concluded, might have supplied a Bible for every person on the globe and have spent no more than they put into the military for one year.

The committee then attempted to solve the problem of the causes of the wars recorded in history since Constantine's adoption of Christianity. They assumed, with the same naïveté as in the former instances, that their analysis was correct and that they had grasped the essentials of the problem. Of the two hundred and eighty-six wars listed, only five were ascribed to commercial reasons; most wars were judged "unsuccessful."[12]

---

[12] *First Report of the Committee of Inquiry of the Massachusetts Peace Society,* Boston, 1817; *Second Annual Report of the Committee of Inquiry,* Cambridge, 1818; *Third Annual Report of the Committee of Inquiry* in *Friend of Peace,* vol. ii, no. 10, pp. 32 ff.

Fantastic as such inquiries appear to be, they nevertheless represent the beginnings of the realistic study of war, and they indicate the character of the arguments used during the early period of American peace agitation.

Of the public issues of the day, none so much concerned the Massachusetts Peace Society as the Holy Alliance. Early in 1817 Worcester expressed the hope that the United States government would not be the last to accede to "the pacific alliance." At the same time William Ellery Channing prepared a memorial to Congress soliciting that body to make professions of peace corresponding to those made by the sovereigns of Europe. The memorialists further urged Congress to institute a special inquiry for the purpose of determining methods which the Government might follow in order to exert on human affairs "that happy influence" which President Madison had referred to in his eighth annual message. The memorialists themselves suggested the reference of disputes to an impartial umpire, national compacts for the express purpose of reducing "the enormous and ruinous extent of military establishments," and milder principles in the conduct of actual hostilities. The failure of this memorial to result in any official action did not discourage the Massachusetts Peace Society. Worcester presently printed in the *Friend of Peace* the text of the Holy Alliance and the Imperial Manifesto, and hoped that nothing would be found in the Constitution of the United States or in the disposition of the American government to prevent adherence.[13]

It was not unnatural, therefore, for the secretary of the Massachusetts Peace Society to write to the Emperor Alexander, and the Czar was thus informed of the formation and objects of the Massachusetts organization. On July 4, 1817, Alexander replied, cordially approving of its purpose. At the same time Prince Galit-

---

[13] *Friend of Peace,* vol. i, no. 6, p. 39; no. 8, pp. 27 ff.; no. 10, pp. 23 ff.; W. H. Channing, *A Memoir of William Ellery Channing,* vol. ii, pp. 111-112. For a discussion of the relation of the Holy Alliance to earlier pacifist thought see W. A. Phillips, *The Confederation of Europe,* New York, 1914, pp. 16-36.

zen, to whom Worcester had also written, accepted honorary membership in the Society.[14]

When the sovereigns who had subscribed to the Holy Alliance identified themselves with a policy of reaction and intervention, the peace men suffered bitter disappointment. Worcester spurned the casuistry of the manifestos of the Congresses of Troppau, Laibach, and Verona, pointing out at the same time that Napoleon and even our own people had adopted the delusive pretext of "fighting for peace." It was hard indeed for him to admit his disappointment in the Holy Alliance, and even when Alexander died in 1825, he was still inclined to be charitable. This faith in the Holy Alliance and this slow bitter disappointment were duplicated in England. The London Society had even gone so far as to send Thomas Clarkson to the Congress of Aix-la-Chapelle for the purpose of memorializing the Czar to establish a perpetual congress of nations for the arbitration of disputes between states. After being closeted two hours with Clarkson, Alexander expressed high approval of the peace societies and bade them godspeed in their work.[15]

If the friends of peace were deceived by these wolves in sheep's clothing, they were on better ground in recognizing the significance to their cause of the Bagot-Rush Convention of 1817. This agreement provided for the maintenance of small and equal armed forces by Great Britain and the United States on the Great Lakes. Both in argument and reasoning, Worcester observed, this agreement ran counter to the maxim that "preparations for war are the best means of preserving peace." It was hoped that this was only a beginning, that the principle would be extended to embrace the armed vessels on the oceans as well as on the lakes, and that the time of terminating such agreements would be extended from six months to sixty years. For, Worces-

---

[14] *Friend of Peace,* vol. i, no. 10, p. 27.

[15] *Ibid.,* vol. i, no. 10 pp. 22 ff.; vol. iii, no. 8, p. 233; no. 10, pp. 312 ff.; vol. iv, no. 4, pp. 112-113; no. 8, p. 248; *Herald of Peace,* vol. i, January, 1819, pp. 20 ff.; no. iii, April, 1821, pp. 97 ff.

ter went on, sixty years was not too long a time "for governments to reflect before they resolve on making war."[16]

Yet Noah Worcester, the spokesman of the Massachusetts
Peace Society, found more in our public policy to condemn than
to approve. His pen denounced the government's policy towards
the Seminoles and Cherokees. The injustice of the wars against
these tribes was the theme of almost countless remarks and
allusions as well as of longer editorials and articles in the *Friend
of Peace*. With fearless energy he denounced these interminable
conflicts as a "foul reproach on our national character." Nor was
his sympathy for the Negro slaves any less pronounced. Slavery
and the slave trade, he pointed out, were both the genuine off-
springs of war. By humanizing and improving the moral sentiments of the white population Worcester believed that the
Colonization Society would aid the peace societies. Why not
divert money from military expenditure to emancipate the slave
gradually and thus weed out the danger of a future slave
insurrection?[17]

Privateering was another public question which the Massachusetts Peace Society did not overlook. In May, 1819, it circulated a memorial to Congress urging that this custom was
"utterly abhorrent to religion and humanity, and inconsistent
with sound national policy." The House committee turned the
question over to the executive, but whether its report or the
memorials had anything to do with the negotiations with foreign
powers presently begun by John Quincy Adams is not clear. At
any rate, the use of memorials praying Congress to initiate measures for the abolition of privateering furnished a precedent for the
method of which peace men later became so fond in their efforts
to influence political action.[18]

---

[16] J. M. Callahan, *Agreement of 1817*, in American Historical Association *Report*, 1895, pp. 369-392; *Friend of Peace*, vol. i, no. 10, pp. 19 ff.

[17] *Friend of Peace*, vol. ii, no. 4, p. 23; vol. i, no. 12, p. 21; vol. iii, no. 6, p.
182; vol. iv, no. 5, p. 150; no. 7, p. 215; *Herald of Peace*, vol. iii, November,
1821, pp. 349 ff.

[18] Channing, *Memoir of William Ellery Channing*, vol. ii, pp. 117-118; *Friend
of Peace*, vol. ii, no. 5, pp. 29-30; no. 7, pp. 36 ff.; Holland, Ms. *History of the*

Meantime the Massachusetts Peace Society followed the same procedure in regard to compulsory service in the militia. As early as 1816 a petition was addressed to the Massachusetts legislature praying for the exemption "not only of Friends and Quakers but of all that believe with them that war is inconsistent with Christianity." The *Friend of Peace* attacked the militia system as wasteful and useless and rejoiced that the abolition of two of the annual trainings of the militia lifted a burden from the backs of the poor and removed a cause of vice.[19]

Nothing was said in the *Friend of Peace* of the failure of the Congress of Panama, though its possible significance had been appreciated and though the President of the Congress had won praise in an annual report of the Massachusetts Peace Society for favoring the uniform reference of disputes to negotiation and for advocating a better code of international law.[20]

Though the Massachusetts Peace Society continued for a while after the formation of the American Peace Society in 1828, its work was over even before that. A contemporary outsider, certainly not unsympathetic, summarized that work. At each anniversary on December 25 a lecture was read to a small audience, and the report of the secretary, Dr. Noah Worcester, listened to and accepted. Although its message was apparently heard "by the multitude with a sort of complacent incredulity," it none the less "arrested the attention of many, and gave conviction to some, and excited active zeal in a few."[21]

The sister organizations of the Massachusetts Peace Society prospered even less than that historically important organization. Surprisingly little came from the New York Peace Society. Dur-

American Peace Cause, vol. i, p. 16; *House Executive Document,* 111, no. 16, 34 Congress, 1 session.

[19] *Friend of Peace,* vol. i, no. 3, p. 39; vol. iii, no. 1, p. 21; no. 7, p. 201; no. 11, p. 343; no. 8, p. 256. Ladd felt the militia system was falling to pieces as fast as its enemies could wish and that "any exertion on their part to accelerate the fall will only produce a reaction," Ladd to Samuel J. May, January 1, 1827, *William Ladd Papers.*

[20] *Friend of Peace,* vol. iv, no. 8, p. 249; no. 11, pp. 340-341.

[21] *Christian Examiner,* vol. xxxiii, January, 1843, p. 296.

ing the year ending in 1819 the Society seems to have distributed only one hundred copies of the *Friend of Peace* and an unstated number of copies of its last annual report. Lack of funds was the apology given for this small showing. Indeed, the New York Peace Society seems barely to have maintained its precarious existence. In 1823 William Ladd could not find any person in New York who knew that a peace society existed there. It was with great difficulty that he managed to keep up, thereafter, a languishing correspondence with its officers; by 1828 he regarded it as "dead as a herring." Long before this, as the brittle notes of the secretary's minutes show, its meetings were irregular and badly attended, and its indebtedness was constantly increasing.[22]

Elsewhere in the state of New York, however, there were signs of activity, though the metropolitan organization seems to have had no hand in it. Matthew Simpson, of Ballston Spa, distributed during the year 1822 almost two thousand peace tracts, chiefly the *Friend of Peace* and the *Solemn Review*. Out of this came two societies, one in Saratoga County with twenty-five members and another at Ellisburg numbering sixty. The circulation of the *Friend of Peace* in the neighborhood of Cayuga resulted in the birth of a society, and by 1826 four numbers of a magazine, *The Peace Advocate*, had appeared at Buffalo. Yet these local societies seem to have made no pretense of lending support to the Quakers who, through memorials, were at this time trying to secure exemption from fines for non-attendance in the militia.[23]

In contrast to this unenviable record, the Ohio Peace Society vigorously circulated copies of the *Friend of Peace*. Oberlin had its peace society, and a female peace society functioned near

---

[22] *Report of the New York Peace Society,* New York, 1818; *Friend of Peace,* vol. iii, no. 1, pp. 27-28; Ms. *Minutes of the New York Peace Society, 1825-1828,* in the archives of the American Peace Society, Washington, D. C.; William Ladd to Samuel J. May, June 11, 1827, in *William Ladd Papers.*

[23] *Friend of Peace,* vol. iii, no. 4, p. 122; no. 9, p. 287; vol. i, no. 9, p. 40; vol. iv, no. 2, p. 63; vol. ii, no. 12, p. 37.

Cincinnati. In fact, by 1818 as many as eight peace societies in Ohio reported activity, and at Mount Pleasant Elisha Bates was publishing the *Moral Advocate,* which devoted itself to the cause of peace along with other philanthropic enterprises. And Ohio was not the only western state to manifest antiwar sentiment. At Salem, in Vigo County, and in Wayne County, Indiana, peace societies testified to the westward migration of pacifist sentiment.[24]

In the South, too, there was some organized activity during this period. As early as 1819 a peace society at Raleigh, North Carolina, reported thirty members. Its president, Calvin Jones, had resigned the chief office in the state militia because of his convictions of its uselessness on the one hand and the righteousness of the principles of peace on the other.[25] Though its motives were suspected, this society distributed literature, corresponded with the organizations of like nature in Ohio and Indiana, and stimulated the formation of one or two branch societies. A handful of friends of peace in Virginia, hearing of the existence of the Massachusetts society, corresponded with it and longed for the happy hour when a peace organization could be formed in their community. At Augusta, Georgia, the Reverend W. T. Brantly recommended in the *Georgia Advertiser* a volume of peace sermons by the Reverend Henry Holcombe of Philadelphia. Out of the convictions aroused by the sale of some five hundred copies of this book, a peace society appeared at Augusta and became auxiliary to the Pennsylvania Peace Society.[26]

It was this Reverend Henry Holcombe, a Baptist pastor, who was responsible for the formation of the Pennsylvania Peace Society at Philadelphia in December, 1822. Although a veteran of the Revolution, this man, like Worcester, renounced war as incompatible with Christianity and used his pulpit to advance

[24] *Ibid.,* vol. i, no. 9, p. 40; vol. ii, no. 5, p. 38; vol. iii, no. 2, p. 62; no. 3, p. 86; vol. ii, no. 8, p. 37; no. 4, p. 39.

[25] *Ibid.,* vol. ii, no. 5.

[26] *Ibid.,* vol. ii, no. 5, p. 32; vol. iii, no. 2, p. 48; vol. iv, no. 4, p. 118; vol. i, no. 10, p. 36; vol. iii, no. 8, p. 210.

his point of view. Among the hundred odd members of the Pennsylvania Peace Society at least eight were distinguished Friends. Meetings were appropriately held on Christmas and on the Fourth of July, and within a year the membership doubled. Probably, however, the Society was not very active. Its example may have suggested the reorganization of the African Baptist Association of Philadelphia into the Africa Peace Society, with a hundred and twenty black friends of peace.[27]

In Rhode Island, Quakers seem to have affiliated with the state peace society, formed on March 20, 1818, in greater proportions than in Philadelphia. Two of their number, Moses Brown and Thomas Arnold, bestowed on the society enough means to enable the publication of 28,704 tracts within three years. The Rhode Island Peace Society continued to be one of the best supported and most flourishing of the local groups.[28]

During this period the most active society in the neighboring state of Connecticut owed its existence to the Reverend Samuel J. May, a Unitarian divine who became a convert to the cause while a student at Harvard. In August, 1826, the orthodox clergy of the community joined him in forming the Windham County Peace Society. May corresponded with leading British pacifists, as well as with American promoters of the cause, distributed tracts, and held meetings in the several towns of the county. Under his leadership the Windham Peace Society became the center of the Connecticut peace movement. Two years later the Hartford Peace Society was formed with a hundred and two members.[29]

[27] William Ladd, *History of the Peace Societies*, p. 176, in *Scientific Tracts for the Diffusion of Useful Knowledge*, Boston, 1836; Henry Holcombe, *The Martial Christian's Manual*, Philadelphia, 1823, *passim; Friend of Peace*, vol. iii, no. 11, p. 339.

[28] *Friend of Peace*, vol. i, no. 12, p. 38; vol. iii, no. 2, p. 51; vol. iv, no. 11, p. 352; vol. iv, no. 4, p. 128.

[29] G. B. Emerson, Samuel May and T. J. Mumford, *Memoir of Samuel Joseph May*, Boston, 1873, pp. 83, 102, 115; S. E. Coues, Ms. *Peace Album*, testimony of Samuel J. May; *Friend of Peace*, vol. iv, no. 14, p. 431; Appendix, no. 4, p. 110; and no. 2, p. 110.

While the peace movement was thus making its way in southern New England, some progress could be noted in Vermont and Maine. In 1819 the Vermont Convention of Congregational ministers approved the objects of peace societies, and in the same year the Vermont Peace Society was organized at Montpelier with fifty members.[30] It was in Maine, however, that the more striking development took place. No little prestige came to the Maine Peace Society by virtue of its distinguished officers, including the Reverend Jesse Appleton, president of Bowdoin College, Samuel Longfellow, Simon Greenleaf, Dr. Edward Payson, and the Honorable Samuel Freeman.[31] Like so many other peace societies it fell into apathy, but had it not existed the American peace movement might not have gained one of its three most valuable organizers, William Ladd.

As the commander of one of the largest ships that ever put out from Portsmouth, William Ladd had visited many parts of the world. No one would have suspected that this bluff, florid, robust, almost excessively good-humored man had a Harvard degree and had attempted to carry out a free-labor experiment in Florida, which he hoped would lead to the peaceful abolition of slavery. Abandoning the sea because of the War of 1812, he turned to agriculture and settled down on a farm inherited from his father at Minot, Maine. Until he stood at the deathbed of the Reverend Jesse Appleton, president of the Maine Peace Society, he had never heard of the organization. Indeed, since giving up the sea he had any number of times thought of entering the navy. Yet Appleton's eloquent plea for peace began his conversion, and at forty-one William Ladd felt his "call" to be an apostle of peace. It was reading Worcester's *Solemn Review* that settled the question, and henceforth this cause became his chief object in life. He began modestly enough by lecturing before the Maine Agricultural Society and by contributing a series of articles to the *Christian Mirror*. He urged

[30] *Friend of Peace,* vol. ii, no. 7, p. 38.
[31] *Ibid.,* vol. i, no. 8, p. 40.

women to coöperate in the peace movement and emphasized its international character. In 1825 he was asked to give the annual address before the Massachusetts Peace Society, and this address was widely circulated in England as well as in his own country.[32]

Even before this Ladd had begun to correspond with English peace men, especially with Thomas Hancock, secretary of the London Society. "I strongly reciprocate those feelings of attachment and fellowship which bind together all the friends of peace, of all nations, kindreds, tongues and languages," he wrote to Hancock on August 3, 1825, making clear at the same time his belief that the harvest must be left to their successors to reap.[33] Meantime Ladd kept up his contributions to the *Christian Mirror*, attacking the vainglory displayed in the building of Bunker Hill Monument, which seemed to him calculated to deepen American prejudice against the British. These essays were incisive, practical, and realistic in their arguments, and Ladd performed a real service to the cause by collecting them and having them brought out as *Essays on War and Peace by Philanthropos*.[34]

The letters of this man bear adequate witness to his energy, enthusiasm, and prodigious work. Up and down the land went his communications to the secretaries of the local peace societies, exhorting the negligent, encouraging the doubtful. But he did not stop with exhortations. Careful plans for capturing the press and the pulpit, for circulating tracts, forming peace societies, making addresses, and interesting teachers of the youth in church and public schools—these were the means he advocated in season

[32] John Hemmenway, *Memoir of William Ladd*, Boston, 1872, pp. 9, 38, 142-143, 51; *Friend of Peace*, vol. iii, no. 9, pp. 259-260; *Christian Mirror*, August 19, October 21, 28, November 24, 1825, May 5, 1826.

[33] John Hemmenway, *Memoir of William Ladd* Ms. (second) edition revised and enlarged, November, 1890, in the archives of the American Peace Society, pp. 68, 105.

[34] *Christian Mirror, passim;* Ladd to May, January 1, 1827, in Ms. *Letter Book of William Ladd;* William Ladd, *Essays on Peace and War by Philanthropos,* Exeter, 1828.

and out and employed with never-flagging zeal in his own work. By 1827 he was lecturing in Connecticut, New York, and Pennsylvania, trying to wake up dormant peace societies. A number of new organizations owed their existence to him. This incessant activity, Ladd wrote a friend, was "meat and drink," not a sacrifice, to him. The partial success he met gave him more heartfelt satisfaction than anything else in his life.[35]

Although Ladd realized well enough that the friends of peace were rowing against the stream, he persisted in faith and deed. "The current at length will turn, the tide will change, the wind of popular favor will blow, and then we may lay in our oars and catch the favoring gale, but until then I would impress it on every friend of peace that he must act as though the peace of the world depended on him alone. This is the most auspicious moment that ever occurred in the cause of peace, and I grudge every moment that is not devoted to it."[36] It was inevitable that such a man should soon find himself the recognized leader of the American peace movement, and scarcely less in the order of things that he should father the idea of a national organization for peace and realize it.

While the American peace movement was still decentralized, the local societies quite definitely felt themselves part of an international movement. It was natural for the peace societies of New England to concern themselves first of all with their Canadian neighbors. Through merchants, literature of the Massachusetts Peace Society reached Canada, and this resulted in the formation of a peace society in Rawdon, Nova Scotia, which kept Noah Worcester constantly informed of its work. By 1826 there were twelve societies in Upper Canada.[37]

The Massachusetts society furthermore sent its publications to Great Britain, France, Holland, Russia, Calcutta, Ceylon, the

[35] Ms. *Letter Book of William Ladd, passim;* S. E. Coues, Ms. *Peace Album,* testimony of Samuel J. May.
[36] Ladd to May, July 5, 1827, in *Ladd Letter Book.*
[37] *Friend of Peace,* vol. i, no. 10, p. 37; vol. iii, no. 5, p. 159.

Sandwich Islands, and South America, and this was not a mere casting of bread upon the waters. The President of Haiti expressed warm approval of the movement, and the chaplain of the West India Company sent a hundred dollars to Worcester and applied for membership in the Boston society.[38]

While thus crusading in the far places of the world, the American leaders did not neglect keeping in touch with the peace men in England. Scarcely a number of either the *Herald of Peace,* the organ of the London society, or of Worcester's *Friend of Peace* appeared without references to the work being done on the other side of the Atlantic. The Americans were glad to learn that by 1819 the London society had eight auxiliaries in different parts of the kingdom and forty correspondents who acted as agents for the committee of the central society. Organizations had also been formed in Glasgow and in Ireland. Occasionally American and British friends of peace met and resolved to use all their personal influence to promote good feelings between the two nations. The London Peace Society frequently sent its tracts to the American societies, which often reciprocated. In both countries the societies published and distributed the leading pacifist literature of the other country. Besides, there was scarcely an anniversary address to an American peace society which was not reproduced in the *Herald of Peace,* while the *Friend of Peace* filled scores of its pages with excerpts from the English periodical. Likewise both journals printed in part or in full the annual reports of the peace societies across the Atlantic.[39]

The British friends of peace admired the progress of the cause in America. In reporting the foundation of the Pennsylvania Peace Society the annual report of the London organization observed that it was the thirty-fifth such society in America.

---

[38] *Ibid.,* vol. ii, no. 1, p. 36; vol. iii, no. 8, p. 255.

[39] *Herald of Peace,* vol. i, January, 1819, p. 10; *Friend of Peace,* vol. i, no. 5; "Thoughts on Universal Peace," vol. iii, no. 1, p. 26; vol. ii, no. 9, pp. 36-37; vol. iii, no. 4, p. 123; E. M. Gallaudet, *Life of T. H. Gallaudet,* p. 109.

"Our transatlantic friends," the report went on, "are moving forward in their most honourable course with unabated zeal and ardour; and removed as they are from the scenes of bloodshed, your Committee hope that peace will find a safe and serene asylum in the land which was peopled by our sires, and which we would fain regard as possessed by our brethren." Similarly Dr. Thomas Hancock, in a letter to Worcester arranging for an exchange of peace periodicals, felt that there was something in American institutions "more favourable to the progress of pacific principles" than in British institutions. Perhaps this feeling in England that American soil was peculiarly adapted to the spreading of peace principles helped the Americans to develop the idea that it was their country's peculiar and special mission to introduce peace into the world.[40]

On the other hand, the American peace men felt they could not hold a candle to the London society with its superior resources and begged Americans to emulate its greater zeal. Worcester pointed out that the British friends of the cause had a natural advantage in the fact that their people had wearied of war during the long struggle with France, and he urged his American colleagues to double their efforts. By 1825 the annual receipts of the London Society for the Promotion of Permanent and Universal Peace totaled two thousand dollars, twice that of the Massachusetts organization in its most flourishing days.[41]

This friendly rivalry, which acted as a stimulus to both American and British workers, did not in the least lead to their overlooking the Continent of Europe as a field for proselyting. Both British and American peace men had a hand in the formation in 1821 of the Société des Amis de la Morale Chrétienne et de la Paix, the object of which was to apply the precepts of

---

[40] *Friend of Peace*, vol. iii, no. 10, p. 309; vol. iv, no. 2; Thomas Hancock to Dr. Worcester, London, July 7, 1824, p. 58. For the idea of an American mission to propagate peace, see *post.*, pp. 53-54.

[41] Hemmenway, *Memoir of William Ladd*, p. 44; *Friend of Peace*, vol. iv, no. 1, pp. 13-14; no. 6, p. 182.

Christianity to social institutions, "in a word, to seek after, and to obtain, Peace." From the President of the Society, the Duke de la Rochefoucauld-Liancourt, down, the personnel of the organization was less popular in character than that of the English and American peace societies. In a short while even the French ministers and the King himself were enrolled as members. The Society established a periodical, the *Journal de la Société de la Morale Chrétienne,* which kept its readers informed of the activities of the English and American peace movement. Though it was not primarily a peace society, both English and American enthusiasts insisted on regarding it as such. British pacifists attended its meetings from time to time, and the two societies, French and British, fraternally resolved to remain united in the work of promoting the happiness of mankind. Beginning in 1822, the Massachusetts Peace Society was also in communication with the Society of Christian Morals, and Worcester rejoiced with his British brethren that through their joint efforts the peace movement had made a beginning, though a small one, in France.[42]

The London Peace Society attempted further to stimulate peace sentiment on the Continent by translating some of its tracts into Dutch, Spanish, French, and Italian, and the kings of France and Spain received these tracts. One of the tracts was republished in Madrid, and the Spanish Athenaeum made cordial offers to aid in their distribution. A correspondent at Gibraltar undertook to circulate the Spanish and Italian tracts in the south of Spain, in northern Africa, and in Italy. The Madrid *Gazette* printed a lively account of the American peace societies. Perhaps, as the government organ, it had in some way

---

[42] Hirst, *The Quakers in Peace and War,* p. 244; Ladd, *History of the Peace Societies, loc. cit.,* p. 176; *Calumet,* vol. i, no. 1, p. 7; vol. ii, no. 6, p. 188; *Records from the Life of Sampson Vryling Stoddard Wilder,* American Tract Society, New York, 1867, p. 176; *Herald of Peace,* vol. iii, September, 1821, pp. 266-267; *Journal de la Société de la Morale Chrétienne,* in New York Public Library, numbers, 4, 5, 7; *Friend of Peace,* vol. iii, no. 6, pp. 183-184; no. 12, p. 372; no. 8, pp. 252 ff.

got word of Noah Worcester's criticism of his country's policy in the negotiations with Spain regarding West Florida.[43]

In Germany, too, the peace movement made an entering wedge. Some of the tracts of the London society, translated into German, circulated in that country, while a German edition of five thousand copies of Worcester's *Solemn Review* was put on the market in 1820 at the great fair in Leipzig, the center of the German book trade.[44]

Aware of the limitations of their work, the peace men made no great claims for their efforts. They felt the need for the gradual organization of an international, united movement. "There must be beginnings," said the Reverend J. Allen in an address to the Peace Society at Northboro, Massachusetts, in 1827. "Gradually as individuals in this and other countries, by work and coöperation, the peace workers may some time make their voices heard. We do not expect that we shall be able to remove at once those prejudices of years, so interwoven with the existing institutions of society. We beg to be acquitted of so egregious a folly."[45] In commenting on the peace address of Dr. John Ware before the Massachusetts Peace Society on Christmas Day, 1824, the editor of the *North American Review* felt that few were affected by such arguments. "How small a portion of the public will ever hear them! If it depended upon reason, and truth, and religion merely to decide, war would long since have fallen into disuse; but men's passions and interests are too powerful for such restraints, and till these can be enlisted for peace, we fear that all the efforts of the peace societies will be ineffectual."[46] Out in Cincinnati Timothy Flint, the editor of a less well-known periodical, the *Western Monthly Review,* expressed pleasure in the progress of the cause of peace abroad as

[43] *Herald of Peace,* vol. iii, February, 1821, p. 54; *Friend of Peace,* vol. ii, no. 10, p. 40; and no. 2, p. 10.

[44] *Herald of Peace,* vol. ii, January, 1820, p. 13.

[45] *Friend of Peace,* vol. iv. no. 1, Appendix, p. 23.

[46] *North American Review,* vol. xx, April, 1825, p. 456.

well as at home, and prophesied that the time would come when thousands would "shout acclamations in praise of peace societies."[47] Whether this would be true depended to some extent on whether the fifty-odd incoherent and struggling societies from Maine to Georgia and from New York to Indiana could be united in a national organization, and whether, ultimately, this national organization could become part of an international organization for the promotion of peace.

[47] *Western Monthly Review*, Cincinnati, vol. ii, 1828-1829, p. 567.

III

THE AGITATION FOR PEACE, 1828-1841

As in the period between 1815 and 1828 Noah Worcester was the dominant figure in the American peace movement, so in the succeeding period of national organization William Ladd was the chief source of its vitality until his death in 1841. Apparently father of the idea of a national peace society, without him it could scarcely have been realized. "The objects of such a society," he wrote, "are to give a tone of prominence, unity, and strength to all the exertions of all the friends of peace in the United States, and indeed of all the inhabitants of North America."[1] Had this not been done, the development of the American peace movement must inevitably have been greatly retarded.

The odds against Ladd were so great that it seemed as if he might be called on to abandon his cherished Maine farm and devote himself entirely to travel. Great as such a sacrifice would be, he was ready to make it. At his instance the peace societies of Maine, Massachusetts, and Portsmouth, New Hampshire, passed during the winter of 1827 resolutions favoring the formation of a national society and appointed Ladd as their agent to achieve that end. Armed with a proposed constitution drawn up by Noah Worcester, he visited peace meetings and secured its endorsement. He had hoped for support in New York, but the largest of his five audiences there numbered only seven persons. Such indifference made his task seem almost hopeless. "I assure you," he wrote to the Reverend Samuel J. May, "it requires no small degree of perseverance to bear up against all the discouragements which I meet with, but I do not and I never will despair of its final success." Though in Philadelphia no one would serve without pay as corresponding secretary of the proposed national society, he took hope from the fact that one of

[1] William Ladd to the Rev. Samuel J. May, March 1, 1827, in *William Ladd Letter Book*. For a brief sketch and excellent bibliography of Ladd, see *Advocate of Peace,* vol. 89, no. 11, November, 1927, pp. 608-611.

his hearers resolved to break his boy's wooden soldier on returning home from the lecture. With bodily infirmities that made
lecturing, to say nothing of traveling, extremely painful, Ladd
visited Connecticut, where he met with just as discouraging
responses to his appeals.[2]

Nevertheless, on May 8, 1828, the American Peace Society
was organized in New York. Ladd, its founder, modestly refused to accept the presidency, although he consented to act as
chairman of the Board of Directors, the governing council. With
a few alterations Worcester's constitution was adopted.[3] This
stated the object of the organization to be the diffusion of "light
respecting the evils of war, and the best means for effecting its
abolition." In this general statement lay seed for future dissensions regarding the problem of so-called defensive war,[4] which
was not specifically condemned. The Declaration of Principles
made it clear that the American Peace Society would not consider the question of the Scriptural legality of defensive war.
"We receive into our communion all who seek to abolish war."[5]
Such were the humble beginnings of the American Peace Society.

Most of the local peace societies became auxiliaries of the new
national organization, yet some remained independent. Although
there are no records concerning membership, its income during
its first year suggests that there could not have been more than
three hundred paying members. Only $618 was paid into its
treasury in that first year, while the income of the American
Temperance Society for the same period was $13,311, of the
American Tract Society, $45,134, of the Prison Discipline So-
ciety, $2,444, and of the American Bible Society, $75,879.[6] Yet

---

[2] Ladd to May, January 1, 1827, February 12, 1828, April 28, 1828, in *William Ladd Letter Book*.

[3] John Hemmenway, revised manuscript edition, *Memoir of William Ladd*,
p. 154.

[4] Cf. *post.*, p. 69.

[5] *Harbinger of Peace*, vol. i, no. 1, May, 1828, pp. 6-7.

[6] *The Missionary Herald*, vol. xxiv, pp. 129, 248, 325, 360.

this year saw a better record in the distribution of tracts than any previous year of the peace agitation.

Though the annual income of the society averaged less than $400 during the first four years, by 1838 it was $3,600; and for the year 1841-1842, the year of Ladd's death, 1,500,000 tract pages, or sixty times the number circulated during the first year of the Society, were distributed. There had been only seven life members in 1829; there were now two hundred and thirty-two.[7]

It is true that this growth was partly the result of the work of valuable lieutenants whom Ladd had interested in the peace movement, but the bulk of the accomplishment was his. Except when paralysis made it impossible, he journeyed about as general agent of the Society, lecturing, getting subscriptions, soliciting aid from colleges, churches, individuals, offering prizes for peace essays, corresponding, talking in season and out of season. During the year ending in 1835, for example, Ladd traveled 1300 miles, delivered forty public addresses, collected over $982, wrote on peace for several periodicals and newspapers, and corresponded widely with peace societies, besides editing the *Calumet*, the periodical of the Society.[8]

Despite the growth during these fourteen years of the American Peace Society, much remained to be done. The movement was practically confined to New England, New York, and Pennsylvania. Even in those states agents of the Society met with "lamentable apathy." This was attributed mainly to the "want of proper information respecting its claims and its wants."[9]

During the early career of the national organization a few of the older local peace societies showed surprising energy, but their story is for the most part one of steady decline, and, in many instances, death. Only a few of the local societies in ex-

[7] *Advocate of Peace*, vol. iv, no. 7, June, 1842, pp. 159 ff.

[8] *American Advocate of Peace*, vol. i, no. 5, June, 1835, pp. 223 ff.

[9] *Advocate of Peace*, vol. iv, no. 2, August, 1841, pp. 40 ff.; and vol. ii, no. 10, March, 1839, p. 238.

istence in 1828 weathered the gales and maintained even the semblance of an organization in 1860.

When the Massachusetts Peace Society in 1828 decided to become an auxiliary of the national organization, it advised its branches to follow its example. Its own life constantly became more precarious. In 1830 the total membership was only 168, not more than a fourth of what it had been in its heyday. It ceased to publish any tracts save the annual reports and anniversary addresses. Each annual report seemed to reflect less achievement and a greater, if veiled, discouragement. By 1845 the long-discussed merger with the American Peace Society had been apparently accomplished.[10] This decline of the Massachusetts organization resulted in part from the fact that its strength had been sapped by the national organization and also because its most ardent member, Dr. Noah Worcester, retired from active peace work in 1828, due to his advanced age. One of its newer members, Amasa Walker, a banker who was to contribute greatly to the American peace cause, felt that its stagnation resulted from the fact that the Society refused to take "the higher ground of condemning all wars, and persisted in a compromising and expedient policy which justified so-called defensive wars."[11] When the Massachusetts Peace Society could not keep above water, it was scarcely to be expected that the rank and file of local societies in the state could last, though sometimes, indeed, the influence of an alert friend of peace kept alive a local society.

Of the New England societies founded in the early period, the Rhode Island Peace Society alone seems to have maintained a continuous existence down to 1860. Probably this was due to the fact that it was endowed and, in 1847, incorporated. In 1844 it was sending the *Advocate of Peace,* the organ of the national society, to all the ministers of the state and to an equal number

[10] *Fifteenth Annual Report of the Massachusetts Peace Society,* Boston, 1831, *passim; Nineteenth Annual Report,* Boston, 1835; *Advocate of Peace,* vol. vi, June and July, 1845, p. 84.

[11] S. E. Coues, Ms. *Peace Album,* testimony of Amasa Walker.

of clergymen in the West. But by 1860 its endowment had dwindled to only $86.[12]

In 1837 some three hundred sympathetic persons answered the call of the Reverend Thomas A. Merrill, a Congregationalist minister of Middlebury, Vermont, to reorganize the defunct Vermont Peace Society, but the attempt failed. Thereafter the national organization, which had assisted in this ill-timed renascence, did little to stimulate the formation of new auxiliaries. It was felt to be a futile effort to help lame dogs over stiles.[13]

In the Middle States the situation was no brighter than in New England. The old New York Peace Society merged itself into the American Peace Society in 1828. An auxiliary society, begun in New York City in 1837, boasted within a year five hundred members and held meetings in twenty churches. At the instance of its energetic secretary, Origen Bacheler, it circulated petitions to Congress for the arbitration of our claims against Mexico and for a Congress of Nations, but by 1844 the Society's wings were certainly clipped. A new group of men in 1844 organized a second New York auxiliary society, but it apparently went to the wall like the rest.[14] Nor was anything more heard from the Pennsylvania Peace Society, organized in 1839.

The anti-war societies of Ohio seem to have had no hand in the formation of the American Peace Society, and though an auxiliary at Worthington was reported in 1832, the cause was not popular. Among the Quakers peace sentiment was from time to time apparent, but there seem to have been no peace societies at all active until, in 1850, a state society, auxiliary to the national organization, was founded.[15]

[12] *Advocate of Peace,* vol. v, July, 1844, pp. 226, 240; vol. xiv, September and October, 1860, p. 130; *Christian Citizen,* November 1, 1844.

[13] *Advocate of Peace,* vol. i, no. 2, September, 1837, p. 94; F. W. Holland, Ms. *History of the American Peace Cause,* vol. i, p. 9.

[14] Ms. *Minutes of the New York Peace Society,* May, 1828, in archives of American Peace Society, Washington, D. C.; *Advocate of Peace,* vol. i, no. 3, December, 1837, p. 143; *Christian Citizen,* May 18, 1844.

[15] *Calumet,* vol. i, no. 8, July and August, 1832, p. 245; vol. ii, no. 5, January and February, 1835, p. 156; Valentine Nicholson to Martin Van Buren, Warren

By all odds the most important local association during this period was the Connecticut Peace Society, which did not become an auxiliary of the national organization. It was formed in 1831 by federating several local societies, which did not forfeit their independent existence. Members of Congress and of the federal and state governments received its pamphlets, and it sent peace addresses to the libraries of every American college. The Society's periodical, the *American Advocate of Peace,* took its place with the best American magazines in regard to subject matter, literary form, and appearance. In 1835, in fact, it became the organ of the American Peace Society, which moved its headquarters to Hartford and was thus all but captured by the Connecticut organization. Indeed, its annual reports show that it rivaled the accomplishments of the national society, both in the amount of literature circulated and in the number and size of its meetings. As many as twelve hundred attended its annual meeting in 1833, and the meeting of March 4, 1835, was the largest and most impressive peace demonstration held up to that time in America. The Connecticut Peace Society was also in correspondence with peace advocates in London, Paris, and Geneva.[16]

This remarkable record was the result of the work and enthusiasm of a small group of men, many of whom became interested in peace through William Ladd. The Reverend Samuel J. May, Thomas Gallaudet, the Reverend Francis Fellows, C. R. Henry, and, above all, William Watson, general agent of the Society, were chiefly responsible for its vigor. The manuscript diaries of William Watson show him to have been a most agile person of wide acquaintance and incredible energy.[17] Through

County, Ohio, August 14, 1848, in *Van Buren Papers,* vol. 55, Library of Congress; *Christian Citizen,* March 22, March 29, 1851.

[16] *Calumet,* vol. i, no. 9, September and October, 1832, pp. 268-270; *Advocate of Peace,* vol. i, no. 4, March, 1835, p. 194; *American Advocate of Peace,* vol. ii, no. 9, June, 1836, p. 43.

[17] These manuscript diaries are in the possession of Miss Elizabeth Dana, of Cambridge, Mass. Extracts are to be found in *New England Historical and Genealogical Register,* vol. lxxx, January, 1926.

his efforts every county in Connecticut had its peace organization by 1834. But as if by magic the Connecticut Peace Society vanished with the death of Watson in 1836. No one else could or would replace him. After 1836, therefore, the American Peace Society had none to rival it in the virgin fields open to cultivation, save the ephemeral societies whose life at best was precarious.

In its lonely battle to end war the American Peace Society tried to affect public opinion by winning as allies the churches, the press, and the colleges. Although a large proportion of life members of the Society were ministers, only a relatively small number of the American clergy were open advocates of peace. Ladd distributed an abundance of literature in theological schools and at ecclesiastical synods and considered a great point won in 1827 when he managed to form a peace society at the Andover Theological Seminary. By 1836 this work was telling, for "almost every ecclesiastical assembly in New England, and many out of it," had given "their testimony against war."[18] By 1838 it was claimed that more than a thousand ministers had pledged themselves to preach at least once a year on peace. Many women responded to the appeal to make their minister a life member of the American Peace Society. In 1840 William Ladd, traveling through Massachusetts and New York as far as Rochester, reported that pulpits were generally open to him, "a great advance on former times." Not long since, he observed, peace was considered a purely temporal subject, "not suitable for the Sabbath," and this testimony is borne out by the reports of other peace agents.[19] Though there was nothing like a thorough penetration of the churches, yet a substantial beginning had been made.

[18] William Ladd to Samuel J. May, March 1, June 11, 1827, in *Ladd Letter Book;* William Ladd, *History of the Peace Societies,* p. 189.

[19] *Advocate of Peace,* vol. ii, no. 1, June, 1838, p. 12; vol. i, no. 1, June, 1837, p. 12; vol. ii, no. 11, February, 1839, pp. 202, 213 ff.; vol. iii, no. 11, December, 1838, pp. 145 ff.; Hemmenway, Revised Ms. *Memoir of William Ladd,* pp. 91-92.

While the Congregational, Baptist, and Methodist denominations led in extending sympathy to the cause, the Quakers remained for the most part as detached and negative as they were during the earlier period. Ladd, confessing his inability to understand why Friends were so rarely enrolled as members of peace societies, appealed in the *Calumet* in 1833 for their support. When the distinguished British Friend, Joseph John Gurney, visited the United States in 1838, Ladd urged him to induce the American Friends to show their colors,[20] but except as individuals they did not coöperate with the peace societies. Some of the Quaker periodicals, it is true, now and then printed extracts from the peace societies' periodicals. The editor of *The Friend* suggested in 1830[21] that the American Peace Society, in not specifically condemning *all* wars, had taken a temporizing position, and this was apparently the only explanation offered by the Friends for their aloofness.

Scarcely less important than the Church as an ally was the press. By 1838 the *Advocate of Peace* reported that more than twenty religious periodicals were inserting articles on peace, some as often as once a week, and at about the same time Ladd was pleased to observe that the religious press was no longer, as formerly, "closed against this subject."[22] The secular press, however, was less sympathetic. Some of the educational journals showed their good intentions, and occasionally newspapers made out a mild case for the cause.[23] But by and large there was little headway in making capital of the secular press.

To stimulate the interest of college students Ladd for many years offered in several institutions prizes for the best essays on

[20] *Calumet*, vol. i, no. 15, September and October, 1833, pp. 449 ff.; *Advocate of Peace*, vol. ii, no. 9, February, 1839, p. 215.

[21] *The Friend*, vol. iii (1830), p. 10; see also, *The Friend or Advocate of Truth*, vol. viii, December 27, 1834, p. 96.

[22] Hemmenway, *Memoir of William Ladd*, p. 83.

[23] *Common School Journal*, vol. ii, November, 1840, p. 349; *Calumet*, vol. i, no. 1, May and June, 1831, p. 8; no. 6, March and April, 1832, p. 166; no. 10, November and December, 1832, p. 310; *Advocate of Peace*, vol. i, no. 1, June, 1837, pp. 32-33; vol. iii, no. 11, June, 1839, p. 6.

peace, and frequently visited colleges to talk on the subject so dear to him. According to Dr. Potter of Union College, the students never tired of hearing the anecdotes by which he made his point.[24] Nor were all these efforts fruitless, for peace societies appeared at Waterville College, Maine, at Dartmouth, at Middlebury, and at Amherst. At this last-named institution the society, which had been founded in 1836 and which numbered at the outset one hundred and forty members, students and instructors, held on each Fourth of July for several years a peace celebration with an appropriate address.[25] By 1835 Ladd's own Alma Mater, Harvard, reported "exercises and discussions" on peace, while at Union College one of the professors remarked that "no books in the library were in greater demand by the students than the volumes on peace." From the college at Georgetown, Kentucky, the President, a friend of the cause, wrote that "nearly every student of the college is on our side." At Oberlin College the cause of peace flourished along with other varieties of idealism, and the President of the college at Galesburg, Illinois, actively supported the movement. The secretary of the London society, desiring American college students to familiarize themselves with the problem, sent in 1841 a file of the *Herald of Peace* to Harvard College.[26]

Peace men also saw the value of controlling the textbooks which students read. William Jenks insisted that history must be rewritten "on peace principles" and advised that this be done "with matured experience, sterling talent, extensive reading, deep study and research."[27] In the *Common School Journal* Horace Mann pointed out the duty of educators to "preserve peace" by their instruction. It was not until 1852, apparently, that a history

---

[24] S. E. Coues, Ms. *Peace Album*, testimony of Aaron Foster.

[25] *American Advocate of Peace*, vol. ii, no. 10, September, 1836, p. 93.

[26] *Advocate of Peace*, vol. v, December, 1844, p. 286; vol. iv, July, 1843, p. 84; vol. v, November, 1844, p. 275; Ms. letter from the Rev. N. Morgan Harry, London, November 24, 1841, to "The Professors of Cambridge University," in vol. i, of *Herald of Peace*, in Harvard College Library.

[27] Coues, Ms. *Peace Album*, testimony of William Jenks, November 8, 1844.

distinctly written for the purpose of peace propaganda was put on the market.[28]

While seeking the churches, the press, and educational institutions as allies, the peace cause did not slight the development of pacifist arguments, and during this period constantly reiterated all those which Noah Worcester had marshaled earlier. There was no yielding in the contention that appeal to the sword was unscriptural; and more and more effort was made to reconcile the Old and New Testaments on the question of war. If God had commanded war in the Old Testament, it was employed as a special means of punishment, and there being no longer an equally clear command, the Gospel of Christ must take precedence. To others it was a thorn in the flesh that war brought violation of Sabbath observance, and they made much of the immoral character of the whole institution.[29]

Fighting was held to be unnatural as well as unscriptural. With much effectiveness the point was made that war was by no means an inevitable force in nature, like lightning, but that it rather depended solely on human custom, human opinion, and human feeling. Beasts, it was said, seldom fought their own species, as did men.[30]

With increasing frequency the relation between peace and other benevolent reforms assumed importance. In a well-thought-out article Professor L. P. Hickock argued that peace was an indispensable condition for the success of the antislavery, temperance, foreign-mission, and tractarian movements. When it was said that specific efforts for peace could be withheld, since, with the advance of Christianity, peace would triumph, there were those to reply that the same reasoning held just as truly in the case of temperance, slavery, and moral reform. The asso-

[28] *Common School Journal*, vol. i, July 15, 1839, p. 221; *Advocate of Peace*, vol. x, September, 1852, p. 160.

[29] Cyrus Yale, *War Unreasonable and Unscriptural*, Hartford, 1833; S. E. Coues, *War and Christianity*, Boston, 1842, *passim*.

[30] *Ibid.; Harbinger of Peace*, vol. i, no. 3, July, 1828, pp. 53 ff.

ciation between war and drunkenness further suggested that the causes of peace and temperance were closely akin.[31]

The appeal to history, begun in the earlier period, came in for elaboration. William Ladd loved to trace the history of war from before the Flood, contrasting its ill effects with the peace policy pursued by Numa Pompilius, ancient China, and the Loo-Choo Islanders, while descriptions of the horrors of Napoleon's battles continued to swamp the pages of the peace periodicals. Pacifists also studied the historical development of international law and hailed its progress since Grotius as full of promise for the ultimate victory of peace. At the same time they emphasized the growth of civil jurisprudence and its inroads on private war-- fare, feuds, and vengeance. From the records of the past, examples of the influence of military discipline in converting free citizens into slaves were piled up, and the testimony of warriors against war was made to render account.[32]

In the discussion of the relation of the peace argument to past conflicts, the outstanding question to be introduced was that of the Revolutionary War, which was first widely discussed during this period. It is true that as far back as 1821 Worcester had called in question that struggle and deprecated the sentiments promoted by erecting Bunker Hill Monument, and William Ladd had held women up to scorn for their part in sanctifying that "patriotic" spectacle. In this period, however, more direct evidence was brought forward to show how the Revolution had encouraged licentiousness, intemperance, and irreligion. Yet many peace advocates held with John Lord that the principles of the Revolution were so true and important that they had been worth the sacrifices. In 1841 the Reverend Sylvester Judd,

---

[31] *American Advocate of Peace*, vol. i, no. 3, December, 1834, pp. 105 ff.; *Calumet*, vol. ii, May and June, 1834, no. 1, p. 24; *Harbinger of Peace*, vol. ii, no. 10, February, 1830, pp. 232 ff.

[32] William Ladd, "A Brief Illustration of the Principles of War and Peace," *American Advocate of Peace*, vol. i, June, 1834, pp. 33-47; vol. i, no. 6, September, 1835, pp. 263 ff.; *Advocate of Peace*, vol. i, no. 4, March, 1838, "The Testimony of Statesmen Against War"; vol. iii, no. 3, October, 1839, pp. 67 ff.

of the Unitarian Church in Augusta, Maine, attacked the patriotic and blind exceptions made in lauding that struggle and was dismissed from his office as chaplain of the legislature.[33] His tract, *The Moral Evils of Our Revolutionary War,* widely circulated by the American Peace Society, touched some to the quick, and its influence among pacifists was so marked that but few continued to exonerate the Revolution.

One of the most important developments in the arguments in behalf of peace was the emphasis put on the special mission of the United States to lead a world crusade against war. "The free and enlightened citizens of America," said the Rev. N. S. Wheaton, "have given proof that they are breaking through the trammels of an accursed delusion, under which the world has lain spellbound for ages."[34] William Ladd never tired of reiterating the peculiar duty of the United States, free as they were from the incumbrances obstructing the march of the mind in the Old World, to cast off the shackles of war. Such was the burden of the argument of Samuel E. Coues in his articles in the *Democratic Review.* "It is in this country that the martial spirit has receieved its greatest check. It is here that the pacific principles will be first adopted." This was the more true, Coues continued, because war ran counter to the democratic principle of elevating the people, to which principle America was above all else devoted.[35] No nation, William Jay argued, had less reason to covet possessions of others or to apprehend loss of her own, and none could experiment with peace with greater

[33] *Friend of Peace,* vol. iii, no. 2, p. 65; Hemmenway, Revised Ms. *Memoir of William Ladd,* p. 477 ff.; *Advocate of Peace,* vol. iii. no. 4, December, 1839, pp. 73 ff.; John Lord, *Address to the Peace Society of Amherst,* July 4, 1839; *Advocate of Peace,* vol. iv, no. 7, June, 1842, p. 156; Sylvester Judd, *A Moral Review of the Revolutionary War;* F. W. Holland, Ms. *History of the American Peace Cause,* vol. ii, p. 49; Ms. *Minutes of the Executive Committee of the American Peace Society,* May 23, 1842.

[34] N. S. Wheaton, *Address before the Hartford Peace Society,* p. 6.

[35] *Calumet,* vol. i, no. 7, May and June, 1832, p. 217; S. E. Coues, in the *Democratic Review,* vol. x (1842), p. 116.

advantage.[36] This special peace mission of the United States was vividly put by Walt Whitman,[37] but it was Emerson who in 1838 in his *Address on War* filled up the measure. "Not in an obscure corner, not in a feudal Europe, not in an antiquated appanage where no onward step can be taken without rebellion, is this seed of benevolence laid in the furrow, with tears of hope; but in this broad America of God and man, where the forest is only now falling, or yet to fall, and the green earth opened to the inundation of emigrant men from all quarters of oppression and guilt; here, where not a family, not a few men, but mankind, shall say what shall be; here, we ask, Shall it be War, or shall it be Peace?"[38] Instances of such an appeal to the American "mission" to elevate mankind could be multiplied, and similar arguments were being advanced by temperance workers. Although now and then an English or a French pacifist found reasons why his country was peculiarly destined to introduce peace to the world, such arguments were less frequent in the Old World.[39] This fact suggests that the peace movement in America bore a direct relationship to the American philosophy of the uplift of the common man and to the self-consciousness with which Americans repeated that conviction.

Another important development in this period was the increasing attention given to economic arguments against war, which Worcester and others in the early period had treated in a rather general way. On the basis of Federal Treasury Reports the expenses of the military and naval establishments and the amount of the public debt due to war were calculated and set forth in simple and telling terms. Strong appeals to the laboring

[36] William Jay, *War and Peace: the Evils of the First and a Plan for Securing the Last*, p. 79.

[37] Cleveland Rogers and John Black, *The Gathering of the Forces*, vol. i, p. 250 (editorial in the *Brooklyn Eagle*, November 16, 1846).

[38] R. W. Emerson, *Works*, vol. ii, p. 552, "A Lecture Delivered in March, 1838."

[39] *Herald of Peace*, vol. iii, February, 1821, p. 53; F. Duran, *Des Tendances Pacifiques de la Société Européenne et du Rôle des Armées dans l'avenir*, vol. i, p. 214.

man urged him to consider specifically what the average worker paid for the war system, while elaborate analyses of statistical evidence in regard to war and its effects on the wealth of nations marked a real advance over the earlier loose and general indictments.[40]

While arguments against war were thus being rounded out, plans for substitutes for war did not at all lag behind. In general, the seventeenth and eighteenth century projects for a federation of nations advocated either a perpetual and forcible union or an ineffective and entirely voluntary association, and thus, opposed as they were to existing conditions, they lacked a substantial basis for erecting realistic structures.[41] It remained for Americans to develop these plans, to work out details in a practical way, to popularize them, and to take steps for their realization. Indeed, the earlier European plans for a Congress of Nations became so metamorphosed in the hands of the Americans that Europeans in the first half of the nineteenth century generally spoke of the resultant scheme for a Congress and Court of Nations as "the American plan." In this work William Ladd was preëminent, though he was not the only important figure.

It was not until the foundation of the American Peace Society that any official action was taken on a Congress of Nations, though, as we have seen, Noah Worcester in the *Solemn Review* suggested a Congress of Nations "to devise means for organizing a High Tribunal for the adjustment of disputes," to "agree on reciprocal terms for the reduction of standing armies and navies," and "to form a solemn compact that in the future no armed force by sea or land shall be employed by one nation for the annoyance of another." Since one of the objects of the

---

[40] *Harbinger of Peace*, vol. ii, no. 9, January, 1830, pp. 193 ff.; *American Advocate of Peace*, vol. i, June, 1834, pp. 19 ff.; George W. Beckwith, *The Peace Manual*, p. 27; William Jay, *War and Peace*, p. 17; Samuel E. Coues, Ms. *Notebook*, Lecture 3, "Avarice and Other Causes of War" (American Peace Society).

[41] For a brief but excellent summary of these early projects see James Brown Scott, *Introduction* to his edition of *An Essay on a Congress of Nations by William Ladd*, xi-xxxviii.

American Peace Society from the first had been to work towards this end, it was appropriate for an early number of its periodical to print a prize essay on a Congress of Nations, crude and sketchy in comparison with later plans, but none the less important as the first dissertation on such a subject ever published in America. In 1832 Ladd himself brought out a pamphlet discussing the project, which, though lacking the details of his subsequent essay on the same subject, none the less deeply interested Chief Justice Marshall, who found the argument, if not conclusive, at least "well arranged and well supported." From 1830 to 1833 Methodist, Congregational, and Baptist organizations in Massachusetts approved the idea of a Congress of Nations, urged ministers to speak on the subject, and advised peace societies to submit memorials to Congress for such an end.[42]

As a result of a petition from William Ladd and Thomas Thompson asking for an expression of opinion on a Congress of Nations, the Massachusetts Senate adopted resolutions advising the establishment of some mode of just arbitration for all international disputes and requesting the governor to invite other states to advance the object in view. This was the first legislative action in the United States, and probably in the world, distinctly favorable to a Congress of Nations. In 1837 and in 1838 both houses of the Massachusetts legislature adopted similar resolutions by overwhelming majorities; and in addition these resolutions called the attention of the President of the United States to the subject, recommending "a negotiation with such other governments, as in its wisdom it may deem proper, with a view to effect so important an arrangement."[43]

---

[42] *Harbinger of Peace*, vol. i, no. 1, May, 1828, p. 10; vol. iii, nos. 9-10, January and February, 1831, pp. 193-223; *Calumet*, vol. i, no. 10, November and December, 1832, p. 290.

[43] *Harbinger of Peace*, vol. ii, no. 11, March, 1830. p. 254; vol. iii. no. 2, June, 1830, pp. 31 ff.; *Advocate of Peace*, vol. vi, November, 1845, p. 124; *Massachusetts Senate Documents*, 1837, Document 94; *Massachusetts Resolves*, 1834-1838, p. 762.

It was the New York Society, however, which, early in the year 1837, anticipated the national organization in carrying the subject of a Congress of Nations, through memorials, to the legislative branch of the federal government. Presently petitions from these societies, as well as from others and from 135 members of the Legislature of Massachusetts, bearing in all 1427 signatures, were sent to the House, and a number to the Senate as well. For the most part the memorials to the House were forwarded to John Quincy Adams, who reported that they were "viewed by the majority of the House with great jealousy, as abolition petitions, or petitions against the annexation of Texas, in disguise." On June 13, 1838, Legaré, of the House Committee on Foreign Affairs, ended a report on a number of these memorials by a resolution discharging the Committee from a further consideration of the subject. It thought the establishment of a permanent international tribunal "under the present circumstances of the world" undesirable. Ladd felt that this report showed how little public men understood the subject, but he was not discouraged.[44]

When an able memorial refuting Legaré's reasoning was presented to the House the following year, it was clear that the project was not to be laid on the shelf. In April, 1839, just after the close of the session in which for the second time peace memorials for a Congress of Nations came to naught, William Ladd interviewed members of Congress, heads of departments, and the President himself. Van Buren felt that it would be unwise for the American government to suggest such a plan to the Cabinets of Europe until they were sufficiently enlightened on the subject to receive the proposal with favor.[45]

Despite these discouragements American friends of a Congress of Nations urged their English colleagues to follow their

[44] William Ladd, *Essay on a Congress of Nations,* p. 69; F. W. Holland, Ms. *History of the American Peace Cause,* vol. i, pp. 36-37; *Congressional Globe,* 25 Cong., 2 sess., vol. vi, Senate, March 19, 1838, pp. 245, 449; *Reports of Committees,* no. 979, 25 Cong., 2 sess.

[45] *Memoirs of John Quincy Adams,* vol. x, p. 97; *Cong. Globe,* 25 Cong., 3 sess., January 17, 1839; *Advocate of Peace,* vol. ii, no. 11, April, 1839, p. 264.

example and memorialize Parliament. Such suggestions were evidently effective, for in 1839 the London Peace Society petitioned Parliament to take steps towards the establishment of a Congress of Nations, but apparently they might as well have spared their pains.[46]

To further the campaign of education on this subject of an international tribunal, two friends of peace in 1833 offered a premium of one thousand dollars for the best essay on a Congress of Nations. The committee, consisting of ex-President Adams, Chancellor Kent, and Daniel Webster, could not agree on the successful competitor, and the American Peace Society printed the best five of the forty essays submitted. William Ladd, after reading all the essays, took from those not chosen for the volume such ideas and illustrations as seemed worth preserving and wove these into his own classic *Essay on a Congress of Nations*. This was the sixth essay in the volume on the Congress of Nations, published by the American Peace Society in 1840. It was by far the most important contribution to the volume.[47]

Ladd, indeed, claimed that his only originality lay in having separated the subject into two distinct parts, which were, first, a Congress of Ambassadors from all civilized nations for the purpose of settling the principles of international law by compact and agreement and of devising and promoting plans for the preservation of peace; and second, a Court of Nations, composed of the most able civilians of the world, to arbitrate such cases as should be brought before it by the mutual consent of two or more contending parties. Such a separation of judicial from diplomatic functions, Ladd felt, would obviate previous objec-

[46] *Advocate of Peace,* vol. ii, no. 11, April, 1839, pp. 262-263; vol. iii, no. 3, October, 1839, p. 61; Ms. *Minutes of the Executive Committee of the American Peace Society,* September 20, 1838. The London Society was officially requested to coöperate with the American Peace Society by petitioning Parliament for a Congress of Nations.

[47] *Calumet,* vol. i, no. 13, May to June, 1833, p. 414; New York *Observer,* July 6, 1833; Ladd, "Advertisement," in *Prize Essays on a Congress of Nations,* Boston, 1840.

tions to similar schemes: the Court could not be controlled by a political body. This original contribution to international thought played a part in the arguments for America's rejection of the League of Nations and for her reservations to the World Court protocol. Ladd also recognized the impracticability of providing armed forces by which the projected international organization might enforce decisions against recalcitrant members. In a careful analysis Dr. James Brown Scott has pointed out that Ladd's plan was, in all its essentials, realized in the Hague Conference of 1899 and the resulting tribunal.[48] Any attempt to summarize this realistic, practical, and carefully planned scheme is unnecessary because of its conciseness and accessibility. If William Ladd had done nothing but write this essay, his place in the history of the peace movement would have been a significant one. As Elihu Burritt said, Ladd was the first to give an American shaping to the idea of an international assembly.[49]

In circulating the volume of *Prize Essays* Ladd stopped at nothing. Copies were sent to the President of the United States, the heads of departments, the governors of the states, the foreign ministers at Washington, and to the cabinets of the Latin American states and to those of Europe. All but two of the foreign ministers at Washington received the volume with fine words. The Danish representative said that it would mark an era in "the cause of peace and human improvement." Palmerston wrote to Ladd that her Majesty was graciously pleased with the *Essays*. Although the London Peace Society printed ten thousand copies of Ladd's own essay, British pacifists did not in general take to the idea. It seemed to them to be like the wings of the wind, and few would have agreed with John Quincy Adams's remark to Ladd that the project would be realized within twenty years.[50]

[48] James Brown Scott, *Introduction to an Essay on a Congress of Nations,* William Ladd, iv, xxxix, xl, xliii.

[49] Elihu Burritt's "Introductory Notes" to John Hemmenway's *Memoir of William Ladd,* p. 14.

[50] Hemmenway, *Memoir of William Ladd,* pp. 86-87; *Advocate of Peace,* vol. iii, no. 11, February, 1841, p. 259; no. 24, August, 1840, p. 182.

Yet the publication of the *Prize Essays* stimulated activity. Several periodicals spoke of the project. Petitions to Congress continued, and J. L. O'Sullivan introduced in 1842 into the New York Assembly resolutions urging the federal executive to act. But the petitions came to nothing, and O'Sullivan's resolutions were tabled.[51] April 9, 1841 found William Ladd almost at the end of a wearisome nine months' journey through the Middle States and west as far as Buffalo, a journey made chiefly to popularize the idea of a Congress of Nations. He had anticipated this venture for six or seven years. Despite his wretched physical condition not a day passed without tremendous exertions—exertions which physicians warned him would hasten the end. At Canandaigua, New York, his legs were so badly ulcerated that he had to ask for a stool on which to sit in the pulpit. But he did not fear death in the field. "If men will venture their lives to procure some earthly good, which will soon perish with the use, why should I be unwilling to risk my life in the cause of that dear Redeemer who laid down his life for me?" Well could the secretary of the London Peace Society, writing from England, beg him, for the sake of the cause of peace throughout the world, not to be "so incessant in the harness." Two days after the letter was written, Ladd, sick as he was, addressed a huge audience in Boston. The next day he died.[52]

Had William Ladd lived, a Congress of Nations would certainly have been urged more vigorously than it was by the Reverend George C. Beckwith, on whom his mantle fell. When, however, Elihu Burritt became interested in the peace movement, Ladd's plan appealed to him as the most practicable undertaking the movement had sponsored, and both in this country and in Europe he was to do for it yeoman's service.

[51] *Christian Examiner*, vol. xxix, September, 1840, pp. 83 ff.; *American Review*, vol. v, no. 4, April, 1847, pp. 341 ff.; *Advocate of Peace*, vol. iv, no. 3, October, 1841, p. 67.
[52] Hemmenway, Revised Ms. *Memoir of William Ladd*, pp. 214 ff., 525-530.

At the same time that American peace sentiment had entered the political forum to work for a Congress of Nations, it continued to take issue with passing political events. For the most part peace men regretted the use of force in the Revolutions of 1830, even though much was at stake. To the realistic editors of the *American Advocate of Peace* it appeared that true and reasonable freedom was an indispensable condition for world peace, and they felt, therefore, that the Revolutions of 1830 were a step towards that end. In England the position of the editor of the *Herald of Peace* closely resembled that of the American peace group.[53]

Close on the heels of the Revolutions of 1830 came the threat of civil war in the South Carolina nullification controversy. Though friends of peace generally refused to enter into discussion of the merits of the question, they agreed that the affair both tested the extent and energy of pacific opinion and demanded their remonstrances. One of the members of the American Peace Society, Thomas S. Grimké of Charleston, South Carolina, a distinguished philanthropist and classical scholar, urged his fellow citizens to remember that civil contest was "absolutely and unchangeably antirepublican," and that the character of the warrior, from every point of view, was unchristian. He concluded his appeal by resolving never to bear arms in a civil contest. Although he had good reason to fear that his house would be attacked because of the pacifist sentiments in a pamphlet addressed to the leaders of the nullification movement, Grimké held his ground, making it clear that he deprecated the show of federal coercion quite as much as he disapproved South Carolina's military threats.[54] It was believed at the time in peace

<hr/>

[53] *Calumet*, vol. i, no. 2, July and August, 1831, p. 39; William H. Channing, *Memoir of William Ellery Channing*, vol. iii, p. 300; *Harbinger of Peace*, vol. iii, no. 11, March, 1831, pp. 241 ff.; *American Advocate of Peace*, vol. i, no. 2, September, 1834, pp. 73 ff.

[54] *Calumet*, vol. i, no. 12, March and April, 1833, pp. 358 ff.; no. 13, May and June, 1833, pp. 393-394. For a sketch of Grimké's life see *Calumet*, vol. ii, no. 5, January and February, 1835; T. S. Grimké, *To the People of the State of*

circles that his efforts were in no small measure responsible for averting a catastrophe, and whether or not justified, this belief was significant, for it encouraged pacifists to take a stronger stand in succeeding episodes which threatened war.

No sooner had the nullification affair calmed down than war clouds descended upon the country as a result of the French claims controversy. William Ellery Channing appeared before his people with an eloquent discourse on behalf of peace, while Francis Fellows pointed out, in the *American Advocate of Peace,* that a fight costing more than the total debt was ridiculous. He insisted that the controversy could have been settled if President Jackson had outlined the case dispassionately, and then said: "We address the citizens of France as our brethren. We invoke them to dispel the clouds of party prejudice and passion from their national councils and to cause justice to be done to us, their friends."[55]

Nor were European friends of peace entirely unconcerned. From Geneva a new champion of the cause, the Count de Sellon, suggested that an effort be made to induce both parties to consent to mediation by the King of Prussia. Apparently the Société de la Morale Chrétienne did not lift its hand, nor is there any evidence that the London Peace Society, worried though it was lest France and the United States engage in war, stimulated King William IV's informal offer of mediation. His action was commended by the American Peace Society, and its official communication to him was courteously answered by Palmerston.[56]

From 1837 to 1839 the claims of French and American creditors against Mexico led to another war scare. Peace petitions

---

South Carolina, p. 16; *Letter to John C. Calhoun, Robert Hayne, George Mc-Duffie, James Hamilton, Jr.,* p. 11; *Calumet,* vol. i, no. 17, January and February, 1834, p. 516.

[55] W. H. Channing, *Memoir of William Ellery Channing,* vol. iii, p. 21; Channing, *Works,* pp. 654-664; *American Advocate of Peace,* vol. i, no. 5, June, 1835, pp. 202 ff.

[56] *American Advocate of Peace,* vol. i, no. 5, June, 1835, p. 250; *Advocate of Peace,* vol. i, no. 2, September, 1837, p. 96.

to Congress and to President Van Buren urged the American government to accede to the Mexican proposal of arbitrating the claims against that power and to suggest arbitration between France and Mexico for an adjustment of French claims. According to John Quincy Adams, it was the petitions from the New York Peace Society which first called the attention of the federal government to the fact that the Mexican Congress had authorized their executive to agree with the United States for such an arbitration. If the peace societies, continued Adams, had never rendered any other service to their country, they would have deserved the thanks of the whole nation for this. What Adams said is substantiated by debates in the House of Representatives and by the fact that the Mexican minister sent a hundred dollars to the New York Peace Society with his expression of thanks for its instrumentality in causing, indirectly, the American government to accept the Mexican suggestion.[57] At the same time that the American peace movement was making these efforts to prevent war with Mexico over the claims question, its leading spokesmen were deprecating the war fever excited by the Texan rebellion.

During this period the shocking pictures of our conduct in the war against the Florida Indians continued to find a prominent place in the pages of peace publications. To prove the crass extravagance of American army officers extracts were made from quartermasters' reports, while evidence was brought forth to show that the war was protracted because of contractors' speculation. At least one Georgian raised his voice in public against the Seminole War, and his arguments were those of a pacifist. Was it not a shame, asked the editor of the *Calumet*, to create "an American Poland" by dispossessing the Cherokees and to ex-

---

[57] *Senate Journal*, 25 Cong., 2 sess., p. 511, p. 544; *House Journal*, 25 Cong., 2 sess., p. 1028; *House Document*, no. 50, 25 Cong., 2 sess.; *House Journal*, February 14, 1838, 25 Cong., 2 sess., p. 407; *Van Buren Papers* vol. xxxii, Origen Bachelor to President Van Buren June 6, 1837; *Congressional Globe*, 25 Cong., 2 sess., vol. vi, pp. 31, 54, 62-63; *Memorials of John Quincy Adams*, vol. ix, pp. 458-459; *Advocate of Peace*, vol. ii, no. 9, February, 1839, p. 214.

terminate a people at home, while lamenting the downtrodden Greeks or Poles in Europe?[58]

Nor did the peace men dodge the connection between their cause and that of the abolition of slavery. Abolitionists appeared more responsive to the appeals of peace than any other group, which seemed to show that all reforms went forward together. This alliance, which John Quincy Adams's peace address on July 4, 1837, strengthened, might have continued had it not been for the antislavery riot at Alton, Illinois, in that very year, a riot in which Lovejoy used force to defend his press and met his death. This use of force the editor of the *Advocate of Peace* could not sanction; and even amongst the abolitionists themselves there was opposition to the abandonment of the pacific policy of the Antislavery Society. Persons like the Reverend Samuel J. May, Sarah Grimké, Lewis Tappan, and, in a less clear-cut way William Ellery Channing, finding their pacifism and antislavery sentiments in conflict, deprecated the use of force even for the sake of the Negro.[59]

The same issue aroused the antislavery men in England, many of whom also held pacifist principles. Joseph Sturge shrank from supporting the new antislavery society of Liverpool unless it outlawed resort to arms. Thus leading peace men met the public questions which faced them without singeing their wings, and, as their behavior in the French claims question went to show, forged ahead in their determination to stay the war tide.[60]

As the American peace men became more active and resolute at home, they also carried on with increasing zeal their correspondence with the London Peace Society. In 1830 two British

[58] *Advocate of Peace*, vol. ii, no. 5, October, 1838, p. 113; vol. iv, no. 2, August, 1841, p. 45; John L. Flournoy, *An Earnest Appeal to Peace*, Athens, Ga., 1838; *Calumet*, vol. i, no. 9, September and October, 1832, p. 263.

[59] J. Q. Adams, *Oration at Newburyport*, July 4, 1837, in *Advocate of Peace*, vol. i, no. 2, September, 1837, pp. 86 ff.; vol. ii, no. 3, August, 1838, pp. 57-58, 60, 67.

[60] Henry Richard, *Memoirs of Joseph Sturge*, London, 1864, pp. 207-208.

peace advocates accepted honorary membership in the American Peace Society, and in both countries the leaders took courage from each other's work. Having larger resources the British made great headway, so that in 1837 the corresponding secretary of the London Society could write Ladd that it was astonishing to see "what a change has been effected during the past ten years." In 1835, a typical year, subscriptions reached £514, while 47,795 copies of publications were sent out.[61] Possibly petitions to Parliament in 1836 expressing pleasure at the recent mediation offered by Great Britain in the Franco-American claims question and asking for an extension of such a policy may have suggested the action of the New York and other peace societies in 1837-1838. On the other hand, it would be hard to overemphasize the stimulus which the Americans gave to the British workers in the cause. In 1838 the London Society adopted the American precedent of employing a special agent to distribute literature and to lecture. Ladd's congratulatory letter to William IV for having offered mediation between the United States and France in the claims dispute was hailed as "one of the most auspicious events in the history" of the peace movement.[62]

While British and American friends of the cause thus saw eye to eye with each other, there was a tendency for the French Society of Christian Morals to go its own way, a tendency entirely natural, perhaps, since peace was but one of its aims. The London Peace Society kept up its end by sending its publications, but the Parisians gave them little publicity, nor were they more active in keeping in touch with the Americans.[63]

On the other hand the work of the Count de Sellon at Geneva proved a real compensation for the indifference of the Society of Christian Morals. This genuine philanthropist formed the Geneva Peace Society in 1830, taking his cue from information

[61] *American Advocate of Peace*, vol. i, no. 5, June, 1835, p. 220; *Advocate of Peace*, vol. i, no. 1, June, 1837, p. 19.

[62] *Advocate of Peace*, vol. i, no. 3, December, 1837, pp. 139, 141-142.

[63] *Calumet*, vol. ii, no. 6, March and April, 1835, p. 20; *Advocate of Peace*, vol. iii, no. 11, June, 1839, p. 3.

about similar societies in America and England. Its periodical, *Archives de la Société de la Paix de Genève,* paid tribute to fellow workers abroad and encouraged them to feel that a second line of defense was taking shape on the Continent. Probably American enthusiasts were oversanguine in choosing to think that the activity of this pacifist member of the sovereign council of Geneva prevented the outbreak of a threatened civil war in Switzerland. But it was natural for them to make the most of his communications with the potentates of Europe on the subject of general disarmament and systematic recourse to arbitration, and to approve his contest for a prize essay on the establishment of a permanent and universal tribunal for keeping the peace. These and other activities took on the more validity when reported directly to Americans by Henry Barnard, a young Connecticut educator, whom de Sellon cordially received at Geneva.[64] The death of de Sellon in 1839 was a real blow to the American foes of war. Decades were to pass before Americans interested in world peace again turned their eyes towards Geneva with an equal expectation. In the interval many battles were to be fought, and none was more dramatic than one within the ranks of the movement itself.

[64] *Calumet,* vol. i, no. 3, September and October, 1831, p. 74; no. 16, November and December, 1833, pp. 500 ff.; no. 11, January and February, 1833, pp. 329-330; no. 13, May and June, 1833, p. 402; *American Advocate of Peace,* vol. ii, no. 10, September, 1836, pp. 81-84.

IV

THE LIMITS OF PACIFISM

THE PEACE movement, like the temperance crusade, had its moderates and its extremists. The friends of peace were never unanimous in their attitude towards defensive war, and therefore the American Peace Society only haltingly advanced towards the position of condemning *all* wars, whether offensive or defensive. The period preceding this nailing of the flag to the topmast was marked by an active conflict of ideas. On the one hand this conflict helped to clarify the pacifist position, but on the other hand it led to a dissipation of energy and finally to a rupture within the peace movement.

As long as the movement was dominated by Noah Worcester and the Massachusetts Peace Society, the moderates, who admitted the Scriptural legality and justifiableness of defensive wars, more than held the field. Indeed, Joshua P. Blanchard later observed that he had the "misfortune to be alone among the respected founders of the cause in Boston" in his thoroughgoing stand of condemning all wars.[1] His colleagues, in merely denouncing war in general terms, thus differed both from the London Peace Society and from Dodge, who from the first had taken the ground that all war was contrary to Christianity. Dodge claimed the half-heartedness of the Massachusetts Peace Society as an excuse for not working very vigorously with it. At Philadelphia, as we have seen, the *Friend* referred to the half-way convictions of many peace societies as a cause of Quaker indifference towards them.

It was perhaps the temperate personality of Worcester which kept him from committing himself squarely on the issue of defensive war. Though the *Friend of Peace* for the most part kept silent on this question, its editor in 1822 admitted into the pages of his periodical—and perhaps even wrote—a Socratic dia-

[1] Coues, Ms. *Peace Album,* testimony of J. P. Blanchard.

logue between "Erasmus" and "Beza."[2] The latter clearly went to the wall in his attempted support of defensive war. "Erasmus" held that every combatant always insisted that he was waging defensive war, and that the term therefore was without any meaning. When it was argued that men might lose their lives by the hand of violence while obeying the laws of love, it was shown that they might also meet with a similar fate while violating those laws on the pretext of self-preservation.

William Ellery Channing, on the contrary, had no sympathy whatever with the doctrine of non-resistance, whether applied to individuals or to nations. He felt that the doctrine would retard the cause of peace in the public mind.[3] Yet he made it plain that he was even less willing to tie himself to the "over-prudent peace men who, loud and zealous in hours of tranquility, are unseen and unheard in times of peril." He maintained that the presumption was always against the necessity and justice of war and that an individual must refuse to support a war if in his conscience it was not justified by "unquestionable wrongs which, as patient trial has proved, can in no other way be redressed."[4]

As for Ladd, his position for some time after his conversion to the peace cause in the early twenties resembled that of this great Unitarian divine. But about 1830 a study of the Bible seems to have brought about a change of opinion. According to Elihu Burritt, Ladd found that by admitting the right of defensive war he stood not on the rocks but on the sands, for the inch he allowed brought in all the evils that a Bonaparte could desire.[5] For even that instigator of wars suavely contended that they were all defensive! Yet it was by no means easy for Ladd to come to the conclusion that *all* war was unlawful for a Christian.

[2] *Friend of Peace*, vol. iii, no. 6, p. 169.

[3] W. H. Channing, *Memoir of William Ellery Channing*, vol. iii, pp. 18-20.

[4] William Ellery Channing in the *Advocate of Peace*, vol. vii, March and April, 1847, p. 28.

[5] Elihu Burritt, *Introductory Notes to Memoir of William Ladd*, pp. 12-13, and pp. 58-59.

As late as 1833 Henry C. Wright, a thorough Non-Resistant, felt that Ladd needed more "sternness and earnestness in showing up all war, and rebuking all who tolerate it."[6] It is not unlikely that Wright, who during this period frequently urged on Ladd the radical position, deepened his growing conviction that defensive war was itself indefensible.

Under Ladd's editorship the *Harbinger of Peace* reflected the position of the American Peace Society. The Society, its founder explained in 1830, neither approved nor condemned wars "strictly defensive, if carried on with Christian principles." He hastened to add that there had never been such a war and that in too many instances members of peace societies merited reproaches because of their temporizing stand. While the third number of the *Harbinger* printed a sermon by Dr. Appleton admitting the right of defensive war, it gave more space to the refutation, which appealed to Biblical argument and which pointed to the peaceful career of Penn's colony.[7]

Although the Connecticut group of peace men preferred, like the American Peace Society, to let members differ quietly in their views on this subject, several factors determined that the controversy begun in the *Harbinger* should be threshed out in its successor, the *Calumet*. One was the visit of H. C. Howells, an Englishman, during the year 1832. This British pacifist's keen logic convinced some of the hesitating friends of the cause that war in every form was incompatible with Christianity.[8] At the same time the writings of the British Quaker, Jonathan Dymond, were coming to be better known in America. His thorough-going condemnation of all war converted Thomas S. Grimké, of Charleston, South Carolina, to the same position; and Grimké, by preparing an American edition of Dymond's *Inquiry into the Accordancy of War with the Principles of Christianity*, stimulated widespread interest in that doctrinaire

---

[6] H. C. Wright, *Autobiography*, Boston, 1849, p. 328.
[7] *Harbinger of Peace*, vol. ii, no. 12, April 30, 1830, pp. 283-284.
[8] *Calumet*, vol. i, no. 7, May and June, 1832, p. 211.

pacifist. Dymond's *Essays on the Principles of Christian Morali-ties,* which left no place in Christian ethics for any kind of war, began to replace Paley's *Evidences* as a text in seminaries.[9] In preparing an address which he delivered at New Haven, May 6, 1832, Grimké drew freely from Dymond and courageously attacked the American Revolution, a sensitive point to all patriots. A steady and protracted appeal to the magnanimity of the British people, Grimké contended, would have enlisted them in our favor. This address stirred the waters of the peace movement. In commenting on it, the *Calumet* sympathetically reminded its readers that there was no natural connection between war and independence and that even independence was not always a blessing, as the case of Ireland and Scotland bore witness.[10] Though in the same breath the *Calumet* reiterated the position of the American Peace Society, which merely declared that war was an evil which it was the duty of all men to combat, it was clear that the controversy as to the limits of pacifism had entered a new stage.

The *Calumet* was open to both the moderates and the radicals. To the ranks of the latter came the Reverend R. V. Rogers of Circleville, Ohio, who tendered effective aid in 1833. Rogers gained a point by admitting that the Scriptures said nothing definitely about defensive war, but he maintained at the same time that their whole spirit opposed it. The injunction in Luke, "He that hath no sword, let him sell his garment and buy one," was interpreted by this Episcopalian divine in a figurative sense. Later, when the sword had been used, Rogers reminded his readers of Jesus' words, "Put up thy sword into its place, for all they that take the sword shall perish by the sword."[11] It was from England, however, that the radicals had most comfort. The *Calumet* culled any number of arguments from the *Herald*

[9] *Ibid.,* vol. ii, no. 2, July and August, 1834, p. 42; J. Gurney, *A Voyage to North America,* Norwich, England, 1841, p. 238.

[10] *Calumet,* vol. i, no. 8, July and August, 1832, pp. 232-233.

[11] *Ibid.,* no. 14, July and August, 1833, p. 442.

of Peace, some of which were highly evangelical. It was pointed out that forcible resistance to aggression might involve the awful responsibility of sending a man to eternity in the midst of his sin. If a whole nation refused to fight the invader, it would involve a sublime martyrdom and an earlier entrance into Heaven![12]

Perhaps the ablest champion of defensive war was Dr. William Allen, president of Bowdoin College. This scholar undertook to refute Grimké's argument in an article entitled "Defensive War Vindicated," which the *Calumet* printed early in 1834. Making free use of Scriptural texts to prove that the Bible sanctioned wars of defense, this paper further maintained that Thomas Clarkson had totally failed to prove his propositions regarding the abstinence of early Christians from war. With much force Dr. Allen held that there was no judgment of a conclusive nature on this point during the first two centuries of Christianity. Turning to the argument by example, he insisted that the security of the Quakers in Ireland in 1798 and in colonial America did not merit such broad conclusions as those of Hancock, Dymond, and Grimké. Perhaps Allen's strongest ground was his skillful maintenance of the right of defensive war as a principle of political science. Both by Scripture and by historical experience the magistrate was, he maintained, justified in using the sword against evil doers; and he referred to piracy as an outstanding example of an evil that should be suppressed by force.[13]

Though Ladd, who at this time had only a nominal connection with the *Calumet,* had doubted the wisdom of printing Allen's article, those in immediate charge of the periodical held that both sides deserved a candid hearing. Hence the conservative had to reckon with the rebuttal of Grimké. Turning his attention chiefly to Allen's insistence on the right of civil magistrates to protect the community, Grimké maintained that there

[12] *Ibid.,* pp. 333 ff.
[13] *Ibid.,* no. 17, pp. 524 ff., "Defensive War Vindicated."

was a great difference between the operations of a government within its own jurisdiction and in its foreign relations. An individual residing under a government was held to a contract to obey it or to pay forfeiture. But there was no such contract between governments. If an individual trespassed on laws, he was tried by a judge and jury of his peers. In war, on the other hand, a nation was judge, jury, and executioner. War was thus not at all comparable to capital punishment. Grimké went on to urge that even if it were analogous, still the so-called right of government to take life was not itself a mathematical axiom, but open to question, from the point of view of both ethics and expediency.[14] Grimké's views, challenging as they did the theory that human life was at the mercy of the state, were indeed forward looking.

This South Carolinian's prediction that before many years the principle of the wrongfulness of defensive war would become an article in the constitution of the American Peace Society was, in fact, prophetic. In the early months of 1835, when Grimké's arguments appeared in the *Calumet,* its editor announced that the majority of those who conducted the affairs of the national peace society were decidedly opposed to all war, offensive and defensive, although many of the local peace organizations still felt that defensive war could be conducted on Christian principles. The Massachusetts Peace Society, for one, refused in 1834 to condemn defensive wars. On the other hand, the new Bowdoin Street Peace Society of Boston in 1835 took the extreme position.[15] Ardent peace men increasingly believed that the failure of the movement to arouse the sort of opposition essential for the healthy growth of any proselyting reform was due to the temporizing position of organized pacifism. The *Military and Naval Gazette of the United States* all but ignored the peace movement. Hardly a report of an agent of a peace society came in that did not lament the prevalent apathy towards the cause.

[14] *Ibid.,* vol. ii, no. 6, March and April, 1835, pp. 165 ff.
[15] Coues, Ms. *Peace Album.*

It was felt that while a mere general disapproval of war permitted military leaders and kings to adhere to the cause, stricter ground might stimulate opposition and growth. The emphasis on the evils of war, which were generally acknowledged, was said to have served the cause as much as it was capable of doing. Henry C. Wright told Ladd in 1833 that if the American Peace Society would take the responsibility for the logical deductions from the peace argument and declare against *all* war, the question would "shake the world as nothing else ever has."[16]

Radicals found other reasons for believing that the wind was blowing in their direction and that the peace movement must bring itself to outlaw defensive war. In the spring of 1835 the influential *Christian Examiner* held that the "nominal division of wars into aggressive and defensive has long presented a barrier to the diffusion of right ideas on the subject." The only distinction was in reality "a greater and lesser degree of provocation," and this journal claimed that the path of peace would almost inevitably be the path of safety.[17] It was this difficulty of drawing the line between defensive and offensive war which gave point to the position of the extremists. As Stebbins put it, "men see wars right, when they think they are in their interest. The fact that, in war, might gives right, makes it impossible to define defensive war."[18]

Yet there can be little doubt that a large body of the friends of peace was not ready for a formal assumption of this logical ground. After an agency of three months in Connecticut in 1836 the Reverend William Ely reported that there was no opposition to the course the Peace Society had pursued in avoiding commitment on the issue of defensive war. It was his opinion that the Society would be seriously hampered by putting defensive war and offensive war in the same category. In 1835

---

[16] F. W. Holland, Ms. *History of the American Peace Cause,* vol. i, p. 9; H. C. Wright, *Autobiography,* p. 328.

[17] *Christian Examiner,* vol. xviii, July, 1835, Boston, pp. 368 ff.

[18] Rufus Stebbins, *Address before the Bowdoin Young Men's Peace Society,* 1836, pp. 15-17.

there were but two members in the parish of the Reverend A. P. Peabody who followed him in denying the Scriptural legality of defensive war, and among his clerical acquaintances he enjoyed the sympathy of but a single man.[19]

The experience of the Reverend Henry C. Wright, who acted as an agent of the American Peace Society during the summer of 1836 in central New York, throws interesting light on the public's attitude towards the issue of defensive war. In this agency he traveled over nineteen hundred miles and lectured sixty times. There was reason for Ladd to fear that Wright, thoroughgoing Non-Resistant that he was, would antagonize public sentiment. Though he persuaded the New England Methodist Episcopal Conference at Springfield to adopt radical resolutions against defensive war, he had to apply to five Christian ministers in Albany before receiving permission to preach in the pulpit of one of them. Even at this church the parson, Brother Kirke, objected to his extreme views on the ground that they endangered civil government. After a week's stay in Albany Wright discovered only two men prepared to accept his own position, but at Schenectady and Saratoga he enjoyed a better reception. In the latter place he recorded in his *Commonplace Book* that "the whole village is in a blaze, everyone talking about peace. Much division of opinion." He wrestled with Dr. Eliphalet Nott, the president of Union College, who, approving the principle of non-resistance, still feared it might lead to "things not allowable" and knew not which turning to take. On the railroads and canals the single-minded Wright seized every opportunity to promulgate peace ideas and to test the issue of defensive war. While he was preaching in the Presbyterian Church in Rochester, a general and an elder, unable to endure his extreme doctrine, left the church in a flurry, the elder threatening to fight some one! What with his advanced ideas and his unwillingness to compromise, it was natural for Wright to

[19] *American Advocate of Peace*, vol. ii, December, 1836, p. 142; Coues, Ms. *Peace Album*, Peabody to Coues, Portsmouth, October 2, 1844.

stir up a good deal of opposition. The Executive Committee of the American Peace Society took him to task for his manner of condemning all wars.[20]

It would have been as easy to make water run up hill as to make Wright hold his peace. At the annual meeting of the American Peace Society in 1836 he boldly and ably urged the Society to take up the gauntlet against defensive war. The result was that a committee, including Ladd, was appointed to draw up a new constitution. During the year Wright left no stone unturned to have the radical position incorporated into the Society's constitution. He all but won over Angelina and Sarah Grimké, sisters of Thomas Grimké, who carried on their brother's work after his death in 1834. He solicited aid from the English Quaker, Joseph Sturge, and from Lewis Tappan. He wrote for *Zion's Herald* and lectured in Massachusetts, central New York, and Philadelphia, everywhere condemning, root and branch, the idea of a defensive war. On March 11, 1837, he suggested to Ladd the formation of a peace society based entirely on non-resistance.[21] The pressure exerted by Wright may have been one of the influences which finally pushed Ladd to the conclusion that unless the Society took more positive ground in regard to the limits of pacifism, such extremists as Wright might abandon the task of trying to cleanse the Augean stable and go their own way.

Meantime Ladd's committee pondered. It sought advice from the most "active and intelligent" peace men in all parts of the country and was also influenced by the position of friends of the cause in England. At length the committee decided to incorporate in the proposed new constitution a declaration against

[20] Wright, Ms. *Journal*, vols. xv-xxviii, March 15, 1835, to June 23, 1836; Ninth Annual Report of the American Peace Society in the *Advocate of Peace*, vol. i, no. 1, June, 1837, p. 25; no. 3, December, 1837, p. 123; Ms. *Minutes of the Executive Committee of the American Peace Society*, August 22, 1836.

[21] Wright, Ms. *Journal*, vol. xxviii, May 12, 1836; vol. xxxiii, February 3, March 11, 1837; *Advocate of Peace*, vol. i, no. 3, December 1, 1837, p. 120; Ms. *Minutes of the Executive Committee*, May 11, 1836.

defensive war. No advance notice of this decision was given out to members of the Society; it was thought best to leave the whole matter to be threshed out at the annual meeting.[22]

When the American Peace Society duly assembled in annual meeting on May 11, 1837, the committee on revision of the constitution declared: "This Society, being founded on the principle that all war is contrary to the spirit of the Gospel, shall have for its object to illustrate the inconsistency of war with Christianity, to show its baleful influence on all the great interests of mankind, and to devise means for insuring universal and permanent peace."[23] No amendment was offered; the report was adopted. Thus, without any opposition on the part of those present at the ninth annual meeting, the American Peace Society took the ground that *all* war was contrary to the spirit of the Gospel. It was urged that the step was less a change than a distinct avowal of sentiment long cherished. It is true that the Society had never taken any ground at variance with this position. It had merely left the point to be settled by individual members. Ladd felt called on to disclaim any influence of the ultraism of the age in this action. Few persons of less thorough views had been found who would or could labor in the cause with "much zeal or success." Some of the best friends of peace could not in conscience join a society, Ladd went on to say, which did not take this "high ground," and some of the recently formed local societies had refused to affiliate with the national organization because its constitution did not consider this vexed question of defensive war. "It is a momentous question and we have decided in the light of the Gospel alone." The course of the Society was not to be changed materially, since it had always directed its efforts against the whole war system. Ladd, thoroughly convinced of the wisdom of more distinctly avowing the position of the Society, spared no efforts in trying to forestall opposition.[24] Perhaps the vigor of his efforts in this direction was partly a reflection of an uneasiness he may well have felt at not having issued due warning that the change would be proposed at this particular meeting. Had the advocates of the more general and conservative policy been better prepared, they might by attendance and argument have prevented the change.

It was not, indeed, to be the fortune of the peace movement to enjoy a truce in the battle of principles which had been waging. One of the vice-presidents of the Society, the Reverend Dr. William Allen, of Bowdoin College, addressed a public letter to Ladd in which he virtually withdrew from the Society, taking the view that he was not bound to a ship which had deserted its old moorings. Allen made the point that he was not alone in his position, that at least one other gentleman whose name appeared on the list of officers of the Society felt the same way about what had been done. The new principle, he insisted, would prove an insuperable obstacle to any great results from the Society. "Statesmen will look on it as a body of visionaries, ignorant of the world's affairs. Society will regard it as it has regarded Quakerism—a dream of weak benevolence." The honest carrying out of the policy, went on the irate Allen, would mean the annihilation of civil government, for the governor of Massachusetts could not defend the city against pirates. Besides, the principle had not been supported by the voice of the Church in any age. Allen concluded by holding that the American Peace Society had surrendered to the age of radicalism. "In its present form," he contended, it is "to all important purposes and results dead."[25]

In replying to Allen's objections, Ladd admitted that for many years he himself had been swayed by like considerations. He had been forced to admit, just the same, that a peace society which allowed the right of defensive war was one to which a Tamerlane or a Napoleon might consistently belong. The subject had

[24] *Ibid.*, p. 8; Hemmenway, *Memoir of William Ladd*, p. 63.
[25] *Advocate of Peace*, vol. i, no. 3, December, 1837, p. 119.

been well aired, he went on, and the committee on revision had taken lessons from the ground gained by the temperance movement's assumption of the consistent policy of advocating total abstinence. He took especial pains to point out that in taking the new ground the Society did not deny the right of the civil magistrate to punish crimes. The controversy, Ladd concluded, reflected the opposition between Paley's doctrine of expediency and Wayland's doctrine of uncompromising and literal adherence to Gospel implications.[26]

Writers in the *Advocate of Peace* urged that no difference of principle in respect to the issue should lessen efforts to persuade nations to settle disputes without the sword, quite apart from the question of aggression and defense. George C. Beckwith, who at Ladd's request became secretary of the Society in 1837 and editor of its periodical, took the lead in trying to appease all shades of opinion, especially the conservative group which had been alienated by the amendment to the Constitution outlawing defensive war. Beckwith had been a professor at the Lane Theological Seminary, and pastor of Congregational churches in Portland, Maine, and in Lowell, Massachusetts. In pursuance of his policy of compromise, he reminded American peace men that the London Society, while discarding every species of war as contrary to a religion of love, had still welcomed the coöperation of those who believed in defensive wars. What was even more to the point, the peace societies of Massachusetts, Connecticut, and Rhode Island had also accepted as members peace men of all shades of opinion. The late revision of the constitution, Beckwith held, was "neither designed nor expected to exclude from coöperation any that are willing to use means for the promotion of universal and permanent peace."[27]

At the tenth annual meeting, May 30, 1838, these sentiments were incorporated into a series of resolutions designed to explain Article II, by which the constitution had been amended

[26] *Ibid.*, pp. 119 ff.
[27] *Ibid.*, pp. 106-107.

GEORGE BECKWITH

in 1837. The article was interpreted in the resolutions as designed "to assert that all national wars are inconsistent with Christianity, including those supposed or alleged to be defensive." It was made clear, however, that the article had no reference "to the right of private or individual self-defense, to a denial of which the Society is not committed." Finally, the active support of "all persons seriously desiring the extinction of war, regardless of their convictions on the issue of defensive war," was earnestly solicited.[28]

The first effect of this change in policy was to bring the American peace movement into greater harmony with the British movement. The Reverend J. Hargreaves, secretary of the London society, felt that raising the standard would "promote the cause, as it will provoke opposition and promote discussion." It was the opinion of Elihu Burritt, after close acquaintance with English peace men, that the adoption of this principle by the American Peace Society gave to their British coworkers moral strength and encouragement.[29]

In the second place, the controversy clarified the whole peace argument and in so doing performed an educative function. The very opposition which Wright stimulated, and which in a lesser degree the action of the Society aroused, made the peace cause more widely known and thus lessened popular indifference towards it. In 1842 the Reverend A. P. Peabody felt that the peace movement gained much influence by its action, and this was also the opinion of others.[30] When Ladd died in 1841, the election to the presidency of the Society of Samuel E. Coues, an outspoken advocate of the new ground, testified to its strength in the Society.

[28] *Ibid.*, vol. i, no. 4, March, 1838, p. 192; Ms. *Minutes of the Executive Committee of the American Peace Society,* November 9, 22, 1837, May 30, 1838.

[29] *Advocate of Peace,* vol. ii, no. 9, February, 1839, pp. 213-214; Burritt, Introductory Notes to Hemmenway's *Memoir of William Ladd,* pp. 12-13; Ms. *Journal,* September 25, 1846.

[30] John Lord, *Address before the Amherst Peace Society,* 1839, p. 7; Coues, Ms. *Peace Album, loc. cit.*

Despite Beckwith's pleas for harmony, the amending of the constitution did not settle the question. By not going so far as to condemn private self-defense and capital punishment, issues brought into prominence by the discussions, the action of the Society led to discontent on the part of extreme radicals. Their opposition emphasized the lack of unity in the movement and led to an even more serious rupture in the ranks of peace.

The leading Non-Resistants, Henry C. Wright, Adin Ballou, the Reverend Samuel J. May, and William Lloyd Garrison, weighed in the balance the amendment to the American Peace Society's constitution and found it too conservative. Garrison laughed to scorn the national Peace Society for "enrolling upon its list of members, not converted but belligerent commanders-in-chief, generals, colonels, majors, corporals, and all." To him it was radically defective in principle and "based on sand." In August, 1837, Garrison gave notice of his intention to part company with the peace societies, as he had done with the Colonization Society, unless "they alter their present course."[31]

At the anniversary meeting of the American Peace Society on May 29, 1838, Garrison and Wright took counsel. They felt Beckwith's annual report was without vital principle and over-emphasized conservative reform. Its appeals for harmony and moderation betrayed a timid fear of offending public opinion, and the whole performance left a decidedly bad taste in their mouths.[32] The very next day, at the business meeting of the Society, Beckwith showed his colors by offering a motion to strike out of the constitution the newly adopted article on the inconsistency of wars with the Gospel. Though the motion met defeat by a large majority, its introduction led Wright to offer one for calling a convention during the coming year to discuss the principles and means of securing peace. This motion carried, and Ladd, as presiding officer, named a committee on arrange-

[31] F. J. and W. P. Garrison, *William Lloyd Garrison: the Story of His Life Told by His Children,* New York, 1885, vol. ii, p. 52, p. 222.

[32] Wright, Ms. *Journal,* vol. xxxviii, May 29, 1838.

ments. It included the Reverend Samuel J. May, Edmund Quincy, H. C. Wright, and Amasa Walker, all Garrisonian abolitionists, who, though differing in their peace views, leaned decidedly towards the left.[33]

The next day the Antislavery Convention also appointed a committee, including Wright and Garrison, to call a peace convention. Women were invited to attend, deliberate, and vote.[34]

During the next few weeks a series of meetings was held at the Town Hall, in which the radicals had the upper hand. They discussed theories of government and gave special attention to the doctrine of the inviolability of human life. Wright saw to it that similar meetings were held during the summer in nearly all the towns of eastern Massachusetts.[35]

Such preparations naturally gave moderate peace men something to think about. On September 17, 1838, the day before the Convention was to assemble, they put their heads together at one of the offices in the Eagle Bank. They determined to prevent the extreme non-resistant measure from coming before the Convention. Beckwith urged that the cause of peace be spared the extravagance of the radicals.[36]

On Tuesday, September 18, 1838, in Marlboro Chapel, Boston, the Reverend Samuel J. May called to order the long-anticipated Convention. Among the 170 enrolled, none took more outstanding parts than Garrison, Wright, George Benson, Wendell Phillips, Adin Ballou, A. Bronson Alcott, Abby Kelley, William Ladd, Charles Whipple, and Amasa Walker.[37]

After the preliminary organization, women, on Garrison's suggestion, were admitted to the full privileges of voting and

[33] *Advocate of Peace*, vol. ii, no. 2, July, 1838, pp. 46-47; Ms. *Minutes of the Executive Committee*, May 30, 1838.

[34] Wright, Ms. *Journal*, vol. xxxviii, May 30, 1838.

[35] *Ibid., passim.*

[36] F. J. and W. P. Garrison, *William Lloyd Garrison*, vol. ii, p. 222.

[37] Wright, Ms. *Journal*, vol. xxxvii, September 21, 1838; *Proceedings of the Peace Convention*, Boston, 1838; Coues, Ms. *Peace Album*, testimony of the Reverend Samuel J. May.

serving on committees. Unable to stomach this action, Beckwith, Baron Stowe, and others asked to have their names erased from the roll of the Convention. Clearly trouble was brewing.

Wright himself opened the discussion by offering a resolution declaring that, according to the Gospel of Christ, no man and no government had the right to take the life of man, on any pretext whatever. Dr. Charles Follen argued ingeniously against the principle of this resolution, and the battle was on. Walker offered a slightly moderated substitute motion to the effect that "human life is inviolable and can never be taken without sin against God." In support of this Ladd remarked that to doubt the safety and expediency of the principle of non-resistance was to deny the wisdom and goodness of Jehovah. Finally, Wright's original motion was passed, and Garrison was appointed chairman of a committee to draw up a Constitution and Declaration of Principles. When the Constitution and Declaration were reported, only twenty-eight voted favorably, and these were all Garrisonian abolitionists.[38]

The members of the new organization, which took the name of the New England Non-Resistance Society, went far in their efforts to cut off the hand that offended. They concurred in the opinion that no man or body of men, however constituted or by whatever name called, had the right to take the life of man as a penalty for transgression; no man could sue another for redress of injuries, or thrust any evil-doer into prison, or fill any office in which he would be liable to execute penal enactments, or take part in military service, or acknowledge allegiance to any human government, or justify any man in fighting for defense of property, liberty, life, or religion. Members were to obey the "powers that be" except when they bade them violate their conscience, and then they were meekly to submit to the penalty

[38] Hemmenway, *Memoir of William Ladd*, pp. 73-75; Coues, Ms. *Peace Album*, testimony of Amasa Walker; *Proceedings of the Peace Convention, passim; Advocate of Peace*, vol. iii, December, 1840, pp. 232 ff.; vol. ii, no. 5, October, 1838, pp. 117-118.

of disobedience. The constitution opened membership to all persons, without distinction as to sex, and members held equal privileges.[39]

Garrison said that never before had a more "fanatical" or "disorganizing" instrument been penned by man.[40] To the new Society he devoted an ever larger portion of the *Liberator,* and at the same time he edited, with Edmund Quincy and Maria W. Chapman, the *Non-Resistant,* the organ of the Society.

It was only the extreme left in the peace movement that cast its lot with the new organization. Amasa Walker, while in fundamental agreement with its principal idea, did not become a member, since he could not see the propriety of refusing to vote or take part in the civil duties and responsibilities of society. As for Ladd, he had tried hard during the Convention to pour oil on the troubled waters. Even Garrison admitted that the "deep solemnity of the occasion was somewhat disturbed by the broad and irresistible humor of William Ladd—a huge and strange compound of fat, good nature, and benevolence." The new constitution was too much for him, and he felt compelled to give his vote, reluctantly, in the negative. "I fully agree with many of their statements," he wrote to a friend, "and I bid them God-speed so far as they follow Christ. I consider the new society as ultra high; but almost the whole world are ultra low on this subject, and, if I must choose between the two ultras, give me the ultra high one; for I have always found it more easy to come down to the truth, than to come up to it." Ladd none the less felt called on to explain his position in a letter to the *Liberator.* Though he believed that *all* war was contrary to the spirit of the Gospel, and that capital punishment ought to be abolished, he did not feel that it was necessary to attach these questions to the cause of peace any more than to temperance or the antislavery question. While it was his duty to vote for the

[39] *Principles of the Non-Resistance Society,* Boston, 1839; *The Non-Resistant,* vol. i, no. 1, January, 1839.
[40] F. J. and W. P. Garrison, *William Lloyd Garrison,* vol. ii, p. 228.

best man, it was not his duty to pay tribute when exacted professedly to support war, or to take part in military service, or to hold any office that might compel him to take life. With such opinions it was not strange that Ladd attended the annual meetings of the Non-Resistance Society and finally concluded, shortly before his death, that while the Society was not likely to do either much harm or good, its existence was perhaps justified as a reminder that there was no ultraism so bad as ultraconservatism.[41]

Nor was Ladd the only prominent officer in the American Peace Society who gave qualified approval to the non-resistance cause. Samuel E. Coues, who was to succeed Ladd as president of the American Peace Society, spoke at the first anniversary of the Non-Resistance Society, and Wright felt satisfied that he, as well as his friend Amos Dresser of Oberlin, Ohio, were at heart Non-Resistants. The Reverend Samuel J. May also aided the radical organization, preaching non-resistance from many pulpits. Gerrit Smith, who had the impression that its principles were right, was confirmed in his mind during the following year.[42]

With such prominent peace men in sympathy with the non-resistance position, its advocates not unnaturally insisted that their conclusions followed inevitably from the premises laid down by the American Peace Society in its declaration that *all* war was contrary to the spirit of the Gospel. Indeed, the *Democratic Review* held that, in reducing peace principles to their ultimate implications, the New England Non-Resistance Society had rendered service to the older organization.[43]

[41] *The Non-Resistant*, vol. i, no. 2, January 19, 1839; Coues, Ms. *Peace Album*, testimony of Amasa Walker; F. J. and W. P. Garrison, *William Lloyd Garrison;* Wright, Ms. *Journal*, vol. xxxviii, September 22, 1838; Hemmenway, *Memoir of William Ladd*, pp. 73, 74, 76; Hemmenway, Revised Ms. *Memoir*, pp. 470-477; Wright, Ms. *Journal*, vol. xiii, April 27, 1840.

[42] Wright, Ms. *Journal*, vol. xli, September 28, 1839; Coues, Ms. *Peace Album*, testimony of the Reverend Samuel J. May; *The Non-Resistant*, vol. i, no. 9, May 4, 1839.

[43] *Democratic Review*, vol. v, March, 1839, pp. 292-293.

On the other hand, the Beckwith group, which controlled the *Advocate of Peace,* washed its hands of the newly formed society and insisted that not more than one or two members of the orthodox organization had joined the Non-Resistance Society. Beckwith especially took pains to repudiate the anti-government implications of the Non-Resistants and assured everyone that the new society was "an enterprise altogether distinct from our own." It was a good thing, he declared, that their "extraneous views," so often unjustly charged on orthodox peace men, had now found expression in a separate organization. In like vein the New York Peace Society repudiated the followers of Garrison and Wright.[44]

Though Wright indeed felt there was "no vital principle" left in the American Peace Society, he went on attending its anniversaries, and at that of 1840 asked and was given permission to speak. On the whole, however, *The Non-Resistant* expressed the feeling of most of the group when it declared that the American Peace Society had failed to make any marked impress on the warlike character of the nation, and that its mission had ended.[45]

Both the Beckwith group and the Non-Resistants realized the importance of winning support from the English peace movement. Beckwith published a letter from the Reverend J. Hargreaves, secretary of the London Peace Society, obviously in answer to an inquiry, the point of which was to show that a man might be a thoroughly committed, radical pacifist without assuming an anti-government position. Wright also kept in touch with English peace men. He corresponded with the famous abolitionist, George Thompson, with the eminent Quaker, Joseph Sturge, and with the radical peace advocate, John Scoble. Within a few years he was to go to England to labor in the

---

[44] *Advocate of Peace,* vol. ii, no. 6, November, 1838, p. 142; no. 5, October, 1838, pp. 117-118; *The Non-Resistant,* vol. i, no. 2, January, 1839.

[45] Wright, Ms. *Journal,* vol. xl, May 28, 1839; vol. xliii, May 27, 1840; *The Non-Resistant,* vol. i, no. 17, September 7, 1839.

cause, and his comprehensive treatment of the whole non-resistance question was primarily addressed to an English audience.[46]

The New England Non-Resistance Society continued for more than a decade after its organization. As for achievement, it was almost a case of beating bare fists against granite. It came in for no end of bitter criticism. Once a mob made demonstrations of a hostile character while the Society was sitting in annual meeting. Wright, who served as agent, fraternized with the Quakers, and sometimes found young Friends willing to lend a hand. It is clear, none the less, that the hospitality he received in Friends' meetinghouses did not mean that they were, as a body, favorable to the doctrines of the Non-Resistance Society. They even published a disclaimer in the *Advocate of Peace,* a disclaimer which the conservative editor of that magazine was doubtless glad to make public.[47]

No less devoted to the cause than Henry C. Wright was the Reverend Adin Ballou, perhaps its most philosophical and able advocate. At the anniversary of the Non-Resistance Society in 1839, Ballou maintained that if the professed friends of the New Testament were consistent, they would withdraw from all governmental society which was constitutionally committed to the war principle. This address anticipated the founding of the Hopedale Community by Ballou in 1842. A year later he became president of the Society and took measures to resuscitate the *Non-Resistant,* which had been suspended. Besides his editorial work for this periodical, Ballou conducted many debates on non-resistance and, at the request of Theodore Parker, preached to his congregation in Boston on April 11, 1852.[48]

[46] *Advocate of Peace,* vol. iii, no. 4, December, 1839, p. 91; December, 1840, p. 232; Wright, Ms. *Journal,* vol. xl, June 5, 1839; Wright, *Defensive War,* London, 1846.

[47] Wright, Ms. *Journal,* vol. xli, September 25, 1839; vol. xliii, May 27, 1840; *The Non-Resistant,* vol. i, no. 19, October 5, 1839; no. 13, July 6, 1839; *Advocate of Peace,* vol. iii, December, 1840, pp. 232 ff.

[48] Reverend Carlton A. Staples, *A Memoir of the Reverend Adin Ballou,* in *Proceedings* of the Worcester Society of Antiquity, 1890, no. xxxv, pp. 99-112,

In 1846 Ballou published the most thorough exposition of non-resistance made in the pre-Civil War period. In this book, *Christian Non-Resistance in all its Important Bearings, Illustrated and Defended,* he urged that the doctrine was not contrary to nature, since it was a universal law that like begat like and that hence kindness would beget kindness. With innumerable examples Ballou illustrated his argument. His book found some countenance in England.

Except in rare cases, the early enthusiasm of the Non-Resistants waned, and the movement made but little noise in the fifties. During the Civil War the Non-Resistants, with few exceptions, "yielded allegiance to the war-god when with his battle-axe he cleft asunder the fetter of the slave." Ballou kept faith with his idea.[49] As an example of the most extreme peace doctrine, the non-resistance movement bears an obvious relationship to the peace movement as a whole, though its direct influence was never great. It was one of the "ultras" of the day and was shunned by most peace reformers. Its real importance lies in the opposition to the American Peace Society which it aroused in that part of the public which confused the two societies, despite Beckwith's persistent repudiations. It was the desire to meet this difficulty that led to complications in the American Peace Society of so serious a nature that open rupture resulted in the end.

From all signs, as he read them, Beckwith had by 1843 concluded that tolerance of all shades of peace opinion was the only policy for the American Peace Society to follow. He urged that the test of a peace man should be simply his willingness to coöperate with others for the entire abolition of war. The cause would be strengthened, he maintained, by admitting the greatest variety of argument and influence. No single class of peace men, non-resistants, opponents, or supporters of defensive war, could

Worcester, 1890; William S. Heywood, editor, *Autobiography of Adin Ballou,* Lowell, 1896, pp. 307-308, 380, 382.

[49] Ballou, *Autobiography,* pp. 422, 462; M. E. Curti, "Non-Resistance in New England," *New England Quarterly,* vol. ii, no. 1, 1929, pp. 55-56.

meet the wants of all friends of the cause. Coöperation would eliminate many of the causes of jealousy and collision among pacifists who were wasting their breath by fruitless contention. How could the Non-Resistants be refused fellowship in the great work for peace? They were thorough peace men, and might point to the example of William Penn to bear out their peculiar assumptions. On the other hand, if men admitting the right of defensive war were to be struck from the list, Beckwith felt that the largest number of coworkers, honest and active friends of peace, would be cut off. "Worcester and even Ladd himself during the great part of his labors had stood upon such ground." The advantages of a broad platform seemed to Beckwith so obvious as scarcely to need defense. With a catholic platform, no one would be obliged to conceal his principles, no "right" standard would be introduced, no principles would be fixed. In short, the reform would be reduced to its simplest, elementary principles.[50]

To others, however, such a point of view seemed weak, and they determined to fight to a finish the battle over the limits of pacifism. They felt that Beckwith was trying to lower peace principles and in a utilitarian way to compromise the "high ground" assumed in 1837. This group had the support of the president of the Society, Samuel E. Coues, and of the financial agent, J. P. Blanchard, whose generosity was keeping the wolf from the door. Amasa Walker, one of the most valued friends that the cause boasted, Dr. Walter Channing, a prominent Boston physician, long active in the councils of the Society, and the Reverend Frederic W. Holland, a Unitarian clergyman, also took this position. No one, however, gave such firmness and resolution to the "reform group" as Elihu Burritt, who by 1844 was actively identified with the peace movement. This "Learned Blacksmith" had come into it in a strange way, for he had never seen a peace tract nor heard of the American Peace Society

[50] *Advocate of Peace,* vol. v, April, 1843, pp. 37-38 ff.; Beckwith to John Lee, Boston, May, 1844, vol. vi, May, 1844, pp. 193-202.

when he became a pacifist. In 1844 he was busying himself with a lecture on "The Anatomy of the Earth," by which he hoped to supplement his meager earnings as a blacksmith, in order to enjoy more time for his philological studies. The unity of the earth and the interdependency of its parts he found so striking that he ended by writing a peace lecture. In this conversion to pacifism the evidence from his study of languages played a part, for his increasing knowledge of common roots suggested that all men were brothers in body as they were in spirit. War appeared to be the artificial reversal of this interdependency and inter-relationship of the units of the earth and therefore utter folly. It is thus not unnatural that Burritt emphasized the economic implications of peace and war and that he saw in artificial boundaries and restrictions of all kinds a menace to the friendly relations of states and peoples. A deeply religious man, it took no great reflection to convince him that the Bible in letter and spirit condemned all war.[51]

In January, 1843, Boston heard Elihu Burritt on peace for the first time. His lecture at once won the ear of peace men, who enlisted him as a member of the Executive Committee of the Society. During the following years Burritt took occasion to introduce the subject of peace wherever he went, "not only from an increasing interest in the cause, but also with a view of acquiring tact for discussing its merits." These lectures took him as far as Philadelphia, where five hundred people came out to hear him. Everywhere Burritt made warm friends. Of these friends none were warmer than Coues, Walker, and Blanchard.[52]

At the suggestion of Burritt a series of peace conventions was held in several towns of eastern Massachusetts from 1844 to 1846. These conventions, which had nothing to do with the American Peace Society, pointed to the beginning of a separate

[51] Charles Northend, *Elihu Burritt, A Memorial Volume, containing a Sketch of His Life and Labors,* New York, 1879, p. 24.

[52] Burritt, Ms. *Journal,* January 15, 1843, January 2, 1845; Holland, Ms. *History of the American Peace Cause,* vol. ii, p. 51.

organization by the group of men dissatisfied with Beckwith's project of admitting the upholders of defensive war into the fellowship. At all of the conventions the chief subject discussed was that of defensive war. Nearly all the "reform group" took part in them; even the Non-Resistants made a gesture of approval. The formation of the Worcester County Peace Society was one of the results of the convention movement, but its chief importance was to challenge Beckwith's "catholic" policy. Not unnaturally the *Advocate of Peace* gave only stinted praise to these conventions, though it admitted that great spirit and interest characterized many of them.[53] Beckwith was caught between two fires: the conservatives who upheld defensive war and these "reformers" who would have none of his own policy of tolerating all points of view.

After the general meeting of the American Peace Society on May 26, 1845, this "reform group," now fairly coherent as a result of peace conventions and the expression of its views through Burritt's *Christian Citizen,* met in Marlboro Chapel. Burritt, Walker, Blanchard, Coues and Peck, the Reverend Sylvester Judd of Augusta, Maine, the Reverend Elnathan Davis of Ashburnham, and the Reverend E. W. Jackson of Boston spoke enthusiastically and in such a way as to discourage those who desired to retain the coöperation of the apologists for defensive war. It seemed that the reformers were bent on nothing less than separating the goats from the sheep once and for all.[54]

The strength of the new group was marked by its acquisition of the *Advocate of Peace,* which Burritt was now to edit. According to him, Beckwith "took the proposition hard." When the change of editorship was announced in the August, 1845, number of the *Advocate,* Beckwith defended his course of mod-

---

[53] *Christian Citizen,* November 30, December 7, December 28, 1844, February 7, April 26, October 25, July 26, 1845; Burritt, Ms. *Journal,* March 29, January 11, 1845; *Advocate of Peace,* vol. vi, January, 1845, p. 12.

[54] *Christian Citizen,* May 31, 1845; Ms. *Minutes of the Executive Committee,* May 27, 28, June 23, October 27, November 3, 1845.

eration between the two extreme wings of the peace movement and emphasized the need of relief from some of his heavy burdens in connection with the cause. Though it was true that Beckwith's hands were more than full with his work as chief financial agent, general lecturer, and corresponding secretary of the Society, it is clear that depriving him of the editorship of the *Advocate* was in large measure due to the desire of the reform group "to introduce some salutary changes in its character."[55]

Burritt at once began to enlist the best talent on the side which opposed defensive war, writing to Charles Sumner for a contribution and to prominent English pacifists.[56] The magazine appeared under the title, *Advocate of Peace and Universal Brotherhood,* indicative of the international character which Burritt wished it to assume. Its new editor emphasized the idea of a Congress of Nations more than Beckwith had and, what was more to the point, urged the necessity of taking the "high ground" of outlawing defensive war.[57]

Fortune, however, did not smile on the reform group. The *Advocate,* which Burritt had agreed to edit on his own financial responsibility, proved an irritating source of expense. He had meant to make it a publication which would appeal to its subscribers as interested readers, not as donors to a cause. It was accordingly increased in size and the price raised. Regarding the publication as a new and distinct venture, he did not feel justified in sending it to the old list of subscribers without their request. As a result of these changes, he soon found that he had the worst of the bargain. Whether rightly or not, Burritt felt that Beckwith's control of the organization kept it from properly coöperating with him. By November, 1846, he had come to the

---

[55] Burritt, Ms. *Journal,* May 31, 1846; *Advocate of Peace,* vol. vi, August, 1845, p. 95; *Christian Citizen,* September 6, 1845.

[56] Burritt to Sumner, November 19, 1845, *Sumner Papers.*

[57] *Advocate of Peace and Universal Brotherhood, passim.*

conclusion that since Beckwith would "soon have the Society in his own hands," the organ should go with it.[58]

With the outbreak of the Mexican War in the early summer of 1846 it seemed to the reformers that the corresponding secretary's efforts "to lower the standard, to accommodate the peace advocates of defensive war," were lamentably unfortunate. For some time, too, the reformers had felt that Beckwith was managing to absorb all the means of the Society into his own salary, monopolizing, as he did, nearly all the offices of the organization. It seemed to them that he was wedded to the "monotonous routine of money collecting, editing the *Advocate,* arranging annual meetings, with an occasional petition to Congress."[59] Apart from this, Beckwith seemed to resent the possible influence of the Methodists in the government of the Society. To his orthodox Congregational brethren Beckwith made much of the danger certain to result if the reformers were allowed to make of the Peace Society an antigallows or antislavery society. Intent on jealously guarding against an increase of their representatives in the Executive Committee, he addressed an appeal to "all men of moderate peace views," just before the May anniversary in 1846. This appeal called for a declaration of the Society's relation to other reforms and for an invitation to all peace men to adopt a more catholic platform. As a result Beckwith's friends turned out in good numbers for the annual meeting. Not to be outdone, the reformers welcomed Garrison and the Reverend A. Foster, Non-Resistants, who made themselves members of the American Peace Society the night before the anniversary.[60]

In such an atmosphere, it was not unnatural that the unrestrained bitterness and rivalry led, the next day, to something like a riot. "If we had not been informed we were present at a

[58] Burritt, Ms. *Journal,* November 3, 1846, January 9, 1847; *Advocate of Peace,* November and December, 1847, p. 143.

[59] Burritt, Ms. *Journal,* October 31, 1846; Holland, Ms. *History of the American Peace Cause,* vol. iii, p. 85.

[60] Holland, *loc. cit., Advocate of Peace,* vol. vii, January and February, 1847, pp. 2 ff.

Peace Meeting," wrote the managing editor of the *Christian Citizen*, "we should have judged we had got into the wrong room, and beheld only a political caucus in uproar."[61] Beckwith understood Garrison to say that although he had opposed the American Peace Society as not being radical enough for him, he had at length concluded that if its members strictly conformed to the constitution as revised in 1837, then they would go with him against the government of the United States for an immediate dissolution of the Union. The reformers, however, denied that Garrison brought forward such a proposition. One of their number testified that the friends of the constitution were obliged to contest every inch of the ground, and "only with the greatest exertion was the clause which places the Society on the ground that all war is inconsistent with Christianity preserved inviolate."[62]

Though the officers of the Society were exonerated of the charge of having mingled other reforms, such as the abolition of capital punishment, with the cause of peace, a series of resolutions was adopted which must have warmed the cockles of Beckwith's heart. By these resolutions the Society henceforth was to confine itself strictly to the single object of abolishing international war, and its affairs were to be managed in such a way as to be kept entirely distinct from anti-government, anti-capital punishment, and all other "extraneous" reforms. It was further resolved to regard as the proper basis of coöperation in the cause of peace the platform of the First General Peace Convention in London in 1843; namely, the inconsistency of war with Christianity and the true interests of mankind. Finally, a resolution was passed inviting all persons willing for any reason to labor for the abolition of the custom of war to unite with the labors of the Society. The affairs of the Society, moreover, were to be conducted in such a way as to render this coöperation practicable, consistent, and cordial by not conflicting in its operations

[61] Thomas Drew in the *Christian Citizen*, January 16, 1847.
[62] *Ibid*.

with "principles, interests, or institutions which the Christian community hold dear and sacred."[63]

These resolutions, of course, were so distinct a triumph for Beckwith that the reform group was terribly embittered.[64] There was left no uncertainty as to which way the wind blew when it was announced that the Executive Committee was preparing a draft of a new constitution to embody the resolutions passed at the annual meeting. On December 17 Burritt observed in his *Journal* that "the division of the American Peace Society is almost consummated," and presently the entire reform group withdrew from the Executive Committee. This meant the loss of the president of the Society, Samuel E. Coues, the treasurer, Joshua P. Blanchard, who since Ladd's death had personally shouldered the annual five hundred dollar deficit, Elihu Burritt, Amasa Walker, Walter Channing, the Reverend E. W. Jackson, and a number of other outstanding figures in the cause.

The reformers, in resigning, took the ground that they were remaining loyal to the constitution as amended in 1837, and that the votes of the majority could not change their convictions. It was their professed desire to promote harmony in the Society, for the conservatives could now test their catholic program. After all, the joint resignation concluded, the spirit of love must remain the basis of all reform.[65]

In his own farewell in the *Advocate* Burritt likewise desired to part friends, with the feeling that they were all traveling "at least obliquely, in the same direction, though by different roads." But he made it clear why he could not remain connected with the Society "a moment after the prohibition of all war was taken out of its constitution and the lawfulness of defensive war

[63] Holland, *op. cit.*, vol. iii, p. 86; *Advocate of Peace and Universal Brotherhood*, June, 1846, p. 137; Ms. *Minutes of the Executive Committee*, May 25, 26, 1846.
[64] *Christian Citizen*, January 16, 1847; Ms. *Minutes of the Executive Committee*, June 10, June 27, 1846.
[65] Burritt, Ms. *Journal*, December 17, 1846; *Christian Citizen*, January 16, 1847: *Advocate of Peace and Universal Brotherhood*, December, 1846, pp. 276 ff.

admitted," and he maintained that such, in effect, was the meaning of the resolutions and the announcement that a new constitution embodying them was being prepared. If the Society was out for numbers, Burritt went on, it was taking the proper step, since the contemplated changes would make it possible for American and Mexican soldiers alternately to subscribe "to the highest articles of faith remaining in the Society's creed, and that, too, with the points of their bayonets nearly dipped in blood." After all, in a society of reformers, of what use were numbers "gained by sinking it down to the opinions of those it seeks to reform?"[66] Beckwith found solace by endeavoring to prove that the course for which he stood was essentially that of Ladd. He would continue to print in the *Advocate,* and the Society would continue to circulate, he went on to state, the writings of such men as Grimké, Dymond, Coues, and Sumner. "I am sorry that such a course and such writings do not satisfy all our friends; but, if they can find a mode more congenial, whether more radical or not, of advancing our common object, the entire and perpetual abolition of war, we shall rejoice in the success of their efforts, and will hope that a division of labor, and diversity of methods in this cause, as in that of temperance, will be found to hasten its ultimate triumph."[67]

Doubtless Beckwith had the majority of the Society on his side. A draft of a new constitution, embodying the resolves of the annual meeting of 1846, was sent to every known member of the Society. Of the hundreds to whom it was sent, Beckwith testified that only two dissented, one of whom wished it to exclude moderate peace men. The other wished it to exclude radicals! It is true that this apparent unanimity was in part obtained by the clever device of framing the leading question in the questionnaire in such a way as to make those who condemned the proposed "lowering of the standard" condemn the greater part of the labors for peace of Worcester, Channing, and

[66] *Christian Citizen,* January 9, 1847.
[67] Beckwith, letter to *Christian Citizen,* January 16, 1847.

Ladd himself. Still, the *Christian Citizen,* friendly as it was to the reformers, printed only one letter criticizing the proposed change. That was from Amasa Walker, who recalled the exultation of Ladd when "by untiring industry and zeal, and many entreaties and even tears, he had brought the Society up to this mark," which was now to be abandoned.[68]

Beckwith had all along maintained that, if the proper support of moderate peace men could be obtained without amending the constitution, such a step would not be insisted on. Hence it was not an open defeat when at the annual meeting in May, 1847, the Society voted unanimously not to alter the constitution. It was feared that the proposed change might at that time, if carried out, be misconstrued as sanction of the Mexican War. It was also stated that Ladd had specifically opposed any change in the constitution. Besides, and this was an important point indeed, any change might endanger the legacy which Ladd had bequeathed the Society or bring controversies about it. Thus the Society contented itself by unanimously voting that "all its operations be conducted with scrupulous adherence to the principles set forth in the resolutions" passed at the last annual meeting.[69]

Echoes of the controversy of course reached England. The Committee of the London Peace Society refrained from expressing an opinion, on the ground that the one side denied as strenuously as the other asserted that the cause of the rupture was an effort to lower the standard of the American Peace Society.[70]

The fact that the constitution was not altered, after all, permitted the reform party, in spite of its preoccupation with the League of Universal Brotherhood that Burritt was founding, to

[68] *Advocate of Peace,* vol. vii, January, February, 1847, pp. 2-4, 22; *Christian Citizen,* May 15, 1847; Ms. *Minutes of the Executive Committee,* September 25, 1846.

[69] *Christian Citizen,* June 5, 1847; *Advocate of Peace,* vol. vii, July, 1847, p. 94; Ms. *Minutes of the Executive Committee,* May 25, 1846.

[70] *Herald of Peace,* no. 57, April, 1847, p. 255.

follow the fortunes of the older society and to resent Beckwith's control. That official, indeed, had things all his own way, for the Executive Committee, now dominated largely by orthodox Congregational clergy, was quite content to sanction Beckwith's virtually unchecked management. Since the resignation of Blanchard as treasurer, for instance, Beckwith had been allowed complete charge of the Society's funds. Complaints began to be heard that he so managed the funds that no one else, not even the Executive Committee, knew what or where these funds were. Beckwith's hands were the only ones through which moneys of the Society went, since he collected the funds and paid the accounts, including the indebtedness of the Society to himself for his own services. There was no real auditing of accounts. Though most of the Executive Committee saw nothing wrong in all this, here was an opportunity for the reformers to get back at their old foe. An accidental majority of their friends at the annual meeting in May, 1849, enabled them to elect nine new members from their own group to the Executive Committee. The friends of reform seemed now to be in the saddle.[71]

The new Executive Committee set about rectifying what it regarded as financial abuses. The treasurer was "restored" to his control of the funds, and henceforth all money collected was to be handed over to him, while expenditures could be made only by vote of the Executive Committee. Beckwith pretended to welcome this relief from onerous financial responsibilities.

After three months of this new financial system, the Executive Committee was forced to recall Beckwith. It asserted that he had refused, under the new plan, to collect funds. That official, however, maintained that the deficiency in funds was due to the new financial organization itself. This could scarcely be the case, since the new procedure was businesslike and was

[71] *Advocate of Peace,* vol. vii, January and February, 1847, p. 22; Holland, Ms. *History of the American Peace Cause,* vol. iii, pp. 89 ff.; *Christian Citizen,* June 15, 1850; Ms. *Minutes of the Executive Committee,* June 8, July 2, October 10, 17, 25, November 1, 15, 1849.

followed by all philanthropic societies; nor could it have lessened the desire of friends to support the cause. Thus to the reformers Beckwith's "Jesuitical maneuvers" were paralyzing peace operations.[72]

Beckwith made out a good case for himself. By the generosity of friends he had been able, he said, after his recall by the Executive Committee to financial responsibility, to wipe out all the liabilities of the Society and yet at the same time to increase its scale of operations. His enemies, however, claimed that this was accomplished only by ignoring the indebtedness of the Society to Blanchard and cited chapter and verse in support of this contention. Beckwith now assumed the position, in his "Financial Suggestions" in the *Advocate* for June, 1850, that he could no longer carry the heavy burdens he had endured and informed the Society that the policy which compelled him to neglect many of his duties in order to spend three-fourths of his time in collecting money was unfair both to the Society and to him—in short, "suicidal." He proposed that to relieve the situation, friends must contribute a sufficiently large sum regularly upon which the Society might count.[73]

The reformed Executive Committee therefore had reason to believe that Beckwith would not oppose its continued efforts to put the finances of the Society on a sounder basis. Hence they were surprised when, at the annual meeting in May, 1850, Beckwith's friends took advantage of the fact that the conservatives, outnumbering the reformers by two, voted, in an entirely unprecedented way, to substitute the Executive Committee of 1848 for that of 1849. This meant nothing less than that Beckwith would again have things just as he wanted them. The *Christian Citizen,* the mouthpiece of the reformers, announced that such

---

[72] *Advocate of Peace,* vol. viii, May and June, 1850, pp. 224-225; Holland, *op. cit.,* vol. iii, pp. 89 ff.

[73] Beckwith, "Financial Suggestions," *Advocate of Peace,* May and June, 1850, pp. 224 ff.

conduct could not be tolerated and that a new peace society would be formed.[74]

It was decided, however, to wage another battle within the ranks of the organization. Things came to an acute crisis at the next annual meeting, in May, 1851. When the Annual Report was read, it seemed to Blanchard that the financial section was "a very ingenious and plausible endeavor" to show that the system of the existing Executive Committee, to which the reformers objected, was "the most economical and effective one ever pursued." Blanchard, in a published statement, pointed out several errors of fact in this part of the report.[75]

Both factions had made every effort to pack this annual meeting. Beckwith charged the reformers with having brought in thirty-two men between the Tuesday evening session, which opened the anniversary, and the Wednesday morning business meeting. It was admitted that these thirty-two had paid their dues for the privilege of voting to reform the Society, though the reformers denied the secretary's charge that they had never before contributed jointly as much as ten dollars to the Society.[76]

After the anniversary address on the evening of May 26, most of the reform group, supposing that the usual custom of delaying business until the meeting of the next day would be followed, withdrew. Beckwith then suggested that the Society proceed to business at once, on the pretext that there were so many anniversary meetings the next day that it would prove difficult to secure an adequate number to conduct business. Blanchard at once objected. The unfairness of conducting business at a time which had not been set for the purpose was so patent that even the conservatives refused to stand back of

[74] *Christian Citizen*, June 15, 1850; Ms. *Minutes of the Executive Committee*, May 29, 1850.

[75] *Advocate of Peace*, vol. ix, July and August, 1851, pp. 33-34; (J. P. Blanchard) *To the Members of the Peace Society*.

[76] *Advocate of Peace*, vol. ix, July and August, 1851, pp. 36-37; Ms. *Minutes of the Executive Committee*, May 28, 1851, June 2, 1851.

Beckwith, and the meeting was adjourned until the day after the next.

What a memorable meeting—the adjourned one of May 28, 1851! Even with the thirty-two newcomers designed to swell the ranks of the reformers, the conservatives enjoyed a slight majority. Beckwith tried to keep the newcomers from voting, but this attempt failed. When a motion was made to reëlect the old officers, the Reverend E. W. Jackson, the reformers' candidate for Beckwith's place, obtained the floor and lodged a series of complaints against his rival. The disorder all but ran into a riot. Bitterness, uproar, and excitement prevailed. Some one announced that the police had been sent for! When at last Jackson yielded the floor, a motion was put and carried to adjourn *sine die*. Jackson's voice warned the dispersing crowd that the reformers would be on hand to carry the day at the next annual meeting.

Since the form of adjournment was equivalent to a dissolution of the meeting, there was an open question as to whether existing officers could continue to hold their office. In the opinion of four "eminent lawyers," three being members of the Society, all officers, by the constitution, ceased to hold office, save the Directors of the Society. At a meeting of the Board of Directors Blanchard alone represented the reform group, and it was resolved to keep the Society in what that vigorous reformer called its "present inconsistent and illegal position." By vote they put it out of their power to meet again, as Directors, save at the call of the corresponding secretary, George C. Beckwith. Thus his absorption of powers was confirmed and strengthened.[77]

During the attack on Beckwith's integrity made in the meeting of 1851, it was voted to appoint a committee from different religious denominations to investigate the charges preferred against him. Although the chief persons on whom the reform party relied were unable or unwilling to serve, the Committee's

[77] *Ibid.*; Holland, Ms. *History of the American Peace Cause,* vol. iii, pp. 85 ff.

report, made at the annual meeting of 1852, was by no means an unalloyed victory for the arch official. It is true that it exonerated him of the charges made against his financial integrity, and that a tribute was paid to his industry, talents, and fitness for the office he had held for thirteen years. Yet it was admitted that he had not "always observed that strict *mercantile* method in keeping his accounts, which the circumstances render especially desirable." It was further pointed out that under the system which had existed it was in the power of one man to control the entire policy of the Society. The embarrassment caused by the financial experiment during the few months of 1849 had been due, the Committee held, to the fact that Beckwith interpreted it as limiting his functions to those of corresponding secretary, and hence he had collected practically no funds. The Committee greatly regretted the misunderstanding of that period, to which, it added, "may be traced a great part of the subsequent opposition to the management of the Society, and the alienation of many from it who previously were friends." The investigating committee then outlined a plan for future operations which provided for careful auditing of all accounts by the treasurer, to whom all funds collected were to be paid, and who alone could dispense funds. To lessen Beckwith's control of the organization, a committee on publications was also recommended.[78] The Society's unanimous adoption of this entire report therefore established something like the limitations on Beckwith for which the reform group had so long contended. At the annual meeting in May, 1854, the Society, in accepting the report of a committee on the revision of the constitution, decided to make no change in that document.

Thus the long controversy was in part healed. Beckwith continued to enjoy the chief duties and emoluments of the most important offices of the Society, although the reformers had won

[78] Ms. *Minutes of the Executive Committee,* May 28, October 8, 1851, March 10, April 20, May 24, 1852; *Advocate of Peace,* vol. x, June and July, 1852, pp. 119 ff; September, 1852, pp. 159 ff.

a point in achieving supervision of his activities. But they held that the Executive Committee failed to represent any shade of opinion save that of Beckwith. They were never entirely reconciled, and as late as 1860 one of their members, in writing the history of the American peace cause, made no efforts to conceal his rancor.[79]

Beckwith, too, regarded the affair as one which resulted in evil that could never entirely be erased. It was natural for him to feel that the attacks against him were in effect efforts to cripple the essential operations of the Society by crippling its chief servant. Friendly outsiders agreed with the *Christian Examiner* that the discord within the American Peace Society was "painfully inappropriate to its harmonious objects."[80]

It is quite true that other benevolent societies, especially the Prison Discipline Society, suffered similar experiences. But by the nature of the cause there could be in no other movement such evil consequences of dissension as in the peace movement. Its effectiveness was sadly lowered in a quarrel which, marked by a conflict of personalities, yet really involved the fundamental question of what the limits of pacifism should be, and how peace might best be obtained.

[79] Ms. *Minutes of the Executive Committee,* May 24, 1852, May 20, 1853; Holland, *op. cit.*

[80] *Advocate of Peace,* vol. x, September, 1852, p. 159; *Christian Examiner,* vol. lxii, July, 1852, p. 146.

V

THE CRUSADE TESTED, 1837-1852

FROM THE MIDDLE of the thirties to the outbreak of the Civil War the peace movement was tested almost without break by wars and rumors of war. Although its leaders constantly pointed to its achievements in these crises, they admitted at the same time the weakness of the movement. In 1842 the *Advocate of Peace* boasted that the press had of late "teemed with many able and pertinent articles on peace," but close examination of this claim indicates that at best the list of secular journals admitting peace principles was unimpressive and remained so.[1] Quite likely the press only reflected the apathy of the general public towards the cause.

Bad as this indifference was, that of the professed friends of the cause was even worse. Other benevolences seemed to absorb the major energy of humanitarian idealism. While many gave verbal approbation to the cause of peace, few contributed, and fewer still were genuinely convinced. This lamentable apathy accounts for the constant complaints of the editors of the *Advocate of Peace* and the *Christian Citizen* that peace workers seldom reported their activities, and that this made it impossible to keep their readers informed of what was being done. Samuel Plant of Northampton, Massachusetts, had labored as a member of one or another peace society for twenty-eight years, but in 1846 he had come to despair of ever witnessing, through the efforts of the peace movement, a change in public opinion on the subject of war. Again and again the leaders admitted lack of progress.[2]

In 1847, Beckwith, secretary of the American Peace Society, outlined causes for this situation. Time and again he heard people arguing that since peace could be achieved only by

---

[1] *Advocate of Peace*, vol. iv, no. 5, April, 1842, pp. 139 ff.; no. 5, pp. 107 ff.

[2] *Ibid.*, December, 1844, p. 285; *Christian Citizen*, July 26, 1845; March 21, 1846.

making all men Christians, their efforts should be put into spreading the Gospel. Others felt that peace could never be obtained until all force, all physical penalties, and even government itself were abandoned. Beckwith felt that such general and extreme points of view hindered the progress of the cause by discouraging more immediate and practical efforts.[3]

Another reason for the ineffectiveness of the movement in America was its failure to enlist the Quakers very actively in its support. As individuals some Friends contributed generously to the peace societies, but Amasa Walker wrote from Philadelphia in 1844, with some truth, that the Quakers had long ceased to bear testimony against the popular sins of the day. Their conservatism and complacency in regard to the organized peace movement may have been conditioned by their feeling that the long controversy over defensive war indicated half-heartedness within the ranks of peace. At any rate, by and large, Friends seemed to look on peace societies as denominational efforts in a good cause which they were not, as Friends, bound to support.[4]

If there had been strong opposition to the peace movement, perhaps it would have gained strength. But the *Christian Citizen* could even quote a speech of General Winfield Scott full of peace platitudes; and the few attacks on peace doctrines came from inconspicuous naval officers, who resented pacifist denunciations of the wastefulness and futility of the navy. Lieutenant Goldsborough, in a pamphlet designed to answer an attack on his branch of the service, felt that the abiding error of peace societies was their "presumptuous impression" that their efforts would ultimately extirpate "evil passions and propensities from the human breast." Sermons preached before "the ancient and honorable artillery companies" also defended war, but on the whole there was not enough opposition to the peace movement to make its propaganda anything like as biting and effective as that of the abolitionists. This indifference on the part of mili-

---

[3] *Advocate of Peace,* vol. vii, July, 1847, p. 51.
[4] *Christian Citizen,* June 28, 1844; *Advocate of Peace,* vols. iii-ix, *passim.*

tarists generally was made worse when not a few wore peace petticoats and became officers in anti-war societies.[5]

Not only did general apathy prevail during this period of trial, but also a few instances of open defection in the peace ranks were reported. Though the spirit of the churches might be willing, the flesh was frequently weak. One clergyman reported that his congregation, which professed the doctrines of peace and friendship to the cause, never wanted him to preach in time of religious indifference, for there were then more important matters at hand, nor in time of religious activity, as the great work of conversion then demanded every effort. It did not want him to preach in such a way as to bring the militia into disrepute. In time of peace it was felt that such preaching was unnecessary, and in time of war it was deemed unpatriotic and unwise. Nor were the principles of Christ ever to be carried out in an "ultra" or "Quaker" fashion. If there were many such friends of the cause amongst church supporters, one can understand Horace Greeley's gloomy observation that peace was as far from realization as it was when Christianity was first promulgated.[6]

With church folk so lukewarm, it was natural for politicians to be even more so. In 1844 Pettit of Indiana, during the debate in the House on appropriations for military and naval chaplains, moved to dispense with their services, because of the incompatibility between the principles of the Gospel and the practices of war. Pettit was attacked, and the debate which followed showed how entirely the nation's representatives in Congress failed to grasp the aims of the peace movement. And yet how naïvely its officers, during this time of test, were to rely on the lip service of public men to their cause! How little the golden opinions which the Reverend Aaron Foster gleaned from this

[5] *Christian Citizen*, August 3, 1844; August 28, 1847; June 15, 1844; August 21, 1847; L. M. Goldsborough, *A Reply to the Attack Made on the United States Navy by S. E. Coues*, Portsmouth, 1845.

[6] *Advocate of Peace*, vol. viii, March and April, 1849, p. 43; *Christian Citizen*, June 12, 1847.

and that Washington politician and set down in his clasp album really meant![7]

In England, the peace movement was in a position little or no better to make effective protests against public deeds or policies pregnant with war. The clergy of the Establishment seldom called war into question, and one Oxford college refused to house the publications of the London Peace Society. Religious periodicals scorned a London advocate's prize essay which was really a notable contribution to peace literature. In common with the American Peace Society, the London organization complained of lack of funds, though it fared as well as other benevolent societies and spent perhaps four times as much as the Americans could. And Parliament did not seem much more favorable than Congress. The Reverend James Hargreaves wrote to Ladd in 1840 that a petition to the House of Lords "too much resembled Jonah's gourd, which came up in a night, and perished in a night."[8]

Apathy, then, prevailed, and yet in both countries genuine efforts were made to prevent threatened wars. During the northeastern boundary dispute both British and American friends of peace pointed out the folly of fighting over such a trivial affair and spared no pains to make their voices heard. They printed all the conciliatory sentiments of public men and the press on the other side of the Atlantic and advised each other to urge arbitration on their respective governments. The ladies of the Essex County Olive Branch Circle sent an address to the ladies of Great Britain inviting their "coöperation, sym-

---

[7] Ms. *Minutes of the Executive Committee of the American Peace Society,* November 20, 1844; *Advocate of Peace,* vol. v, August, 1844, p. 234; vol. vi, July, 1845, pp. 207 ff. Henry Clay, J. Q. Adams, Rufus Choate, and Robert C. Winthrop were among the sixteen signatories mentioned, and so was General Scott.

[8] Henry J. T. Macnamara, *Peace, Permanent and Universal,* London, 1841, pp. 302, 309. Bishop Watson, Bishop Horne, Archbishop Secker and Dr. Whately were cited by Macnamara as favoring peace doctrines. *Advocate of Peace,* vol. iv, July, 1842, pp. 186-187; December, 1841, p. 91; November, 1842, pp. 257 ff.; vol. iii, no. 4, December, 1839, p. 86; no. 8, August, 1840, p. 191.

pathy, and prayers" in efforts to preserve and strengthen peace. During the so-called Aroostook war Ladd, writing for the newspapers on the question, maintained that the whole affair proved the need of a competent tribunal for settling such disputes and argued that the case would long before have found a satisfactory adjustment had such a tribunal existed.[9] Other individuals, in sermons and pamphlets, pictured the frightfulness of an Anglo-American war, its incalculable losses, its grave dangers, its moral and social results. William Ellery Channing, who since 1827 had been trying to foster better relations between the two countries through correspondence with persons of influence in England, redoubled his efforts. In a "plain and pungent appeal" to his fellow countrymen he spoke of a war with England as one between mother and daughter. Charles Sumner, trembling at such a thought, suggested to Lord Morpeth, chief secretary for Ireland, that both do what they could to maintain "peace, amity, and love" between the two countries and wrote an article for *Galignani's Messenger* presenting the boundary dispute in such a way as to be "not disagreeable to England."[10] Still another American, Origen Bacheler, congratulated President Van Buren on the pacific character of his message to Congress and suggested that the two governments select several individuals from the peace societies of their respective countries to act as umpires in the case.[11]

[9] *Harbinger of Peace,* vol. ii, no. 1, May, 1829, p. 7; vol. iii, no. 8, December, 1830, p. 191; *Calumet,* vol. i, no. 6, March and April, 1832, pp. 172-173; *Herald of Peace,* January, February, March, 1835, pp. 9 ff.; *Advocate of Peace,* vol. i, no. 3, December, 1837, p. 129; Hemmenway, *Memoir of William Ladd,* p. 80.

[10] *War with England, The Case Fairly Stated; with an Address to President Van Buren, by an Advocate of Peace,* New York, 1838; *Memoir of William Ellery Channing,* vol. iii, pp. 282, 289; *Correspondence of William Ellery Channing and Lucy Aikin,* ed. Letitia LeBreton, London, 1874, pp. 343, 306, 355, 346; Edward L. Pierce, *Memoir and Letters of Charles Sumner,* 4 vols., Boston, 1876, vol. ii, pp. 82, 87.

[11] *Van Buren Papers,* Library of Congress, Origen Bacheler to President Van Buren, February 28, 1839, vol. 35 (1839).

The American Peace Society, on the other hand, contented itself with issuing "An Appeal to the Friends of Peace throughout the United States," but not one in five of the fifty newspapers that received it, with a request to print, saw fit to do so. It is true that the Society also adopted a resolution at its anniversary meeting in June, 1839, deprecating the war excitement and urging counterstrokes. But these it was willing to leave, for the most part, to its members as individuals. The *Non-Resistant,* which went to great lengths to print anti-war arguments during the controversy, took the American Peace Society to task for its do-nothing policy. Even its secretary, Beckwith, apologized for it by reminding those who read the *Advocate of Peace* that the aim of the Society was not to meet political emergencies, but to disseminate "Christian Principles" that would obviate them.[12]

The London Peace Society, not content to let individuals do the bulk of the work of fighting the war scare, petitioned Parliament for a peaceful settlement of the boundary trouble. It also made the most of the testimony of British travelers in the United States as to that government's sincere desire to avoid war.[13]

Ill feeling between the United States and Canada was accentuated by the contemporaneous events of the Canadian Rebellion. A letter from near the New York-Canadian line begged the *Advocate of Peace* to send literature to offset the jingoism of the "Hunters' Societies." While deprecating the war spirit, neither the editor of the *Advocate* nor the Society apparently did anything to stem the tide. The Vermont State Peace Society,

[12] *Advocate of Peace,* vol. iii, no. 1, June, 1839, pp. 12 ff., 16-20; vol. ii, no. 2, April, 1839, p. 264; *The Non-Resistant,* vol. i, April 6, 1839, p. 7. The Executive Committee of the American Peace Society authorized the issuance of an extra number of the *Advocate of Peace.* Ms. *Minutes of the Executive Committee,* March 13, 1839. The Committee also communicated with the London Peace Society, urging the publication of appeals to prevent the outbreak of war. Ms. *Minutes,* March 12, 1838.

[13] *Herald of Peace,* new series, no. 18, April, 1842, pp. 67 ff.; no. 19, July, 1842, pp. 162-163; *Advocate of Peace,* vol. iv, no. 5; vol. iii, no. 4, December, 1839, p. 92; no. 3, October, 1839, p. 61; vol. xi, April, 1854, pp. 54 ff.

however, requested the help of a well known pacifist, John Lord; he carried the olive branch to northern Vermont and New York. Other peace men reminded their countrymen that if war resulted from American aggression along the border, it would be on our part a violation of the Convention of 1818.[14]

To make matters worse, the McLeod affair and the *Caroline* affair increased the misunderstanding between the two countries. Although peace men were by no means silent, there is little evidence to support a later claim that by diffusing information at this time they prevented war. William Ellery Channing tried to pour oil on the troubled waters, but there is no reason to believe that either his correspondence with English people or his public pleas had any real effect in either country. Nor does the biography of Joseph Sturge show us how his communications with Americans checked "the irritability of public opinion," though such correspondence may have been of some advantage in clearing the atmosphere. It is true that the American Peace Society, in sending a copy of the *Prize Essays on a Congress of Nations* to Queen Victoria, called attention to the danger of war "between the two most enlightened nations of the world" as a result of the cumulation of minor misunderstandings. But there is no evidence that either this seasonable word or the essays themselves or the Queen's gracious reply had anything to do with the negotiations presently begun by Webster and Ashburton.[15]

Webster, for his part, explained to a Faneuil Hall audience, early in 1843, that the northeast boundary and these other dis-

[14] *Advocate of Peace*, vol. i, no. 4, March, 1838, p. 192; vol. ii, no. 2, April, 1839, p. 261; no. 5, p. 116; Wright, Ms. *Journal*, vol. xxxvii, June 12, 1838; *War with England, the Case Fairly Stated, passim.*
[15] *Advocate of Peace*, vol. iv, no. 12, December, 1842, p. 284; vol. iii, no. 12, April, 1841, pp. 280 ff.; no. 12, April, 1841, p. 279; *Memoir of William Ellery Channing*, vol. iii, pp. 286-287, 299, 293, 293-295; Channing, *Works*, pp. 853-907; Henry Richard, *Memoirs of Joseph Sturge*, pp. 398-399; Macnamara, *Peace, Permanent and Universal*, pp. 286-287; Emerson Davis, *The Half Century*, Boston, 1851, p. 182.

putes were settled because the Whigs knew that even the fear of war was bad for business.[16] The editor of the *Advocate of Peace* somehow took this to mean that the influence of the peace movement had erected public opinion as "a new and elevated tribunal to which the disputes of the nations must in all cases be referred." It was, Beckwith insisted, due to the peace movement that a diplomat such as Webster could testify that nations might no longer take up arms unless there were grounds and reasons which would justify them in the general judgment of mankind. The next month Beckwith repeated the claim that there had been "auspicious and important changes in the international policy of Christendom" and that these had resulted mainly from "the blessing of God upon the efforts made by the friends of peace." He added that there was no space to substantiate this statement, though he was fully prepared to do so. But in the next issue he contented himself by saying that had public opinion been what it was a half century before, the arbitrators would have separated at once.[17] Another peace worker stated that he had learned in Washington that the reduction of the army to eight thousand men, at a critical stage of the negotiations, had induced Ashburton to continue the discussions, and it was intimated that this auspicious reduction of the service followed from the peace propaganda.[18] In view of the lack of supporting evidence, these statements are certainly open to question. There is, indeed, not the slightest reason to suppose that Ashburton would have packed up and gone home even had the army maintained its earlier strength. Nothing in the official printed records of the negotiations points to such a likelihood, and a careful student of the question believes that the British negotiator's entire conduct proves the sincerity of his inten-

---

[16] *Advocate of Peace*, vol. v, February, 1843, p. 16; vol. iv, no. 12, December, 1842, pp. 281-284.

[17] *Ibid.*, April, 1843, p. 47; January, 1843, p. 6; February, 1843, p. 14.

[18] *Christian Citizen*, February 15, 1845.

tions.[19] But peace agitators continued to take comfort from what they believed they had accomplished.

The American peace movement, if it blew its own trumpets louder than circumstances merited, none the less appreciated the significance of the final pacific settlement of outstanding disputes. The American Peace Society congratulated Lord Ashburton, gave him a copy of the *Prize Essays on a Congress of Nations,* and made him an honorary member of the Society. How pacifists rejoiced, when accounts were settled, to find the American government reducing its contracts with certain ammunition makers and advertising several thousand guns, "nearly new," at the Watertown arsenal! The *Herald of Peace* claimed part of the credit for the British peace movement and expressed just as great satisfaction at the final outcome.[20]

While these Anglo-American differences were resolved without an appeal to the sword, England meantime found herself pitted against distant foes over opium and Afghans. As early as 1836 William Watson maintained that extorting a treaty from an unwilling nation by show of force was an act contrary to both international law and morality, and that dangerous consequences were in order.[21] Only in 1841 did the London Peace Society wake to the danger of war in the East; it was not until the following year that the British did more than protest against the policies of their government. Then the *Herald of Peace* brought out any amount of material against the Opium and Afghan Wars. Tracts were scattered, and from great public meetings in London, Manchester, Leeds, Glasgow, and Dublin antiwar resolutions poured down on Sir Robert Peel. Efforts to discourage enlistments were not without some effect. Indignant

[19] E. D. Adams, "Lord Ashburton and the Treaty of Washington," in *American Historical Review,* vol. xvii, 1912, pp. 764-782; *House Executive Documents,* no. 2, 27 Cong., 3 sess.

[20] *Advocate of Peace,* vol. iv, no. 11, November, 1842, p. 263; February, 1843, p. 14; June, 1843, pp. 61, 63; *Herald of Peace,* new series, no. 18, April, 1842, p. 67; no. 23, July, 1843, pp. 317 ff.

[21] *American Advocate of Peace,* vol. ii, September, 1836, pp. 69 ff.; Holland, Ms. *History of the American Peace Cause,* vol. i, p. 133.

Joseph Sturge put his shoulder to the wheel, arranged protest meetings, and lectured his fellow citizens on their Christian duties. Another Quaker, John Gurney, reminded his countrymen that when he had taken Calhoun to task as the defender of slavery, that statesman, pointing to China and Afghanistan, suggested that people who lived in glass houses would best not throw stones. Elihu Burritt blessed the peace men who lifted up their voices as against blasphemy when in Parliament a vote of thanks to the army of India was moved. While British friends of peace left no stone unturned to discourage enlistment, induce labor to boycott munition factories, and to besiege the press and government with public meetings and resolutions, their American coworkers drew ample courage and moral precepts for the cause from their example.[22] Before long they were to be called on to join with their English cousins in making out a case for peace in the Oregon dispute.

This new war scare quickened the endeavors of the peace groups in the two countries as had no earlier test. In 1845 the arch pacifist, Henry C. Wright, challenged his British audiences to preserve the threatened peace, while Isaac Collins brought to the London Peace Society word from America urging renewed efforts against war. American friends of peace soon learned that in no previous year had their English colleagues gone to such lengths, for 270 lectures had reached more than 64,000 people, and 6,000 signatures had been added to the Peace Society's Declaration of Principles. On May 11, 1845, at the instigation of the Society, 110 peace sermons were listened to by London congregations. The Society further memorialized her Majesty, urging the Government not to be turned aside from its pacific course by any circumstance of American provocation that might arise. In addition some two hundred petitions de-

[22] Annual Report of the London Peace Society in *Advocate of Peace*, December, 1841, vol. iv, no. 4, pp. 89 ff., 259-260; *Herald of Peace*, new series, no. 19, July, 1842, pp. 121, 114, 144; no. 22, April, 1843, p. 270; no. 23, pp. 317 ff.; Richard, *Memoirs of Joseph Sturge*, pp. 286-287; *Littell's Living Age*, vol. iii, December 21, 1844, p. 517; *Christian Citizen*, April 4, 1846.

ploring the proposed increase in the army and navy were sent to Parliament.

In all this activity British Friends played a prominent part. Joseph Sturge took it upon himself to write to Whittier and to Lewis Tappan, of the New York *Journal of Commerce,* urging them to use their influence to avoid threatened hostilities.[23] When Peel and Aberdeen received a petition from Quakers begging them to make every concession and even suffer rather than do harm, those statesmen suggested that American Friends use their influence in a similar way. Perhaps this may have had something to do with the fact that a deputation from the Indiana Meeting for Sufferings memorialized Congress in April, 1846, pleading for a compromise, and that four English Friends called on President Polk to express their great desire for the preservation of peace.[24]

This activity on the part of the British stimulated American friends of peace. Sumner kept in close touch with his English correspondents regarding the dispute, urging that the substance of British demands was within their reach, and that it was folly to delay a settlement for reasons of diplomatic etiquette. These letters found their way into the hands of Lord Aberdeen and Sir Robert Peel.[25] Individuals communicated their anti-war position to Polk, while the New York Peace Society and the editor of the *Christian Citizen,* Elihu Burritt, urged on the President a moderate policy. They called his attention to similar petitions from British citizens to their Government. S. E. Coues, the President of the American Peace Society, addressed two striking letters to Polk and sent the *Advocate of Peace,* which described British pacifist activity, to each member of Congress. Every mem-

---

[23] *Advocate of Peace,* vol. v, May, 1845, p. 60; *Christian Citizen,* July 5, June 13, August 17, December 27, 1845; Richard, *Memoirs of Joseph Sturge,* p. 404.

[24] *Christian Citizen,* August 23, 1845; Richard, *Memoirs of Joseph Sturge,* pp. 400 ff.; Hirst, *The Quakers in Peace and War,* p. 264; M. M. Quaife, *The Diary of James K. Polk,* Chicago, 1910, 4 vols., vol. i, p. 302.

[25] Jacob Harvey to Charles Sumner, New York, November 22, 1845, *Sumner Papers, 1845;* Richard Rathbone to Charles Sumner, Liverpool, June 2, 1846, *Ibid., Foreign Letters Received, 1844-1846.*

ber of that body also received Elihu Burritt's convincing "Olive Leaves."[26]

By far the greatest achievement of this Anglo-American cöoperation, however, was the Friendly Address movement—a kind of picturesque "People's Diplomacy," which originated with the sending of a peace address from Birmingham pacifists to "the friends of peace in the United States." Although this address was printed in the *Advocate of Peace* and the *Christian Citizen,* the movement might have perished stillborn had not a Birmingham Quaker, Joseph Crosfield, popularized the idea in the British press and taken steps to interest Elihu Burritt in it. Burritt was sending out each fortnight circulars, the Olive Leaves, to some 1,500 American newspapers, and he was therefore just the man to familiarize the American public with the scheme of interchanging Friendly Addresses. According to his own testimony, two hundred newspapers printed his Olive Leaf describing the plan, and by return packet Burritt sent this Olive Leaf to Crosfield. The British press quickly learned of it.[27]

British cities paired off with towns in America whose placenames or whose industries suggested kinship. Addresses, "brotherly letters, breathing with sentiments of friendship and amity, deprecating every expression of unkind feeling and invoking coöperation in bringing their respective governments to an amicable adjustment of differences," were sent from Plymouth and Boston to New England's Plymouth and Boston, from Edinburgh to Washington, from Manchester to New York, and from many more British cities to American cities. Some of the Friendly Addresses, as that from Southampton to Cincinnati, ran to over 1,500 signatures. Perhaps the most interesting one was that from the National Association for Promoting the Political and Social Improvement of the People. Written two years

[26] *Herald of Peace,* no. 43, April, 1846, pp. 59-60; *Christian Citizen,* May 10, 1845, January 16, 1846.

[27] *Christian Citizen,* May 24, 1845; *Advocate of Peace,* vol. vi, July, 1845, pp. 78-79; April, 1845, p. 48; *Christian Citizen,* January 3, 1846; *Bond of Brotherhood,* new series, no. 12, July, 1851.

before the Communist Manifesto, this address appealed to the class consciousness of the laboring brethren of America, urging them not to be "seduced" into a war to enrich the aristocracy, "our enemies and yours." The war spirit, the address went on to say, had already led the rulers of Britain to add to labor's burdens by increasing the length of militia service. Well might Burritt observe that "peace and bread" were associated in the minds of British laborers as intimately as they were in nature.[28]

British workingmen were not alone in responding, from economic motives, to the Friendly Address movement, for several hundred of the leading manufacturers and merchants of Manchester answered Crosfield's appeal to that class to use their influence for peace. Their friendly address, along with that of the merchants of Leeds to the merchants of New York, emphasized the interdependence of nations and held that the "acquisition of Oregon territory by either country would be utterly worthless, in comparison with the evils and cost of war." Many leading British papers, together with men like Cobden, Bright, Lord Morpeth, Dr. John Bowring, Milner Gibson, Douglas Jerrold, and Thomas Clarkson, commended the merchants for their action.[29]

For the most part the Friendly Addresses were framed at meetings in English towns, called by the mayor or leading merchants. At the Manchester meeting over two thousand attended, while at Boston more than a hundred were turned away. Charles Dickens, Douglas Jerrold, and the popular Hutchinson actor-family entered the lists. The movement got into the London *Times,* which thus "carried the subject of the Friendly International Addresses before the whole commercial world, and to the very ends of the earth." When the American responses came to England they were circulated in printed form by the Man-

---

[28] Elihu Burritt, *Thoughts of Things at Home and Abroad,* Boston, 1854, p. 330; *Advocate of Peace and Universal Brotherhood,* April, 1846, pp. 91-95, 103.
[29] *Advocate of Peace and Universal Brotherhood,* February, 1846, p. 56; October, p. 236, March, p. 69; *Christian Citizen,* March 28, 1846.

chester group of Friends, who furnished the chief support for the movement. Often these American addresses also found their way into the British press.[30]

In some cases the British Friendly Addresses were forwarded to the mayor or to some prominent citizen in the town addressed, though many of them went to Burritt. They were then sent, as Olive Leaves, to the press, sometimes in batches numbering as many as seven hundred, to cities "from Texas to Canada." Burritt himself presented the Edinburgh Address to the government of the City of Washington, unrolling it first before a large number of senators. Among them was Calhoun, who expressed great interest. Many cities replied in kind, the address from Boston being signed by the mayor, Josiah Quincy, and by George S. Hillard, president of the Common Council, at the direction of the City Council. Worcester's address to the parent English city contained eight hundred signatures, and as many as 3,525 Philadelphia women responded to Lucretia Mott's appeal and signed a friendly address to the women of Exeter, England. Four hundred New York merchants signed a response to the Manchester Address, circulated by Lewis Tappan, of the *Journal of Commerce*. "As a matter of profit and loss," ran this address, "it would be infinitely better that the whole of Oregon should sink into the bottom of the ocean, than that two such nations as Great Britain and the United States should go to war about it, to the disgrace of civilization, Christianity, and rational freedom."[31]

Burritt, without whom the movement could scarcely have reached very great proportions, expressed the general feeling of the pacifists of both countries in observing that by "this cheap, quiet instrumentality, not a little public opinion was manufactured in favor of peace and brotherhood." It was firmly be-

---

[30] *Christian Citizen*, May 16, 1845, April 25, 1846, citing the London *Times*, March 20, 1846.

[31] Burritt, Ms. *Journal*, September 25, 1846, March 31, 1850; *Advocate of Peace and Universal Brotherhood*, March, 1846, p. 69, May, pp. 124-126; *Christian Citizen*, June 27, 1846.

lieved that the Friendly Address movement not only contributed "greatly to the speedy and satisfactory settlement of the question at issue," but also inspired a friendly feeling "between the peoples of the two countries." While the American Peace Society contented itself with passing resolutions, Burritt, the Methodist of pacifism, appealed directly to the people to stay the war clouds.[32]

Yet this growing reliance on appeals to public opinion did not altogether replace efforts to influence public men. It is not at all unlikely that the propaganda with which Coues and Burritt besieged each member of Congress furnished the stock pacifist arguments with which such senators as H. W. Miller, Rufus Choate, J. J. Crittenden, and Reverdy Johnson garnished their Oregon speeches. Whatever Calhoun's motives in sponsoring peace, it is interesting to note that he used in his address of March 16, 1846, all the arguments most relished by the peace men. Burritt also warned Senator Benton of his duty to posterity as well as to "the impulsive populace of the West," where Manifest Destiny was the cry of the hour; and though this appeal may not have been the cause, Senator Benton's noisy patriotism gave way to a spirit of compromise.[33] What one Congressman, Robert C. Winthrop, owed to the peace arguments was clearly shown in the speech by which he supported his resolutions for the arbitration of the controversy.[34]

In the large volume of pamphlet literature urging peace, there was, for the most part, a repetition of the familiar religious,

[32] *Bond of Brotherhood*, new series, no. 13, August, 1851; *Herald of Peace*, April, 1846, p. 60; Burritt, *Thoughts of Things at Home and Abroad*, p. 331; *Charles Sumner Papers*, Richard Rathbone to Charles Sumner, Liverpool, July 24, 1846; Richard, *Memoir of Joseph Sturge*, p. 402; F. W. Holland, Ms. *History of the American Peace Cause*, vol. ii, p. 51.

[33] Burritt, Ms. *Journal*, March 11, 1844; *Christian Citizen*, March 9, 1844; Thomas Benton, *Thirty Years View*, New York, 1856, 2 vols., vol. ii, pp. 600 ff., 679 ff.; *Christian Citizen*, January 24, March 28, April 13, May 30, 1846; Calhoun's *Works*, vol. iv, pp. 258-290 (ed. Richard Crallé, New York, 1854).

[34] R. C. Winthrop, *A Memoir of Robert C. Winthrop*, Boston, 1897, pp. 38 ff., 46 ff.

philanthropic, and economic arguments. Of the economic arguments the most striking was the appeal to western farmers and merchants not to forfeit the new British markets opened up by the repeal of the corn laws. Without British capital, it was also pointed out, work on our public improvements must stop. During the controversy much importance was attached to combating the war fever in the West, and new plans were devised for opening the door of that region to the appeal of the Olive Branch.[35]

Turning to the expression of opinion in the press, one cannot doubt that pacifists were right in maintaining that it was far more hospitable to their cause than ever before, but this change was not necessarily due, as they inferred, to their own efforts. In 1845 Burritt knew of thirty-seven newspapers which championed peace "in its full radicalism" and, according to him, the columns of many hundreds more were open to a free discussion of the subject. Yet only a few years before, a newspaper in a New England seaboard town refused to admit, even for payment, a notice of the formation of a peace society.[36] Without cataloguing the newspapers, British and American, that came out for peace, one might note that among many others the *New York Tribune*, the New York *Telegram*, the Boston *Recorder*, the Charleston *Mercury*, and the Baltimore *Clipper and American* lent support. Clearly the cause of peace was becoming respectable.[37]

Both in England and America, then, appeared widespread protests on the part of individuals, editors, and public men

[35] "W. G.," Philadelphia, April 20, 1846, to Elihu Burritt, in *Christian Citizen*, May 2, 1846; *Advocate of Peace and Universal Brotherhood*, December, 1846, p. 284; *Christian Citizen*, April 13, 1844, February 15, 1845, September 6; *Advocate of Peace and Universal Brotherhood*, July, 1846, pp. 154-155.

[36] *Advocate of Peace*, vol. vi, September, 1845, p. 101; *Christian Citizen*, July 19, 1845.

[37] *Littell's Living Age*, vol. vi, pp. 251 ff., August 9, 1845; pp. 251, pp. 302 ff., August 16, 1845; vol. viii, pp. 35 ff., 68 ff., 489 ff., 578 ff.; *Christian Citizen*, March 16, June 1, 1844; February 22, May 17, May 24, June 28, July 5, September 6, September 13, 1845; January 3, 1846.

against a possible settlement of the Oregon controversy by war. It is perhaps impossible to determine how much or how little peace workers contributed to these protests and how effective these protests were in influencing the final compromise. Peace leaders honestly believed, however, that their organization and work during the preceding fifty years had so transformed public opinion that peace was as inevitable a solution as war would have been at an earlier time. They went even further and believed that their timely activity turned the scales in the point at issue.[38] They were thus neglecting the consideration that the closer economic ties between the two countries were also working for a changed public opinion, that southern cotton in British mills and British capital in America, to say nothing of less restricted commercial relations, were telling arguments for keeping the peace.[39] Despite the ugliness of the controversy, it is likely that war would have been avoided had peace workers not lifted their fingers. Yet their work seems undoubtedly to have increased the habit of intercommunication of ideas between the two countries, and it may have furnished some convenient arguments to those who, being in public authority, were committed to peace. Whatever pacifist activity contributed to clearing the atmosphere, there can be no doubt that it strengthened the peace movement by giving its leaders the conviction that their practical efforts had at last directly influenced public men.

Not least important in the activities of the peace movement during this time of trial was the Fourth of July Oration of Charles Sumner, delivered before Boston municipal authorities in 1845 and directed against both the Oregon and the Mexican crises. "By an act of unjust legislation, extending our power over Texas, peace with Mexico is endangered, while, by petulant

---

[38] Eighteenth annual report of American Peace Society, *Advocate of Peace and Universal Brotherhood*, June, 1846, pp. 140-141; *Herald of Peace*, no. 49, August, 1846, p. 113.

[39] Joseph Schafer, "British Attitude towards the Oregon Question, 1815-1846," in *American Historical Review*, vol. xvi, p. 294; *Cambridge History of British Foreign Policy*, vol. ii, pp. 258-260.

assertion of a disputed claim to a remote territory beyond the Rocky Mountains, ancient fires of hostile strife are kindled anew on the hearth of our mother country."[40] From these specific references Sumner went on to consider the whole problem of peace and war as they affected the national honor and the true glory of nations. "Can there be in our age any peace that is not honorable, any war that is not dishonorable?" He pointed out the utter and pitiful insufficiency of war as a mode of determining justice, and he analyzed the sundry prejudices by which it was sustained, especially the false prejudice of national honor. He massed statistics regarding the wastefulness of war and preparation for it; he appealed to rational as well as to Christian principles. Rich in historical and literary allusions, the address eloquently synthesized the arguments already familiar to peace workers.

Like an avalanche this address fell upon the military portion of the audience, and its epoch-making significance in the history of the peace movement can be understood only by reading the correspondence resulting from it. Sumner had been a member of the Executive Committee of the American Peace Society since 1841, and naturally his colleagues were the first to congratulate him. "As the cause of peace dates principally from your oration," wrote Elihu Burritt, "you must in a degree father it." Other advocates of the cause were no less expectant. In its next annual report the American Peace Society announced that 9,000 copies of the address had been republished in England and in the United States and took courage from its wide approval. Antislavery men, too, hailed the performance with joy, while more than a dozen distinguished scholars and philanthropists spoke Sumner's praise from their hearts.[41]

On the other hand, a large number of influential men like

[40] Charles Sumner, *Works,* Boston, 1874, 12 vols., vol. i, p. 8.

[41] Ms. *Minutes of the Executive Committee of the American Peace Society,* October 13, 1841; *Sumner Papers,* 1845, S. E. Coues to Sumner, July, 9, 1845; Beckwith to Sumner, July 5, and *passim.*

W. H. Prescott, Horace Mann, the Reverend Andrew Norton, Judge Story, Josiah Quincy, president of Harvard, Nathan Appleton, Richard Henry Dana, and Alexander H. Everett took exception to the tenets of the address, especially to the implication that nations would do well to disarm completely. Some bristled at the thought of what such a procedure might mean, others insisted that the doctrines of the oration were ill adapted to human nature, and many held that war was at times necessary to promote justice to such downtrodden peoples as the Poles and the Negro slaves.[42] An anonymous pamphlet tried to disprove the contentions of the oration; the *Christian Citizen* professed surprise that no stronger refutation could be made.[43]

While the mercantile and conservative journals in general treated the address with indifference, the religious and antislavery papers for the most part spoke of it with respect. The *New York Tribune* thought it a "noble performance," and even the *North American Review* had a good word to say for it. Extracts from the oration appeared in a large number of the newspapers and periodicals of the country, and the publicity thus accruing to Sumner made him henceforth a well known man. His public career had begun.[44]

In England the oration met with a decidedly good reception, for not only the *Herald of Peace,* but Lord Morpeth, Charles Vaughan, R. M. Milner, and Richard Rathbone held a brief for Sumner and determined to turn his oration to good account. It was felt that the "momentous crisis" of the Oregon question justified the freest use of the oration. Without waiting for Sumner's consent, the Liverpool Peace Society printed and circulated 7,000 copies of a collection of extracts from it, sending the pamphlet to the Queen, the Duke of Wellington, Sir Robert Peel, the Earl of Aberdeen, Viscount Palmerston, Lord

---

[42] Pierce, *Memoir,* vol. ii, p. 361 ff.; Massachusetts Historical Society *Proceedings,* April, 1917, pp. 249 ff., "Letters to Charles Sumner on his Oration, July 4, 1845."

[43] Pierce, *op. cit.,* vol. ii, p. 370; *Christian Citizen,* November 15, 1845.

[44] Pierce, *op. cit.,* vol. ii, pp. 362 ff.

John Russell, the Bishop of Norwich, Bright, Cobden, and other members of Parliament and notables.

The London Peace Society sent copies to forty periodicals. Rathbone regretted that he was unable to persuade either Sumner or Burritt to take up the cudgels and answer the criticisms made of the address. In general, both London and provincial papers, however, spoke favorably of the oration, and it must have been flattering to its author to have heard from Cobden that it would be very useful to him in dealing with the armament question in Parliament.[45]

Thus the thoroughness of the views expressed by Sumner at a time when the American peace movement was debating the limits of pacifism served not only to stimulate interest in the peace cause in the United States, but acted as part of the machinery by which English friends of peace sought to allay the Oregon war fever. Sumner took a more active part in the Executive Committee of the American Peace Society and addressed that organization at its annual meeting in 1849.[46] For two hours he held an "overwhelming" audience by what Thomas Drew of the *Christian Citizen* regarded as "the mightiest word for peace that has yet been spoken."[47] In this address on "The War System of the Commonwealth of Nations" Sumner traced the history of the peace movement, advocating its chief specifics, a Congress of Nations and arbitration treaties, as the best means of abolishing war. Possibly the advice of friends to wash his hands of pacifists, "weaklings and one-sided idealists," possibly absorption with the slavery question, accounts for Sumner's waning interest in the peace cause, which, however, he did not entirely forget.[48] Meantime a powerful gladiator had raised his

[45] *Herald of Peace*, new series, no. 38, September, 1845, pp. 338 ff.; Lord Morpeth to Charles Sumner, October 1, 1845, *Sumner Papers, Foreign Letters, 1844-1848;* Charles Vaughan to Sumner, December 28, 1845; R. M. Milner to Sumner, December 29; Richard Rathbone to Sumner, February 1, March 26, April 2, 1846; Cobden to Sumner, March 8, 1848.

[46] Sumner, *Works* (Boston, 1874), vol. ii, pp. 177-277.

[47] *Christian Citizen*, July 7, 1849.

[48] Pierce, *op. cit.*, vol. iii, p. 39.

voice for peace at a time when war clouds hung heavy over the country.

And there was need of support, for suddenly the Mexican War brought home to peace advocates their worst fears. In both the *Christian Citizen* and the *Advocate of Peace* Elihu Burritt had sounded the alarm and warned his associates to consider well their duty should war come. He had denounced Manifest Destiny with both penetration and irony. To counteract the war fever he had commenced to publish a little periodical, the *Bond of Brotherhood,* which he circulated in railway cars and on canal boats, employing four young men for that purpose in the spring months of 1846.[49]

To the American Peace Society the Mexican War seemed entirely unnecessary. At its annual meeting in May, 1846, it passed resolutions deprecating the War and laying it at the door of the American government. War would have been averted, the report of the Society insisted, had there been a Congress of Nations. With characteristic sanguineness the Society, at its next anniversary, ventured to anticipate ultimate good to the cause as a result of the War. In no other school than war itself would people learn that it was as unjustifiable as it was inhuman.[50]

After the *Herald of Peace* called upon the American Peace Society to bestir itself, Beckwith took pains to see that whatever was done came to the attention of the British. By reason of "the whirlwind of excitement" the plan of holding public protest meetings was given up, but the Society petitioned the President and Congress and through communications to a thousand newspapers urged individuals to do the same. New England and Philadelphia Friends, as well as the *Christian Citizen,* entered the lists, and partly as a result of all this activity as many as

[49] *Christian Citizen,* March 30, 1844, August 2, 1845; Mary Howitt, Memoir of Elihu Burritt, the preface to *Thoughts of Things at Home and Abroad,* p. xxiv.
[50] F. W. Holland, Ms. *History of the American Peace Cause,* vol. iii, p. 94; *Advocate of Peace and Universal Brotherhood,* June, 1846, p. 139; *Advocate of Peace,* vol. iii, July and August, 1847, p. 75.

twenty petitions for peace sometimes reached the House of Representatives on a single day. Sometimes these petitions bore as many as nine thousand signatures. At least once an anti-war demonstration in Boston was broken up by soldiers and friends of soldiers.[51]

While a critic of the American Peace Society, the Reverend F. W. Holland, felt that the petitions were tardy, feebly expressed, and altogether ineffective, he approved the offer of a prize for the best book on the Mexican War.[52] The prize of five hundred dollars was awarded to the Reverend A. A. Livermore of Keene, New Hampshire. His book, the *Mexican War Reviewed,* accepted the theory that the war was a conspiracy to extend slavery, explained how the conflict might have been avoided, and emphasized the economic waste which it entailed. It made the most of war atrocities; it urged that the struggle accentuated party and sectional strife and concluded that its only possible good was the lesson it might teach.

The competition also stimulated the writing of other books indicting the War, the most telling of which was William Jay's *Review of the Mexican War.* Funds of the American Peace Society printed and circulated this book, and within five months nine thousand copies had been distributed.[53]

In these books and in the pages of the *Advocate of Peace* every thinkable argument did service in blackening the War. Much was said of military expenses and of how the working and producing classes paid them. Countless letters from American soldiers pointed to corruption in the army, brutality, unnecessary bloodshed, mismanagement. The executive department was arraigned for profiting from the War by increasing its

[51] *Herald of Peace,* new series, no. 66, January, 1848, pp. 5 ff.; *Advocate of Peace,* vol. vii, July and August, 1847, pp. 75 ff.; *Herald of Peace,* no. 57, April, 1847, pp. 250 ff.; *Christian Citizen,* January 9, 23, 1846; June 27, November 28; *Advocate of Peace,* vol. vii, March and April, 1847, p. 47; Ms. *Minutes of the Executive Committee of the American Peace Society,* January 4, 1848.

[52] Holland, Ms. *History of the American Peace Cause,* vol. iii, p. 102.

[53] *Christian Citizen,* September 22, 1849; A. A. Livermore, *Mexican War Reviewed,* Boston, 1850.

despotic hold on the country. Then the *Advocate* also published the Mexican side of the story whenever it could lay hands on documents from south of the Rio Grande.[54]

Ecclesiastical bodies, especially the Unitarians and Friends, joined hands with organized pacifism, and a few advocates of peace among the politicians also took up the glove against the struggle. Though many public men who opposed the War did so by reason of their antislavery sentiments, some advanced purely pacifist arguments. But Beckwith came to believe that hardly a speech in Congress against the War was of any permanent value to the cause, so high did partisanship run among the politicians. Both parties, it appeared to Beckwith, had steeped themselves in the guilt of the War, for the Whigs rushed to its support and boasted of furnishing the best generals and of voting generous supplies.[55]

While most peace men were true to their colors during the Mexican War, some seem to have joined the flag-waving hue and cry. Lowell in the *Bigelow Papers* satirized peace men who presented swords to generals and aided the recruiting sergeants. Ralph Waldo Emerson, poet-pacifist that he was, felt that the centuries would justify the Mexican War, while Walt Whitman, editor of the *Brooklyn Eagle,* abandoned the pacific position he had taken during the Oregon crisis and urged the thorough chastening of Mexico. With romantic idealization of American democracy, he held that our superior civilization justified our absorption of our southern neighbor as the best road to ultimate peace with her and rejoiced that the fraternization of American soldiers with Mexicans was already strengthening the bonds of friendship between the two peoples. It is a matter of special comment that these two courageous idealists found the test of even a jingoistic war too much for their reason to withstand.

[54] *Advocate of Peace,* vol. ii, January and February, 1847, and in succeeding numbers of the *Advocate.*
[55] *Advocate of Peace,* vol. vii, January and February, 1848, pp. 145 ff.; March and April, p. 198.

Thoreau, on the other hand, thought that honest men ought to "rebel and revolutionize" when the invading army of their country unjustly overran and conquered a neighbor. He even went further and arraigned those who opposed the war and yet, indirectly, by their taxes, furnished a substitute and sustained an unjust government. Thoreau hated war all the more because it made of the soldier "a mere shadow and reminiscence of humanity"—a mere machine with "no free exercise whatever of the judgment or of the moral sense."[56]

A respectable number of periodicals gave space to antiwar arguments. But the *Quarterly* of Orestes A. Brownson, a Catholic publicist, dwelt on the necessity of obeying the authority of the state in all cases. Quoting St. Thomas Aquinas as well as the Scriptures, he tried to refute pacifist arguments. Although the Reverend Samuel J. May of Syracuse, New York, was threatened with violence because of his pacific work,[57] most peace advocates seem to have been tolerated to an unusual degree. No doubt this circumstance was related to the existence of widespread criticism of the War by others than peace men.

For years prior to the end of the war peace-loving Americans had urged on the Government the principle of arbitration. Along with other opponents of slavery and of the annexation and prowar sentiment dominant at the time, they had taken part in keeping up the continual flow of anti-war, anti-annexation and arbitration petitions which poured in on Congress and the Administration between the years 1837 and 1848.[58] Although

[56] *The Writings of James Russell Lowell* (Riverside edition, 10 vols., Boston and New York, 1892), vol. ii, p. 55; J. E. Cabot, *Memoirs of Ralph Waldo Emerson,* 2 vols., Boston, 1887, vol. ii, p. 576; M. E. Curti, "Literature and the Synthetic Study of History," *Historical Outlook,* vol. xiii, April, 1920, p. 175; Cleveland Rogers and John Black, editors, *Gathering of the Forces,* 2 vols., New York, 1920, vol. i, pp. 240 ff., 246, 254, 256, 264; *The Writings of Henry David Thoreau,* 20 vols., Boston and New York, 1906, vol. iv, pp. 359, 361, 365.

[57] *Brownson's Quarterly Review,* vol. iii, October, 1846, pp. 497, 517; *Advocate of Peace and Universal Brotherhood,* 1846, p. 175.

[58] See, for example, Miss Adelaide R. Hasse's *Index to United States Documents Relating to Foreign Affairs, 1828-1861,* Washington, 1914, Part I, pp. 60-61, and *passim.*

it has since been claimed[59] that this activity led to the incorporation in the Treaty of Guadalupe Hidalgo of Article XXI, a definite recommendation for arbitration in case of future disputes between the two countries, this assumption is without foundation. The article was in fact a concession to the Mexican desire for an even stronger safeguard in case of future difficulties with their more powerful neighbor.[60]

While American advocates of peace were opposing, however ineffectively, the militaristic policy of their government, their British fellows were also meeting the challenge of the Mexican War. The London Society addressed a memorial to President Polk and to Santa Anna, urging them to accept British mediation. At the same time it begged Lord John Russell to renew his offer of mediation, and a similar request was made of the monarchs of France, Austria, the Netherlands, Belgium, Sweden, and Russia. The English humorist, Douglas Jerrold, joined with the Birmingham philanthropist, Joseph Sturge, in casting his influence for peace between the two American powers.[61]

If it be said that much of the American opposition to the Mexican War was not that of professional pacifists, it must be remembered that the greatest satire of the war, the *Bigelow Papers,* came from a man who had previously expressed sympathy with the peace movement.[62] It must also be remembered that, although the voices of those who opposed the War have outlasted the shouts of their opponents, the loudest and most popular sentiments at the time came from those intoxicated with the war spirit. Even such an antislavery organ as the *National*

[59] For example, Anon., *Arbitration and the United States,* World Peace Foundation *Pamphlets,* vol. ix, nos. 6-7, Boston, 1926, p. 485.

[60] M. E. Curti, "Pacifist Propaganda and the Treaty of Guadalupe Hidalgo," *American Historical Review,* vol. xxxiii, no. 3, pp. 596 ff.

[61] *Advocate of Peace,* vol. vi, September and October, 1847, pp. 117 ff.; vol. vii, May and June, 1848, pp. 213-214; *Herald of Peace,* no. 62, September, 1847, pp. 215 ff.; Burritt, Ms. *Journal,* June 17, 1847; *Christian Citizen,* July 17, 1847; Richard, *Memoirs of Joseph Sturge,* p. 432.

[62] C. E. Norton, *Letters of James Russell Lowell,* 2 vols., London, 1894, vol. i, pp. 106-107, Lowell to Longfellow, August 13, 1845.

Era favored the absorption of Mexico, state by state.[63] Hence the consistent opposition of most friends of peace is truly significant. Horace Greeley's pessimistic prediction at the opening of the war, that the "old women" who talk peace so loudly in time of peace would remain "dumb as oysters" in war, was not borne out. Young men were publicly urged to choose prison, if drafted, rather than service.[64] Not only did the peace movement, torn by factions as a result of the debates on the limits of pacifism, register consistent opposition to the Mexican War; it also tried to convert the facts furnished by the war into "powerful arguments for peace." While it can not be proved that the peace propaganda was responsible for breaking the war morale, it can be recorded that the behavior of the bulk of pacifists was not a matter for apology.

Closely following the Mexican War came another test for peace advocates, the Revolutions of 1848. These revolutions presented a conflict of loyalties, since most peace men were friends of national self-determination as well. How would they now reconcile their sympathies for European freedom with their opposition to war?

At first both English and American pacifists welcomed the victories of the revolutionists, believing that they proved the futility of armed forces for maintaining unpopular authority. They were also inclined to feel that the people's victory meant the success of public opinion, the means by which the triumph of peace would be achieved. Only when it was clear that violence and social radicalism were part of the story did they withdraw their sympathies from the revolutionists. It is true that some friends of peace, such as Horace Greeley and Horace Mann, did not falter in their loyalty to the cause of the revolutionists,

---

[63] C. Fish, *American Diplomacy*, pp. 277-278.
[64] *Christian Citizen*, June 6, November 28, 1846.

but the great majority resolved the conflict of loyalties by remaining true to their peace principles.[65]

When the revolutions were crushed their exiled leaders tried to persuade the governments of England and the United States to make some gesture of sympathy for the new uprisings they were planning. Both the London and American peace societies warned their members not to fall into the trap Kossuth was so eloquently baiting. Overt sympathy with the projected revolutions might involve their governments in continental wars, and these, peace leaders insisted, were by far too big a price to pay for the triumph of national rights. In America "the Kossuth excitement" interfered with peace work, and many abandoned their internationalism and championed Washington's isolation policy, which now seemed the surest guaranty of preserving the nation's peace. Internationalism was now associated with military implications, and peace men would have none of it.[66]

Closely allied with the interventionist movement, which resulted largely from the activities of such men as Kossuth, Kinkel and other refugees, was the movement calling itself Young America. This slogan, Young America, was another name for the spread-eagleism which demanded the immediate realization of America's power in the world, a realization to be achieved through a big army and navy and a defiant foreign policy. It was to achieve our Manifest Destiny by absorbing the whole American continent and to tender aid to peoples struggling for national freedom from the autocratic dynasties of the Old World.[67] Such sentiments, with their blatant chauvinism, were obviously the antithesis of the doctrines of peace. Young

[65] *Herald of Peace*, no. 69, April, 1848, pp. 56 ff.; *Advocate of Peace*, vol. vii, August, 1848, p. 234; October and November, p. 265; Cobden to Sumner, November 7, 1849, *Sumner Papers, Foreign Letters*, 1849-1852.

[66] *Advocate of Peace*, vol. x, January, 1852, pp. 12, 14; Bruitt, Ms. *Journal*, October 30, 1851; *Christian Citizen*, September 8, 1849; William Jay, *The Kossuth Excitement*, 1852, *passim*.

[67] M. E. Curti, "Young America," in *American Historical Review*, vol. xxxii, no. 1, October, 1926, pp. 34-35.

America was a challenge. "We have among us combustible material enough to set a whole continent on fire; and we should take good heed that no spark is ever applied to it," remarked the editor of the *Advocate of Peace*.[68]

Apart from condemning editorially the policies of Young America—filibustering expeditions to Cuba and Nicaragua, and anti-British policies in Central America—the peace group as such took no action, though individuals did. Elihu Burritt sought out the hero of Young America, Stephen A. Douglas, and was surprised to learn that he had attended the Edinburgh Peace Congress while in that city and to hear him admit that he had been impressed by the anti-war arguments of Cobden and Bright. Burritt even penetrated into high places in the administration, which was deprecated in peace circles for its "Young American" character. President Pierce invited him to dinner, and the peace missionary tried to commit the Chief Executive to a policy of securing arbitration treaties with all foreign powers. Burritt left peace literature behind him and apparently succeeded in interesting not only Mrs. Pierce, but the President himself, who later welcomed him with more than formal politeness.[69]

Although such English friends of peace as Joseph Sturge and Richard Cobden regretted the chauvinism of Young America, the British had their hands full in combating the dangers of an Anglo-Continental war. Cobden, it is true, urged Sumner to try to restrain his countrymen from interfering in the Canadian question, but organized friends of peace in England and America apparently felt that the danger of the movement for annexing Canada was scarcely serious enough for a formal protest.[70]

Thus advocates of peace combated not only war but also policies which threatened war. Their attitude and work were

[68] *Advocate of Peace*, vol. x, January, 1852, pp. 1-3.
[69] Burritt, Ms. *Journal*, April 26, 1854, November 17, 1848, May 16, 1854.
[70] Richard Cobden to Charles Sumner, November 7, 1849, *Sumner Papers, Foreign Letters*, 1849-1852.

the more commendable during these troublous times when one considers the essential weakness and limitations of the peace movement. During the period from 1837 to 1852 the Americans were engaged, as we have seen, in the problem of defining their fundamental platform and policies. Encouraged and fortified by their joint activities in combating war and rumors of war, American and British peace workers were at the same time founding a truly international organization.

VI

THE BEGINNINGS OF INTERNATIONAL ORGANIZATION

FROM THE BEGINNING of the peace agitation its international character had to some extent been emphasized. Publications had been interchanged and the periodicals of the societies in England, France and the United States had frequently inserted accounts of the activities of their foreign co-workers. Yet in 1842 there was reason to doubt whether sufficient progress had been made in the cause to justify an attempt at a more formal international organization. There was especially little to hope for from the continent of Europe. Although the Society of Christian Morals at Paris appointed in 1841 a special committee on peace, that organization for the most part was attempting little if any practical work for the cause.[1]

The first move of a definitely international character occurred in 1842, when the London Peace Society sent an agent to work on the Continent and financed a prize essay competition for the Society of Christian Morals. The premium of a thousand francs was divided between M. Bazan and M. Charles Pecqueur. Their essays were published, and medals were awarded three of the twenty-four contestants. Thus the cause of peace was advertised, and both the London Peace Society and the Society of Christian Morals became more widely known on the Continent.[2]

As the American and British peace movements claimed for their respective countries a peculiar mission to lead the world in peace, so French pacifists claimed a similar mission for France. Yet organized French pacifism was far behind that of America

---

[1] *Herald of Peace,* January, February, March, 1835, p. 57; *Advocate of Peace,* vol. iv, October, 1841, p. 71.

[2] *Advocate of Peace,* vol. iv, October, 1841, p. 71; Villenave, Mathieu G. T. de *Société de la Morale Chrétienne, Rapport sur le concours ouvert . . . a l'assemblé . . . le 18 avril 1842,* Paris, 1842; M. Bazan, *Discours couronné par la Société de la Morale Chrétienne,* Paris, 1842; C. Pecqueur, *De la Paix, de son principe et de sa réalisation,* Paris, 1842; P. R. Marchand, *Nouveau Projet de Traité de Paix Perpétuelle,* Paris, 1852.

and England. Villenave, a vice-president of the Society of Christian Morals who especially interested himself in peace, emphasized the importance of converting kings rather than peoples, thus showing kinship with the pacifists who had followed Alexander in his idea of a Holy Alliance and a Concert of Europe. Many of the projects for a federation of Europe showed slight development beyond the plan of Saint-Pierre. Bazan, the author of a prize essay, felt that the chief obstacle to the cause of peace was the likelihood of uprisings on the part of artisans and recommended that peace be secured by keeping them quietly at work on public improvements. Enthusiasm for the national liberty of suppressed peoples and the conviction that they could achieve their independence only through war kept such intellectuals as George Sand from professing sympathy with pacifism.[3]

On the other hand, among French Socialists the economic aspects of pacifism were emphasized to a greater degree than in the peace circles of England and America. Saint-Simon and his followers, especially Enfantin, maintained that peace was a *sine qua non* for the workingman. Constantin Pecqueur, who published in 1842 *De la Paix, de son principe et de sa réalisation,* not only favored arbitration by a permanent Diet with delegates from all nations, but also the organization of permanent peace armies for production, in which the arts of peace, commerce, and industry were to be taught. Such a scheme, Pecqueur thought, would bring peace and justice to all humanity. French Free Traders, like Frédéric Bastiat, Horace Say, Joseph Garnier, and Émile de Girardin were, like Cobden, Bright, and Burritt, beginning to point out the connections between restrictive tariffs and war. It was only later, however, that they began to work with the peace movement, while the Socialists for the most part kept aloof.[4]

[3] Villenave, *op. cit.*; Bazan, *op. cit., passim*; George Sand to George Sumner, April 4, 1846, *Sumner Papers, Foreign Letters Received,* 1844-1846.

[4] C. Pecqueur, *De la Paix, de son principe et de sa réalisation,* III and IV; Pecqueur, *Des armées dans leurs rapports avec l'industrie, la morale et la liberté,*

If the outlook, then, was somewhat gloomy in Paris, it was ominous elsewhere. Stephen Rigaud, an agent of the London Peace Society, found it impossible in 1842 even to hold a meeting in Lyons or to form a peace committee. Despite the work of de Sellon in Geneva, Rigaud could not hold a public meeting because of the militant excitement over a political affair; and the Countess de Sellon had been unable to find a suitable editor to continue the peace periodical provided for in the will of her husband. Elsewhere in Switzerland, to be sure, Rigaud was kindly received by small groups of professors and Protestant pastors. This was true, to a less extent, in the Rhine valley. In these journeys this missionary of the London Peace Society, in spite of discouragements, scattered tracts and introduced Ladd's *Prize Essays on a Congress of Nations* into the Royal Library at Brussels and that of the new University at Athens.[5]

American influence was also presently brought to bear upon peace propaganda in Europe. George M. Gibbes, a South Carolinian and a graduate of Harvard College, in 1842 urged the necessity of a journal, to be published daily in Paris, in French, as an organ for disseminating the arguments already formulated by the British and American peace movements. This was the more necessary, Gibbes urged in his communication to the American Peace Society, since the journal of the Society of Christian Morals had but a few hundred subscribers, and being a monthly, was necessarily slow in its appeals. Except for the government press, every newspaper in Paris hated England. Gibbes went so far as to publish a prospectus for the journal, to be conducted under the auspices of Lamartine, Dr. John Bowring, M. P., and Henry Wheaton, American minister to Prussia, who warmly supported the plan. This international daily journal was to promote peace and international philan-

Paris, 1842, *passim;* J. L. Puech, *Tradition Socialiste en France et la Société des Nations,* Paris, 1921, *passim; Journal des Économistes,* vol. xxiv, August, November, 1849, pp. 101 ff.

⁵ Report of S. Rigaud in *Advocate of Peace,* vol. v, March, 1843, pp. 30 ff.

thropy, cement an alliance between England, France, and the United States, and support the true principles of international law, the abolition of the slave trade, piracy, and maritime war. The journal was further designed to dispel the "profound French ignorance of America" and to make known our great and inexhaustible resources. To promote this object, and to encourage amicable relations between the Old World and the New, an American Athenaeum had already been established at Paris.[6]

Both the London Peace Society and the American Peace Society warmly commended this project and gave it what publicity they could, but neither felt able to support it financially. The mere proposal, none the less, played a part in the preparation for a more definite international organization. The publicity given it in Paris may have had something to do with the establishment in February, 1843, of a weekly paper, *La Paix des Deux Mondes,* by Madame Niboyet. The first number gave an account of the peace societies in America and England and advocated French participation in an international peace organization. This journal reached America for at least two years after its foundation.[7]

While the discussion of an international newspaper was clearing the way for a more formal international organization, a series of exchange visits between English and American peace advocates was promoting the same object. Henry Barnard, representing the Connecticut Peace Society, and the Reverend Dr. Humphrey, president of Amherst College, spoke at the nineteenth anniversary of the London Peace Society in 1835. In announcing the enthusiastic reception of these Americans, the Editor of the *American Advocate of Peace* suggested that a regular interchange of opinions and influence by delegates as well as by cor-

[6] George M. Gibbes, *Letter to the American Peace Society,* Paris, 1842, p. 8.

[7] *Herald of Peace,* new series, no. 21, January, 1843, p. 263; no. 27, April, 1844, p. 67; *Advocate of Peace,* vol. iv, July, 1842, p. 188; vol. vi, November, 1844, p. 274; Ms. *Minutes of the Executive Committee of the American Peace Society,* January 26, 1844.

respondence be established by the peace societies of England, America, and France.[8]

The interchange of visits thus auspiciously begun did not stop. In 1838 the distinguished British Friend, Joseph John Gurney, came to the United States and was sought out by Ladd, who urged him to induce American Quakers to aid in the work of the organized peace movement. Gurney contributed to the publishing of the *Prize Essays on a Congress of Nations,* and peace men felt his travels "would produce much good."[9] In 1841 the Quaker philanthropist, Joseph Sturge, visited America to promote both the abolition of slavery and the establishment of permanent international peace. He proposed to a meeting of the American Peace Society that a conference of the friends of peace from all countries assemble in London "at the earliest practicable opportunity." The American Peace Society favored this suggestion in resolutions which Sturge later presented to the London organization.[10] This was a bold design, for international conferences were as yet unusual and fraught with difficulties.

After a full interchange of opinions in a preliminary conference, at which Richard Cobden favored the proposal as a means of drawing public attention to "the great subject of peace," it was decided to sponsor such a convention. A committee on arrangements decided to hold it immediately after the Antislavery Convention in June, 1843. American readers of the *Advocate of Peace* were informed of every step which the committee in England took. In its pages were reprinted the rules of procedure, constitution, and program of the Convention.[11]

[8] *American Advocate of Peace,* vol. i, no. 6, September, 1835, pp. 269 ff.

[9] Hemmenway, *Memoir of William Ladd,* p. 78; *Advocate of Peace,* vol. ii, no. 9, February, 1839, p. 215; Wright, Ms. *Journal,* vol. xxvii, May 25, 1838.

[10] Joseph Sturge, *A Visit to the United States in 1841,* Boston, 1842, preface, pp. 173, 218; *Advocate of Peace,* vol. iv, no. 3; October, 1841, p. 66; Ms. *Minutes of the Executive Committee,* October 13, 1841.

[11] *Herald of Peace,* new series, no. 19, July, 1842, pp. 113 ff.; no. 21, January, pp. 173, 218; *Advocate of Peace,* vol. iv, no. 3, October, 1841, p. 66; Ms. *Minutes of the Executive Committee,* February 8, 1843.

No efforts were spared by the Committee to make the venture a success. Circulars were sent to all the correspondents of the London Peace Society urging the appointment of delegates. Considerable success resulted from the efforts made to secure notices in the leading newspapers and periodicals. Copies of the circular announcing the Convention, along with William Jay's *War and Peace,* were sent to every member of Parliament, to the ambassadors of foreign nations in London, and to distinguished judges. As a result of correspondence with prominent persons in Amsterdam, Rotterdam, Hamburg, Stockholm, Strassburg, Geneva, Lausanne, Basle, Paris, Brussels, and Lyons, arrangements were made for delegates from Paris, Brussels, and Le Mons. The Executive Committee of the American Peace Society appointed twenty delegates and requested the president and corresponding secretary to attend as official representatives and to make a report on the proceedings of the Convention.[12]

Finally, on June 28, 1843, in Freemasons' Tavern, London, there assembled for the first time in history an international congress of peace advocates. Thus only two years after the death of William Ladd the world saw the beginning of the international organization for which he had so long worked and hoped.

At the opening session attendance ran above three hundred, a number equal to that of the Antislavery Convention which had just ended. The average attendance, however, was not more than one hundred and fifty delegates, although there were many visitors, including a large number of women. Only fourteen of the twenty delegates appointed from the United States were at hand, but impressive letters of regret helped compensate for the absence of the rest. Of the American delegates present, the best known in the peace movement were the Reverend George C. Beckwith, Amasa Walker, John Tappan, Lewis Tappan, Dr.

[12] Henry Richard, *Memoirs of Joseph Sturge,* pp. 347 ff.; *Advocate of Peace,* vol. v, October, November, 1843, pp. 109 ff. (report of the American delegation); May, 1843, p. 60

Thomas Cock of New York, George M. Gibbes, and Isaac Collins of Philadelphia. Of the six French delegates, the most distinguished was the Duke de la Rochefoucauld-Liancourt, president of the Society of Christian Morals. Naturally British delegates made up the bulk of the convention. Perhaps the best known British names were such members of Parliament as Richard Cobden, William Ewart, John Brotherton, Charles Hindley, Joseph Hume, and Dr. John Bowring, and certain religious leaders and philanthropists such as the Reverend John Burney, the Reverend Pye Smith, the Reverend James Hargreaves, William Forster, John Lee, Joseph Sturge, Edward Miall, Joseph Price, John Allen, and Samuel Gurney.[13]

The committee on arrangements had determined the principle on which the Convention should be based—that "war is inconsistent with the spirit of Christianity and the true interests of mankind." Its object was to deliberate on the best means, "under Divine blessing," by which the world might be shown the evils and inexpediency of war and to promote permanent and universal peace. An attempt was made to alter the basis of the Convention by excluding all those who did not believe war to be under all possible or supposable circumstances inconsistent with Christianity, but this proposal was defeated. Apart from this jar, the sessions were remarkably harmonious, a fact noteworthy in view of the heterogeneous personnel.[14]

The rules of the Convention prescribed that all members must devote themselves exclusively to the objects at hand, and to insure relevancy, papers, propositions and items of business had to be submitted in advance to the secretaries of the Convention. Later peace congresses in general followed these precedents.

Two sessions, lasting from four to five hours, were held

---

[13] *Advocate of Peace*, vol. v, September, 1843, p. 97; *Proceedings of the First General Peace Convention Held in London on July 22, 1843, and the following days with the papers read before the Convention, letters read etc.*, London, 1843, *passim*. Report of the American delegation in the *Advocate of Peace*, vol. v, October and November, 1843, *passim*.

[14] *Ibid*.

daily for the three days that the Convention sat. Of the papers read, one dealt with a statistical account of war expenditures, one appealed to Christian ministers and teachers, and another considered "the best practical means of obtaining peace." Resolutions adopted by the Convention elaborated the means for achieving the ultimate goal: the use of teachers, ministers, women; handbills, periodicals, circulars, the press generally; the control of the manufacture and sale of munitions; a Congress and Court of Nations; clauses for arbitration in international treaties; and resistance to threatened war by awakening in every way possible public attention whenever war should threaten. Still other resolutions condemned the wars which Great Britain was then fighting in the East, especially the Opium War, and expressed the hope for a second international peace convention.[15]

Friends of peace felt that the undertaking had been a thorough success. As Beckwith pointed out, it was "a bold and hazardous experiment" fraught with many difficulties. "We made a beginning, and that was all we ventured to hope. Its final results may take ages to disclose."[16]

The first important effect of the London Convention was that which it produced on the friends of peace themselves. For the first time in the peace movement their efforts were guided, stimulated, correlated in joint action. Plans were formulated for later execution. Moreover, the beginnings of a definite international organization were made, while pleasant personal relationships were established between American, British, and French promoters of peace.

Secondly, the Convention made the cause of peace known to a wider public. All the leading papers of London had representatives present to report its proceedings, and, though generally meager, these reports were considered "fair and respectful." The London *Times,* it is true, spoke of "the vagaries and delusions of those unhappy individuals who have just been figur-

[15] *Ibid.*
[16] *Ibid.*

ing before the world under the title of "the Universal Peace Convention." Its pretentions, continued that influential journal, found support only in "good-natured emptiness and commonplace triviality."[17] The London *Morning Advertiser* observed that although it was the first meeting of the kind, it would not be the last, and expressed the belief that peace principles were making rapid headway throughout the civilized world. The *Nonconformist,* the *British Friend, Buck's Gazette,* the *Oxford Chronicle,* and the *Cheltenham Gazette* either gave detailed accounts of the Convention or warmly applauded its object and character.[18]

Nor did the Convention fail to make some impression upon governments. "An Address to the Civilized Governments of the World" was presented by deputations from the Convention to Sir Robert Peel, Prime Minister of Great Britain, to the King of Belgium, to Louis Philippe, and to President Tyler. In each case the delegates received courteous treatment from these government heads, who with soft words expressed approval of the principle of arbitration. "Thank God," Louis Philippe observed to the delegation, which included several Americans, "war now costs too much for nations to afford it." President Tyler told Beckwith that he was sure peace was an especially wise policy for the United States. "Let the people bear sway," he continued blandly, "and they will, if duly enlightened, demand peace as essential to their welfare."[19]

Though the "Address to the Civilized Governments of the World" was presented or sent to fifty-four governments, peace men appealed directly to the people as well. During the summer and autumn of 1843 more than seventy meetings, with an average attendance of over two hundred, were held in the boroughs of London and in the country, at which American delegates

---

[17] *Herald of Peace,* new series, no. 25, October, 1843, pp. 452-453, quoting extract from London *Times,* June 28, 1843.

[18] *Advocate of Peace,* vol. v, January, 1844, p. 151.

[19] Report of the American Delegation, *loc. cit.; Advocate of Peace,* vol. v, April, 1844, p. 192; October and November, 1843, pp. 124-125.

spoke. Ten thousand handbills were circulated in Wales, and fifty-five petitions were sent to the Government to prevent the quelling of an uprising by military force. This activity suffered no hindrance during the entire year, as the annual report of the London Society well showed.[20] In Paris, too, friends of the cause took courage and formed a peace society with fifty members, the Société de la Paix de Paris, with William Jay, George C. Beckwith, and J. P. Blanchard honorary members. In his agency in the provinces of France, in Belgium and in Holland, Rigaud found that the mere fact of the London Peace Convention made it easier to break the ground for his labors.[21]

Americans, too, experienced something of this buoyancy. The American Peace Society circulated eleven thousand copies of the *Advocate* describing the London Convention and, in addition, sent a specially prepared circular on arbitration to all members of Congress and to twenty-eight governors. To this campaign of publicity "a multitude of papers, secular as well as religious," contributed by copying the "Address to the Civilized Governments" and an account of its reception by the British and French governments. The *Christian Citizen* ventured to say that from 1844 to 1845 more had been written and said on peace than during the ten or twenty preceding years. It believed that half a dozen more such congresses, in London, Paris, and Boston, would "make war impossible between the three governments. By a most natural induction they would prepare the way for a new and pacific attitude on the part of Christian governments."

The London Peace Convention thus acted like a tonic. It was natural, considering all that had been said and done, for Beckwith to write to Dr. John Lee, President of the London Peace Society, proposing the formation of a Universal Peace Society, on a broad platform, with its headquarters in London.

[20] *Herald of Peace,* new series, 25, October, 1843, p. 431; *Advocate of Peace,* vol. v, December, 1843, p. 143 (Jefferson to Beckwith, September 2, 1843); August, 1844, p. 236 (Report of the 28th meeting of the London Peace Society).
[21] *Advocate of Peace,* vol. v, August, 1844, p. 237; February, 1845, pp. 17-19.

"We all need a central committee of Vigilance for the peace of all nations; a committee with branches, correspondents and co-workers in every part of the civilized world; a committee on the alert to descry far ahead the gathering storm and able by the prompt coöperation of friends in all parts of the great marts of public opinion, to prevent its bursting on mankind in the horrors of actual war." Such a bond of union of the friends of peace throughout the world would have more influence, he thought, than any local organization. A common universal basis of coöperation was made necessary by the fact that "peace is an object common to the great brotherhood of nations."[22] It remained for another man, however, to realize this suggestion.

[22] *Herald of Peace*, new series, no. 27, April, 1844, p. 59 (Beckwith to the Rev. John Jefferson, December 16, 1843); *Christian Citizen*, July 5, 1845; *Advocate of Peace*, vol. v, May, 1844, and August, 1844, p. 237.

Your faithful friend.
Elihu Burritt.

VII

ELIHU BURRITT AND THE LEAGUE OF UNIVERSAL BROTHERHOOD, 1846-1855

"THE GREATEST value I attach to life is the capacity and space of labouring for humanity." Thus Elihu Burritt wrote in his *Journal* on December 8, 1846. As early as 1838 the idea of universal brotherhood had been one of his "most precious thoughts."[1] To advance this cause he began in 1844 at Worcester, Massachusetts, a weekly newspaper, the *Christian Citizen*. Each number carried as a headpiece across the first page these words: "God hath made of one blood all the nations of men." Devoted to temperance, antislavery, and "self-cultivation," the *Christian Citizen* held no reform so dear as that of universal peace.

Although this venture did not earn its impoverished editor his daily bread, he did not despair. In 1845 he even added to his heavy load by assuming financial responsibility for the periodical of the American Peace Society, which he undertook to edit. He aimed to make the *Advocate of Peace and Universal Brotherhood* an Anglo-American and ultimately a universal periodical, and he secured contributions from prominent English peace men as a step in this direction.[2]

On the evening of July 29, 1846, Elihu Burritt, with knapsack and staff, was walking along an English country road towards Worcester. He had refused the great public welcome by which British friends of peace wished to honor him, for his purpose in coming to England was to serve the cause of peace rather than to be admired. At this moment his mind was on a task at hand—that of writing for the *Christian Citizen* and the *Advocate of Peace and Universal Brotherhood,* for he was still their editor. He therefore decided to stop at the little village of

[1] Ms. *Letter Book of Elihu Burritt,* American Antiquarian Society.
[2] Burritt, Ms. *Journal,* January 1, April 10, 1845; *Advocate of Peace and Universal Brotherhood,* 1846, *passim.*

Pershore. But his thoughts turned rather to his dream of a League of Universal Brotherhood, the secret, half-formulated object of his journey. How warmly English friends of the cause had received him in this short fortnight on their soil! They had aided him with much enthusiasm during the Oregon controversy. Might they not perhaps join with him in a project for an international peace organization? Such a thing was all the more necessary when he remembered the victory of Beckwith at the anniversary of the American Peace Society, May last. He reflected that his friends, Amasa Walker, Samuel Coues, and Joshua P. Blanchard, felt sorely tempted, as he himself did, to leave that organization, now that Beckwith held the reins and could be counted on only to win worldly men who at heart were far from consistent peace advocates. Burritt, moreover, had no sympathy for what seemed to him the exclusive basis of each reform movement. The vital principle beneath the work of the peace men, the temperance crusaders, the partisans of prison reform, the friends of the slave, the insane, the diseased, and prostitutes, was it not fundamentally one and the same? Was it not the "elevation of man, as a being, as a brother, irrespective of his country, color, character, or condition?" How unfortunate that it was unconstitutional on the peace platform to advocate any other reform, lest this might offend some friend of peace who believed in the lawfulness of human slavery or the divine sanction of the gallows! Yet he found in England what he found in the United States, that the most earnest and sincere friends of one reform were at the same time friends of other reforms. The efficiency which would come from the coöperation of related philanthropic enterprises would be incalculably enhanced, he thought, if the scope of their work were international. By the very principle of human brotherhood, which was the spirit guiding all of them, their work, he concluded, must be international.[3]

[3] *Christian Citizen*, February 7, 1846; Burritt to John Jefferson, July 1, 1846, *Herald of Peace*, no. 49, August, 1846, p. 117; Ms. *Lecture on the League of Universal Brotherhood*, in the Library of the American Antiquarian Society.

With these thoughts in his mind, he determined to stay at Pershore for a day or so. It was there that he drew up a pledge as the basis of his contemplated League of Universal Brotherhood. He entered it into a little clasp book which he bought for the purpose:

Believing all war to be inconsistent with the spirit of Christianity, and destructive to the best interests of mankind, I do hereby pledge myself never to enlist or enter into any army or navy, or to yield any voluntary support or sanction to the preparation for or prosecution of any war, by whomsoever, for whatsoever proposed, declared, or waged. And I do hereby associate myself with all persons, of whatever country, condition, or colour, who have signed, or shall hereafter sign this pledge, in a 'League of Universal Brotherhood'; whose object shall be, to employ all legitimate and moral means for the abolition of all war, and all spirit, and all the manifestation of war, throughout the world; for the abolition of all restrictions upon international correspondence and friendly intercourse, and of whatever else tends to make enemies of nations, or prevents their fusion into one peaceful brotherhood; for the abolition of all institutions and customs which do not recognize the image of God and a human brother in every man of whatever clime, colour, or condition of humanity.[4]

The idea of a pledge was suggested by the success which its use had brought the temperance movement. It would provide the personal, individual element which was too often lacking in the abstract propaganda of the older peace societies. Its terms made it certain that the League could not be torn by dissipating arguments in regard to defensive war.

That evening a Mr. William Conn invited Burritt to drink tea with him and some friends in his "little upper room" at Pershore. Some twenty humble artisans and country people gathered, and Burritt, having signed the pledge himself, for some three hours explained it and his mission to England. The

---

[4] Announcement, in *Works of Elihu Burritt*, London (no date).

result was that nineteen "good men and true" signed the pledge, and thus began the League of Universal Brotherhood.[5]

But the League of Universal Brotherhood was not to remain limited to the lowly. At a soirée of the delegates to the World's Temperance Convention, in Freemasons' Hall, London, August 5, 1846, Joseph Sturge introduced the subject of the pledge. Burritt spoke, and the printed pledges were "filled upon the spot with names that stand high, in the estimation of the public, on both sides of the Atlantic." These sixty names included Lawrence Heyworth of Liverpool, a man of great wealth and beneficence; Joseph Sturge, James Silk Buckingham, outstanding religious leaders; and the secretary of the London Peace Society, the Reverend Joseph John Jefferson. Burritt began addressing groups in private houses and in Quaker meetinghouses, and within four months, thanks to his enthusiasm and energy and a hundred pounds from Joseph Sturge, nine hundred and twenty-five persons had signed the pledge.[6] These names appeared in the *Christian Citizen*, which Burritt had left in charge of Thomas Drew. Responses soon came from the *Christian Citizen's* invitation for American signatures to the pledge, among the earliest being those of S. E. Coues, Amasa Walker, and J. P. Blanchard. Each week the *Christian Citizen* printed new lists of signers, alternating an English list with an American list.[7] In this way the League of Universal Brotherhood was founded, without any formal organization, in both England and the United States.

As the unofficial organ of the League of Universal Brotherhood the *Christian Citizen* became a truly international newspaper. Edmund Fry, the son of Elizabeth Fry, in whom Burritt early found one of his most valuable English co-workers, contributed each week a column entitled "A Voice from London," and after 1848 Earnest Lacan, a young French protégé of Burritt,

[5] William Conn to the editor of the *Christian Citizen*, December 11, 1847.

[6] *Advocate of Peace and Universal Brotherhood*, October, 1846, pp. 245 ff.; Burritt, Ms. *Journal*, September 21, 1846.

[7] *Christian Citizen*, September 26, 1846; Burritt, Ms. *Journal*, October 4, 1846.

did the same for Paris. General political news was reported from a pacifist point of view, and fresh as well as familiar peace arguments were introduced. The chatty and intimate tone of the newspaper made it resemble an enlarged family circle's tea-table. It printed countless letters from friends of peace in Europe and America and went into great detail in describing the activities of the League of Universal Brotherhood. Early in 1850 the young Scotch poet-pacifist, J. B. Syme, came to Worcester to help in its editorship.[8]

For a time the *Christian Citizen* flourished. In 1847 it was read in twelve hundred towns. But subscribers were slow in paying for it, and one of the business partners, it seems, drew more out of it than its income justified. It became increasingly a sinking concern, and Burritt lost heart when not "a single dollar return" rewarded his continual slaving for it. Had not Amasa Walker insisted that the League in the United States would crumble without it, Burritt would probably have abandoned the paper before 1851, when, as a result of Drew's mismanagement, it was declared bankrupt. "The Learned Blacksmith" was saddled with new debts.[9]

Burritt, even before the demise of the *Christian Citizen,* had learned to lean on the *Bond of Brotherhood* as the most effective organ of the League. Its short, pithy, and striking arguments gave it an extremely popular tone. Arresting statistics on the cost of war compelled attention no less than the epigrammatic quotations. Although he had begun to publish this sheet in Worcester, Massachusetts, during the Oregon crisis, Burritt printed the *Bond* in England as soon as the League was founded in 1846; and from England it found its way both to America and the Continent. For a time its circulation reached 30,000, but its average monthly issue did not exceed 6,000.[10] It increased from four

[8] Burritt, Ms. *Journal,* February 18, 1850; *Christian Citizen, passim.*

[9] *Christian Citizen,* December 4, 1847; Burritt, Ms. *Journal,* December 17, 1847, March 23, 1849.

[10] *Advocate of Peace and Universal Brotherhood,* April, 1846, p. 104; December, p. 274; Burritt, Ms. *Journal,* June 25, 1847, December 20, 1848.

to sixteen pages, and besides making the work of the League possible, proved an effective agency for peace. Burritt regarded the attack made on it by *Blackwood's Magazine* as proof of its influence, for *Blackwood's* would have spared its virulent invective on a movement "too contemptible for observation." Elihu Burritt was proud of what he called the "first and only international publication ever issued."[11]

While Burritt was organizing the League by addressing groups in Friends' meetinghouses and in "little upper rooms," and writing up its activities for the *Christian Citizen* and *Bond of Brotherhood*, he was broadening his circle of friends and co-workers. Philanthropic Quakers applauded his work for relieving famine-struck Ireland and entered into his activities with great energy. Indeed, it was the support of such men as Joseph Sturge, Edmund Fry, Crosfield, Alexander Brockway, and a number of other Friends that made his work in England possible.[12]

But the Quakers were not his only allies. Free Traders welcomed Burritt's emphatic declaration that unrestricted commerce was inherent in "the constitution of nature" and that commercial competition and war went hand in hand. In 1842, a year after Burritt reached this conclusion, Richard Cobden also saw the connection between Free Trade and the peace movement and urged enlisting Friends to champion the repeal of the corn laws. It does not seem, however, that the English peace movement threw its weight into the free trade campaign.[13]

Cobden and the free trade group must all the more, therefore, have welcomed Burritt's efforts early in 1846 to persuade

[11] *Blackwood's Magazine*, March, 1853, quoted in the *Bond of Brotherhood*, new series, 34, May, 1853; *Christian Citizen*, September 26, 1846.

[12] For Burritt's picturesque but effective famine relief work see *Littell's Living Age*, vol. xiv, July 17, 1847, p. 129, and the *Christian Citizen*, May 23, 1846.

[13] H. D. Bosanquet, *Peace and Free Trade in the Nineteenth Century*, New York, 1924, pp. 48, 71. Charles Sumner in 1844 and John Stuart Mill in 1848 also commented on the relation between peace and free trade. Pierce, *Memoirs and Letters of Charles Sumner*, vol. ii, p. 315, and Mill, *Political Economy* (1848), Book iii, chap. xviii, p. 5.

Western farmers to send their cargoes of wheat to England and to support Free Trade in America. It is interesting to point out that the coöperation of the Manchester School with the peace agitation became much more marked after Burritt's arrival in England. Indeed, George Wilson, president of the Anti-Corn Law League, became one of his loyal and valuable co-workers. In Manchester the Brights made it possible for him to address their great body of factory operatives. It was the friendliness of the Free Trade group that accounted for one of Burritt's earliest English triumphs at the London Hall of Commerce, in November, 1846. When he extended his work to France, his Free Trade convictions were to play an important part in winning the support of such Free Traders as as Bastiat, Michel Chevalier, and Émile de Girardin.[14]

Burritt counted on and won much support from labor as well as from the substantial middle classes. A blacksmith by trade, he felt the necessity of new efforts to elevate the working class as the wealth-producing class; and his lecture on "The Philosophy of Labor" emphasized the dignity of labor no less than its right to a just share of the wealth created. In speaking to the great labor groups that assembled to hear him, the "Learned Blacksmith," he pointed out the financial burdens labor suffered from war establishments. The great cheering and rush of hand-shaking that greeted Burritt after such appeals to crowded meetings of workingmen encouraged him to seize every opportunity to promote the cause of peace among British laborers. After 1848 his efforts in this direction were especially noteworthy in Bethnal Green, London, a district where physical violence ran high during the Chartist riots.[15]

[14] *Christian Citizen*, January 24, 1846, August 15; Burritt, Ms. *Journal,* December 3, October 12, November 24, 1846; Bosanquet, *op. cit.*, p. 7.

[15] Burritt, Ms. *Journal*, October 5, 1846, December 12, 1848, March 18, October 9, 1852; *Christian Citizen,* August 15, 1846, December 5, 1849, January 19, June 1, 1850, December 22, 1849; *Herald of Peace*, no. 70, May, 1848, p. 75; Richard Rathbone to Charles Sumner, November 26, 1846, and April 21, 1846, in *Sumner Papers, Foreign Letters Received*, 1844-1848.

Burritt, moreover, argued that free labor in Great Britain should have as its ally free labor in the United States. His appeals to English workingmen to support his project for boycotting slave-made produce anticipated the kind of appeals that Cobden and Bright made to English labor during the Civil War.[16]

During these experiences with British workingmen Burritt formulated a bold and striking idea. Perhaps the best means of securing peace, he felt, would be "to urge the workingmen to unite and refuse to fight." Since Burritt often noted in his *Journals* books and pamphlets which impressed him, it is not unreasonable to infer that he had not seen the *Communist Manifesto* of Marx and Engel when, in 1850, he began to introduce this appeal to labor in leading German newspapers. He went on nursing this idea, later developed in his pamphlet, *The World's Workingmen's Strike Against War*. Here he urged "a parliament of the workingmen of Christendom" as an instrument of peace, and advocated "an organized strike of the workingmen of Christendom against war" as the only alternative to a Congress of Nations for immediate, simultaneous, and proportionate disarmament. In light of subsequent developments in the labor movement, this early idea of an organized strike to prevent war is of unusual interest. Burritt's realism was also evident in his later work for the codification of international law. With Dr. James B. Miles he originated the International Code Association, which was to develop into a world organization, enlisting distinguished jurists in many lands.[17]

These ideas testify to the intellectual ability of the man who, in organizing a universal peace league, was winning friends and fellow workers among influential Quakers, free traders, and laborers. His burning enthusiasm for his cause no less than

[16] Burritt, Ms. *Journal*, January 19, 1848, October 3, 1846.

[17] Burritt, Ms. *Journal*, November 27, 1850, and *post*, p. 159, for Burritt's peace propaganda on the Continent. *The World's Workingmen's Strike Against War*, New Britain, is without date, and was probably printed after 1855; Northend, *Elihu Burritt*, p. 450.

his modesty and unbelievable capacity for work strengthened the admiration and affection that old and young felt for him. Although not an eloquent orator, Burritt seems often to have magnetized his audiences by his sustained enthusiasm. This was the more remarkable in view of his wretched health during the whole of his labors for peace. Overwork and self-denial undermined his health, and this misfortune was accentuated by extreme poverty. When some kind English friend pressed on him an occasional gift, it was more than likely to come to a man with less than a shilling in his entire possession.[18]

Burritt was as modest as he was energetic and enthusiastic. He shunned efforts to "lionize" him. In spite of adequate proof that his enthusiasm, simplicity, and earnestness caught his audience, he was so modest about his oratorical abilities that on more than one occasion he felt sorely tempted never to mount a public platform again. Such a man characteristically paid no attention to the derisive attacks made on him in the powerful London *Times,* which dubbed him "The Yankee Cobbler" and spoke contemptuously of his work. Only at rare intervals in his *Journal* did he permit himself to reflect upon what appeared to others as singular success.[19]

The man's almost incredible capacity for work led Richard Rathbone to write Sumner that Burritt was working "like a dray horse."[20] His *Journal* alone can testify adequately to the implications of this remark. Besides editing the *Bond* and writing at great length for the *Christian Citizen,* Burritt often wrote as many as thirty letters a day. During his years in England he lectured without let or hindrance, thus absorbing what might be left of his strength after an arduous day.

[18] David Bartlett, *Modern Agitators,* New York, 1855, pp. 107-108; Burritt, Ms. *Journal, passim.*

[19] Burritt, Ms. *Journal,* October 16, November 24, December 19, 1846, December 14, 1848; letter from Burritt to Charles Gilpin, January 8, 1848, in Burritt, Preface to *Sparks from the Anvil,* London (no date).

[20] Richard Rathbone to Charles Sumner, January 29, 1848, in *Sumner Papers, Foreign Letters Received.*

Such was this servant of peace. Awkward in his movements and his pronunciation, he was never quite at ease socially, although he was exceedingly sociable at times. Although his voice lacked flexibility and compass, and the style of his public addresses was too elaborate and literary, he possessed great conversational talents. His large, stout hands might well remind his friends that for years he had swung the hammer on an anvil, but his narrow chest and general frailty would recall that he had also pored over Sanscrit and Hebrew late of nights and early of mornings. His clear blue eyes, his large, sloping forehead, and his fine mouth gave his person the charm which, with his enthusiasm, sincerity, and modesty, caused him to be received and appreciated by a large and influential group of democratic English men and women.[21]

Largely as the result of Burritt's zeal, over 10,000 British and Americans had signed the pledge of the League within five months from the time it was launched at Pershore. Although Burritt was right in fearing that the London Peace Society did not entertain the most friendly feelings towards him and the League, it inserted the pledge in the *Herald of Peace* and outwardly encouraged the project.[22] As one would suspect, the early supporters of the League in the United States came from the ranks of the reform group. Charles Sumner kept aloof, and Beckwith's influence was cast into the scale against the League. Admitting that it was a fine conception, he criticized it as being "altogether too vague and broad for any specific purpose." The editor of the *Advocate of Peace* rather grudgingly admitted that it might be made "for a time very useful in its way." As for the Non-Resistants, Adin Ballou welcomed it and worked with it, but Edmund Quincy, who in Garrison's absence was editing

[21] Bartlett, *Modern Agitators,* pp. 107-109—Bartlett as a young man knew Burritt intimately. Burritt was, as he once observed in his *Journal,* probably at home with more English families than any American had ever been.

[22] Burritt, Ms. *Journal,* December 31, 1846, July 7, 1847; *Herald of Peace,* new series, no. 51, October, 1846, p. 153.

the *Liberator*, declared it to be a "humbug." Although the objection was sometimes raised that the Leaguers were "traitors," there seems to have been no very vigorous opposition, either in the United States or in England.[23]

By the summer of 1847 thirty thousand persons had signed the pledge, and a formal organization was made in England and feebly imitated across the Atlantic. On July 13, 1847, some forty persons answered a call in the *Bond of Brotherhood* to assemble in London for the formation of the English branch of the League. The fifty existing League groups were organized in twelve districts, and annual district meetings as well as a general anniversary in London were planned to give unity and direction to the efforts of the Leaguers. Persons of influence like Henry Vincent, parliamentarian, orator and popular reformer, Douglas Jerrold, humorist, and Charles Gilpin, publisher, as well as smaller fry, aided Burritt in whipping the organization into shape. Burritt noted in his *Journal* that evening: "This is one of the most interesting days that I have ever seen in my life. I have looked forward to it with so much solicitude. It was the issue of my year's labor in England; and such a one as ought to fill me with gratitude."[24]

During the year 1848 Burritt began preparations for the introduction of the League on the Continent. As a result of his work in Paris a Société d'Union des Peuples was formed, with Francisque Bouvet, a member of the Chamber of Deputies, as president. The platform of the society embraced in large part the principles and measures of the League. The first continental signatures to the Pledge, however, came in from Holland. In the spring of 1847 "The Christian Brotherhood" was formed in

---

[23] Rathbone to Sumner, April 2, 1847, *Sumner Papers; Advocate of Peace*, vol. vii, March and April, 1848, p. 191; vol. viii, May and June, 1847, p. 52; *Christian Citizen*, January 12, October 10, 1846, August 28, June 19, December 18, 1847.

[24] Burritt, Ms. *Journal*, July 13, August 27, November 18, 1847; *Christian Citizen*, July 24, August 7, 1847.

Amsterdam, and this group became a nucleus for the operations of the League in German-speaking lands.[25]

The first annual meeting of the British branch of the League took place at the Hall of Commerce, May 28, 1848. Its informal and friendly character was emphasized by preceding the business meeting with tea. Its founder read a report of League activities during the past year to a goodly and enthusiastic audience, made up in large part of Quakers. With the beginning of 1848 Edward Fry became secretary of the English branch of the League, and its work prospered. As many as four thousand not infrequently attended district meetings, and in 1850 it was reported that the League's secretariat was "overwhelmed with correspondence, which it does one's heart good to read."[26] Annual meetings continued to bring out much interest and enthusiasm until 1855, when Burritt devoted himself increasingly to antislavery work in his own country, and when the Crimean War dampened peace activity. By 1853 the voluntary contributions to the English branch of the League reached six thousand dollars, a sum larger than the American Peace Society ever enjoyed. Revenue came largely from a series of annual bazaars, held in London Tavern, Birmingham, or Manchester, and these offered an admirable medium for an intimate, friendly association of League members from different parts of Great Britain, many of whom had become acquainted by correspondence. Frequently Americans attended the bazaars and the soirées, which became annual social events at the anniversary week in London. Sometimes as many as four hundred persons from as many as eighty local League groups foregathered to make merry. Women Leaguers especially rejoiced in this kind of social communion.[27]

[25] Burritt, Ms. *Journal*, April 10, 1848, January 26, April 9, 1849.
[26] *Christian Citizen*, July 29, January 1, 1848; Burritt, Ms. *Journal*, May 30, June 3, 1848.
[27] *Christian Citizen*, January 26, January 12, March 16, July 13, November 2, November 23, 1850; February 26, July 7, 1848; Burritt, Ms. *Journal*, April 28, July 29, 1851, May 4, 1853; *Bond of Brotherhood*, new series, no. 12, July, 1851.

Burritt hoped that this auspicious beginning of the League in England would find a counterpart in the United States. Thus a basis would be given to the "social principle of fraternizing nations through smaller communities coöperating in family communion, of expanding the tea table, the hearthstone, until the largest communities of the world are socialized and cemented by the kindliest affinities of the family circle."[28] By May, 1847, 20,000 Americans had signed the pledge, and this number, within three years, ran up to 25,000. These signatures came chiefly from the back country in New England, and, strange to say, from the West, where Manifest Destiny had such a vogue. Sometimes pledges were secured by house to house canvass, but chiefly it was the *Christian Citizen* that did the work. Visits were exchanged between British and American Leaguers, and a surprisingly voluminous correspondence seems to have sprung up between Leaguers who became acquainted through the pages of the *Christian Citizen* or the *Bond of Brotherhood*.[29]

Although only a dozen local league groups could be formed, a call was issued, in accordance with Burritt's desire, for the formation of an American branch of the League of Universal Brotherhood. On May 26, 1847, a respectable number of delegates, from Western as well as from all the New England states, assembled in Boston, and despite severe criticism of the pledge from people like eccentric old Father Taylor and Origen Bacheler, who insisted that it was no less than a veiled attack on civil government, an organization was made. As a matter of course the old reform wing of the American Peace Society played the leading rôles in the American Branch of the League.[30]

For a time the sky looked bright. State organizations were announced in Maine and Rhode Island, William Lloyd Garri-

[28] *Christian Citizen*, April 3, 1847, March 16, 1850.
[29] *Ibid.*, April 18, May 22, December 18, 1847; January 12, February 16, 1850; February 1, February 15, 1851; Burritt, Ms. *Journal*, August 29, 1847; Burritt, Ms. *Lecture on the League of Universal Brotherhood.*
[30] *Christian Citizen*, June 5, 1847; Burritt, Ms. *Journal*, June 15, 1847.

son and Theodore Parker showed interest, and the Philadelphia Methodist conference and the New England Wesleyan synod recommended that ministers present the pledge to their congregations. Burritt took pleasure in the knowledge that by December, 1847, five hundred ministers had signed the pledge and that several newspapers had "noticed the movement handsomely." Amasa Walker lectured on the pledge in the West, and twenty-seven others, including the Rev. Samuel J. May, S. E. Coues, J. P. Blanchard, Gerrit Smith, and W. H. Channing, volunteered their oratorical services. Though contributions were sent to the English bazaars, the American branch never proved a source of strength to the League. For a time it drew out enthusiastic and large audiences in towns where the American Peace Society had failed, but by 1850 Burritt realized it would be fortunate if the American branch could be kept alive.[31]

Several reasons explain this turn of things. Many felt with Sumner that after all the pledge could not be carried out, since every payment of taxes to a war-making government violated it. Financially the League lived from hand to mouth. After a time Burritt's collaborators on the *Christian Citizen* wearied and turned cold shoulders to the League. But chiefly it failed in America because it possessed no outstanding leader. In England, Burritt was meat and drink to it, and appealing as his letters were, they proved inadequate substitutes for his own unbounded zeal.[32]

How much the success of the British branch of the League owed to Burritt's own personality became evident when he returned to the United States in 1855. Edmund Fry proved unable

[31] Burritt, Ms. *Journal*, June 29, July 17, August 18, 1847; *Christian Citizen*, December 25, November 27, 1847; June 10, 1848; June 16, 1849; May 18, February 16, 1850.

[32] Richard Rathbone to Charles Sumner, April 2, 1847, *Sumner Papers;* Burritt, Ms. *Journal*, October 25, 1847, October 8, November 4, 1850, January 16, 1851, June 12, 1851; *Christian Citizen*, May 13, 1850, September 21, 1851. *The Christian Citizen* was absorbed by the New York *Independent*, Holland, Ms. *History of the American Peace Cause*, vol. ii, p. 32.

to counteract the depressing effect which the Crimean War brought to the Leaguers, and in 1857 the League amalgamated with the London Peace Society. Fry continued to bring out the *Bond of Brotherhood* and hoped, with Burritt, that the spirit of the League, if not its organization, might continue.[33]

During the eleven years of its existence, the League of Universal Brotherhood accomplished a work of no mean proportions. It undertook, almost simultaneously, six projects, all of which were related, directly or indirectly, to universal peace. In 1847 and again in 1852, when war between England and France seemed imminent, the League sponsored the sending of Friendly Addresses to important groups and cities across the Channel; it inserted peace propaganda, in the form of "Olive Leaves," in the continental press; it advocated ocean penny postage to facilitate intercommunication as a means to peace; it assisted emigrants bound for America; it made possible the holding of the international peace congresses; and, finally, it stimulated free labor production.

Shortly after Burritt arrived in England in 1846 it occurred to him and to Crosfield, with whom he had been associated in the Oregon exchange of Addresses, to continue the work by arranging for similar Friendly Addresses between English and French towns. At League meetings in a dozen such cities as Manchester, Birmingham, Southampton, Bristol, Leeds, and Sheffield, Friendly Addresses to towns like Havre, Nîmes, Bordeaux, Strassburg, and Lille were drawn up, and resolutions were passed against the policy of increasing the national defenses. Twenty-five thousand persons signed the Liverpool Address to Marseilles.[34] In general the French cities responded, through the mayors to whom the addresses were sent. Seventeen hundred

[33] Burritt, Ms. *Journal*, May 17, 1854, July 18, 1855; *Bond of Brotherhood*, new series, no. 80, March, 1857, p. 120, July, p. 184.

[34] Burritt, Ms. *Journal*, November 22, 1846, January 27, 1848; Burritt, *Thoughts of Things at Home and Abroad*, pp. 331-332; *Christian Citizen*, July 8, 1848. *The Herald of Peace*, December, 1846 (no. 53, p. 180), also proposed the exchange of Friendly Addresses between England and France.

citizens signed the Address from Bordeaux to Birmingham. This movement came to a head, opportunely enough, with the outbreak of the Revolutions of 1848. Lamartine, Minister of Foreign Affairs, received the delegation which brought the Friendly Address from London to Paris, and promised to insert it in all the government papers and to preserve it in the archives "as the bond of fraternity between the two peoples."[35] The London *Telegraph* gave publicity to the movement, while the Friendly Addresses, printed in pamphlet form, were sent to every member of the National Assembly, to each mayor of Paris, to the chief towns of France, and to every journal in the country.[36]

This picturesque "people's diplomacy" was resumed in 1852 when, as a result of Louis Napoleon's *coup d'état,* England was seized with a widespread and irrational fear of invasion. In the course of a few weeks more than fifty of the leading towns of the United Kingdom had, in public meetings convened by the local branches of the League, taken appropriate action. Although a number of members of Parliament signed the addresses, the movement kept its essentially popular character. Burritt was honored with the commission of delivering these addresses personally to the proper French authorities.[37] The addresses, which denounced the new militia bill rushed through Parliament as contrary to the will of the people, were in general dignified expressions of friendly feeling for the people of France.

Although French bureauracy stood in the way of an official reception of the impressive Address from Edinburgh to Paris, with its signatures of the Lord Provost, members of Parliament, nearly all the magistrates and clergy of the city, as well as eighteen hundred merchants and manufacturers, Burritt fared much better in practically all the twenty-five other cities he visited. At Dijon, Lyons, Avignon, Nîmes, Montpelier, Toulouse, Bor-

[35] Burritt, Ms. *Journal,* March 1, 1848.

[36] *Ibid.,* March 29, August 21, 1848; *Herald of Peace,* March, 1848, pp. 35-36; June, p. 85; *Christian Citizen,* October 7, 1848.

[37] Burritt, Ms. *Journal,* May 15, May 31, 1852; Burritt, *Thoughts of Things at Home and Abroad,* p. 333.

deaux, for example, mayors or even prefects of the department received him with courtesy. Only at Amiens and Orleans did he meet with brusque treatment. Three fourths of the journals of France, Burritt said, noticed these addresses by printing them or commenting on them. Only a few newspapers took exception to the ideas expressed in the addresses or criticized the movement itself. On the whole the French response was one of good will and courtesy, if not of faith in the efficacy of the addresses, but the London *Times* noticed the movement only to poke fun at it.

It is, of course, quite impossible to estimate the amount of influence, if any, which this movement exerted on public opinion in England and France. Burritt believed that perhaps "no petition from Parliament, or other document, ever went forth from it, clothed with more moral power" than did the addresses of this popular movement.[38] If the method was crude, at least it signified a faith in democracy and in the influence of that vague force, "public opinion." At least the League of Universal Brotherhood was trying to practice its precepts.

The second major enterprise of the League was the Olive Leaf mission. Believing the Continent to be almost virgin soil for the seeds of peace propaganda, Burritt in 1849 arranged with his young French colleague, Earnest Lacan, to circulate short tracts in French—Olive Leaves—among the workingmen of Paris. When a new press law interfered with the work of distributing monthly the customary 40,000 Olive Leaves to operatives as they came out of their factories, Burritt resorted to the newspapers. On December 15, 1850, the first Olive Leaf in a European journal appeared in *L'Événement,* the cheapest and most widely circulated paper in France. It was agreed that an Olive Leaf was to appear each month in return for the sum of

---

[38] Burritt, Ms. *Journal,* August 21 to October 4, 1852; *Thoughts of Things at Home and Abroad,* pp. 334 ff.; *Bond of Brotherhood,* new series, no. 28, November, 1852.

a hundred francs. Victor Hugo, Lamartine, and Cormenin heartily approved this unique project.[39]

Obviously, little could be done without funds for such an undertaking. Burritt went from town to town in England, meeting groups of women assembled in the house of some Leaguer with whom he had previously corresponded, and explained the Olive Leaf mission. In the great majority of instances an Olive Leaf Sewing Circle was formed then and there. Quakeresses and Wesleyans furnished the chief membership in these new League Auxiliaries, which seldom ran above thirty-five women. They met in an informal way, plied their needles, drank tea, and listened to reports of the Olive Leaf mission and of sister sewing circles in other towns. The women seem to have been largely drawn from the middle class, though the Circle at Brixton was aristocratic enough to permit some of its members to drive up with footmen. Within five years a hundred and fifty Olive Leaf Circles had been formed in England and Scotland, and in the following year Burritt journeyed to Ireland and organized a half dozen more. Many took no deep root, but some showed much vitality. The Edinburgh Olive Leaf Circle, for example, kept up its monthly meeting for eight years, and others had almost as good a record. Even before the Crimean War, however, the novelty had worn off, and the Executive Committee of the League found it necessary to make a regular appropriation of twenty pounds a month for the Olive Leaf movement.[40]

Since the maintenance of the Olive Leaf Circles depended largely on Burritt's personal efforts, it is clear that less was to be hoped for in the United States, to which he returned only twice, for a few months, between 1846 and 1854. Burritt, however, often spent an entire day in writing to American peace men and women, goading them on to form Olive Leaf Circles. During

---

[39] *Bond of Brotherhood*, new series, no. 7, February, 1851; Burritt, Ms. *Journal*, December 6 and 30, 1848, July 29, 1850; *Christian Citizen*, February 8, 1851.

[40] Burritt, Ms. *Journal*, March 30, 1848, September 6, 1851, February 10, March 14, April 7, 1853; *Christian Citizen*, February 26, 1848, for a description of a meeting of the Southampton Olive Leaf Circle.

the years 1850-1851 Olive Leaf Circles were formed at Worcester and Roxbury, in Massachusetts; at New Britain, Connecticut; Cleveland and Columbus, in Ohio; and in two villages in Maine. Only after three weeks of house to house canvassing could Harriet Henshaw bring together a half dozen persons in Boston to form a Circle. In 1853 and 1854 Burritt, while in the United States for short periods, succeeded in interesting Quakeresses in Philadelphia, New York, Wilmington, and Baltimore to form Olive Leaf Circles. After his visit home in 1853 Burritt concluded that the Olive Leaf mission "did not seem practical" to his fellow countrymen. With one or two exceptions he found the Circles dead. Although he continued to try "to keep them bright and active," he was working against the wind, for antislavery was absorbing most of the benevolent feeling. Still, as late as 1855 the American Olive Leaf Circles were sustaining the publication of Olive Leaves in seven continental papers; and in 1856 the North Brookfield Circle raised a hundred dollars for the support of Olive Leaves in three German newspapers.[41]

Although an Olive Leaf Circle at Hamburg rendered good account of itself for more than a year, Burritt succeeded better on the Continent in winning support from distinguished pacifists than from groups of women. Lacan in Paris, Jules Paradon in Nîmes, the Reverend Adrien Van Andel and Dr. Fabricus of Hamburg, George Meissner of Nuremberg, Dr. Bodenheim of Berlin, Professor Lutken of Copenhagen, and Don Luis de Usozi Rio of Madrid all gave effective aid in translating and securing the insertion of Olive Leaves in journals. At the same time Americans and Englishmen on the Continent, especially those connected with missionary work and some legation officials, made Burritt's work a good deal easier.[42]

[41] Burritt, Ms. *Journal*, December 7 and 17, 1850; April 22, June 8, June 25, November 11, 1851; July 16, 1852; February 10, November 5, 1853; September 1, 1854; January 5, 18, 26, 1855; Holland, Ms. *History of the American Peace Cause*, vol. ii, p. 61; *Christian Citizen*, February 8, January 11, 1851; *Bond of Brotherhood*, new series, April, 1854, p. 134, and February, 1856, p. 110; *Advocate of Peace*, vol. x, May, 1852, p. 79; September, 1853, pp. 350-351.

[42] Burritt, Ms. *Journal*, September 21, August 5, 1850; also April 30, May 3, May 27, June 10, August 12, November 9, October 9, 1850.

The Olive Leaves, which discussed almost every point and principle involved in the subject of peace, ran from fifty to a hundred lines in length. Some issues included material from the pens of Cobden, Sumner, Robert Hall, and William E. Channing.

Within six months after the first Olive Leaf was inserted in *L'Événement* in December, 1850, arrangements had been made for the monthly publication of Olive Leaves in prominent newspapers in Hamburg, Bremen, Berlin, Stuttgart, Cologne, Frankfort, Copenhagen, and St. Petersburg. Within a year Spanish, Italian, Belgian, and Dutch papers were including Olive Leaves, which, indeed, presently appeared in almost forty influential continental newspapers, in seven different languages, from St. Petersburg to Madrid. Two leading German newspapers, the Augsburg *Gazette* and the Cologne *Gazette,* were on this list.[43] The expense of these operations ran up to three hundred pounds a year and was almost entirely borne by the Olive Leaf Circles. The movement was suspended in 1855 largely because Burritt was devoting himself to Free Labor Production and Compensated Emancipation in the United States in order to prevent the calamity of the threatened Civil War.[44]

Burritt estimated that the Olive Leaf mission reached regularly each month at least a million readers.[45] Ignorant of the fact that the insertion of the Olive Leaves had been paid for, readers assumed that they expressed the opinion of the journals. One Olive Leaf so interested a Scandinavian scholar, the Rector of the University of Upsala, that he brought out a complete history of the peace movement. There is no lack of evidence in Burritt's *Journals* that the Olive Leaves were read and that they influenced teachers, minor government officials, workmen, and scholars. A Bavarian correspondent wrote the American mis-

---

[43] *Bond of Brotherhood,* August, 1852. Some of the representative papers were the *Hamburger Nachrichten, Constitutionelle Zeitung* and *Vossische Zeitung* of Berlin, *Weser Zeitung,* Bremen, Stuttgart *Schwabischen Merkur, Koelnischer Zeitung, Journal de St. Petersburgh, El Clamore Publico,* and *E. Barcelones, Madrid, l'Opinione,* Turin, *l'Independence Belge,* and the Amsterdam *Handelsblad.*

[44] Burritt, Ms. *Journal,* February 3, 1851, and *Journal,* 1855, *passim.*

[45] Burritt, *Lectures and Speeches,* p. 310.

sionary of peace that the Olive Leaves were everywhere, in that part of Germany, stimulating anti-militaristic discussion, and this statement is borne out by other testimony.[46]

The vitality of the movement is likewise attested by the opposition it aroused. The Cologne *Gazette* was fined for inserting one Olive Leaf, which was apparently too radical for the government censor. *Kladderadatsch,* the German *Punch,* frequently satirized Burritt, and the caricatures it presented kept some German women from lending aid to the movement.[47]

On the other hand, many English people felt that the Olive Leaf mission exonerated Burritt from the charge of being impractical. *Blackwood's* and the London *Times* expressed scorn and disdain.[48]

Although the ebb had begun in the Olive Leaf Circle enthusiasm before the Crimean War that catastrophe seemed to spell ruin to the movement, and certainly discouraged its supporters. But something had been done. The older peace societies had never begun to carry the word of peace so effectively and on such a scale into the heart of Europe. The enthusiasm and activity of the League was comparable to that of Methodism, and the emphasis put on intimate social communion and hearty fellowship made the parallel striking. Whereas older peace societies sought in general to convert dignified and influential clergymen and government officials, the League aimed to remove "the spirit of war from the hearts of the people."[49]

The other projects of the League, Ocean Penny Postage and Assisted Emigration to America, only indirectly affected the peace cause and, important as they were, can be little more than

---

[46] *Bond of Brotherhood,* May, 1852, new series, no. 34; *Advocate of Peace,* September, 1854, vol. x, pp. 350-351; *Christian Citizen,* January 25, April 12, 1851; Burritt, Ms. *Journal,* October 23, 1852, August 18, August 29, August 30, September 1, September 12, 1853.

[47] Burritt, Ms. *Journal,* April 24, December 27, 1851, August 25, 1853.

[48] *Ibid.,* April 10, March 4, 1851; *Blackwood's Magazine,* vol. 73, pp. 373 ff.

[49] Burritt, Ms. *Journal,* September 23, 1846, June 14, November 3, 1851, March 29, 1852; *Christian Citizen,* July 2, 1848.

mentioned. Burritt believed that Ocean Penny Postage was a project well suited to an international organization like the League and that it was calculated to act as a solvent of prejudices, an instrument of peace, and a bond of brotherhood by making intercommunication between peoples more feasible. He lectured on this enterprise in both England and America, persuaded Charles Sumner to take it up in the Senate, and helped convert Cobden, Milner Gibson, Henry Cole, and Bright. Olive Leaf Circles petitioned the Queen with sixty thousand signatures of British women for a Penny Postage Act. During 1852 Burritt held eighty-five public meetings in England, with attendance varying from six hundred to a thousand, and most of these gatherings sent petitions to Parliament.

Burritt's pamphlet on the subject prepared the way in America for his five-thousand-mile lecture tour in 1853. The Washington *Union* and the *National Intelligencer* printed his articles on Ocean Penny Postage, and he interested Rusk of Texas and other members of Congress in this measure. Though it was not to be realized until 1871, Burritt and the League of Universal Brotherhood were true pioneers in the cause.[50]

The League made even less progress in its program of Assisted Emigration. A few emigrants from England were helped by sympathetic Leaguers in the American West. It was Burritt's purpose to rescue the "great transportation of peoples from the Old World to the New, from the heartless money-making speculators."[51] The idea, at any rate, was an expression of an organized effort to make universal brotherhood a reality.

Although Burritt was also interesting the League during this period in the formation of juvenile peace societies and arranging for correspondence between such groups in England and in America,[52] this work was subordinate to that of the Olive Leaf

[50] Burritt, Ms. *Journal*, December 22, 1852 to June 29, 1854.

[51] *Ibid.*, March 30, 1849; *Christian Citizen*, April 28, 1849.

[52] Burritt, Ms. *Journal*, November 14, 1846; *Christian Citizen*, May 1, February 13, 1847.

movement, the Friendly Addresses, Ocean Penny Postage, and finally, the International Peace Congresses. Burritt and the League of Universal Brotherhood contributed a great deal to the success of these international gatherings of peace crusaders. They were of such importance as to warrant special treatment.

VIII

THE INTERNATIONAL PEACE CONGRESSES, 1848-1851

WITH THE NERVOUS discontent in the Paris clubs and workshops and the tense rumors of plots and demonstrations against the provisional government, probably no one paid much attention on the morning of August 23, 1848, to an American making his way past the liberty trees in the squares and the recently barricaded Paris boulevards to the quarters of an attaché of the American legation. Doubtless the weary, impoverished man—it was Elihu Burritt—was pondering the discouragements he was courting in his eagerness to use this propitious season for holding an international peace congress in the storm center of revolutions, Paris. What a misfortune it would be if obstacles and indifference should prevent a great demonstration, which, like the Friendly Addresses, would lessen the danger of general war and afford a great opportunity for stimulating the peoples of Europe, so aroused and yet so sympathetic with each other, to organized efforts for peace! Five years had gone by since the first international peace convention had met in London. It was high time, he thought, for another, if ever a regular international peace organization were to be achieved. What if he had thus far suffered defeat? What if the London Peace Society had so tardily and reluctantly agreed to send a delegation, or if his own Leaguers had hesitated when faced with the prospect of Paris barricades and cannon? What if the editor of *La Démocratie Pacifique* had insisted on a ticklish commitment to communism before aiding the proposed congress? It was indeed a blow to find that even such staunch friends of peace as the influential economists, Michel Chevalier and Horace Say, were gloomy and doubtful. It was only last year that Francisque Bouvet, M. Ziegler, Frédéric Bastiat, and other members of the Société du Libre Échange had abandoned the idea of forming a peace society, so unsettled were political conditions and so dubious was the privilege of holding meetings. Were these men right, after all, in their insistence that no prominent Frenchman could risk popular disfavor by taking part in a congress which the Paris mob would certainly misinterpret as a British effort to strengthen the French government in its unpopular decision to withhold aid from revolutionary Italy? If Burritt thought at this particular moment of the growing coolness of his influential countryman, George Sumner, things must have looked yet darker. Many of Sumner's friends among the French litterati, like George Sand, refused to lift a finger for peace when it appeared that fighting alone could free the oppressed peoples. Was it such a consideration, perhaps, that explained his failure to hear from the German liberal, Arnold Ruge, whom he had invited to participate in the congress? He had especially counted on Ruge because of his bold championship of a congress of nations on the floor of the Frankfort Parliament.[1]

At any rate, whether or not these doubts darkened the Learned Blacksmith's mind as he sought out Colonel A. Dudley Mann, attaché at the American legation, his *Journal* shows how heavily they hung on him. Would Colonel Mann now accept his invitation to preside over the peace congress? Or would he, too, think it midsummer madness? His fears were well founded. The Colonel, in fact, was at this very time about to embark on an official mission to Hungary, to determine whether the United States ought to recognize its revolutionary government.[2] Thus when Burritt asked his aid on the ground that it was America's mission to lead the world in peace, Colonel Mann was not sympathetic. As a "Young American,"[3] he felt it was the duty of the

[1] This account is based chiefly on Burritt's Ms. *Journal,* from April to October, 1848, and on the *Christian Citizen,* especially July 8, August 10, September 9, October 21, 1848.

[2] M. E. Curti, "Austria and the United States, 1848-1852," *Smith College Studies in History,* vol. xi, no. 3, pp. 150-153; Burritt, Ms. *Journal,* August 23, September 1, 1848.

[3] M. E. Curti, "Young America," *American Historical Review,* vol. xxxii, no. 1, October, 1926, pp. 34 ff.

United States to help the militant revolutionists achieve national self-determination. What a striking coincidence brought together in Paris in 1848 these representatives of American uplift sentiment to disagree on their country's duties to the Old World in this flare of revolutions! What an interesting anticipation of a pattern which in our own time helped to involve the United States in a world war, a war justified on the basis of two conflicting American ideals—that of international peace and that of the self-determination of peoples!

Unable to win support from any save a few Protestant pastors, Burritt waited day after day for leave from the Minister of the Interior to hold the Peace Congress. Nothing he could do hastened an answer. The interminable delay finally led him to suggest to his British friends that the Convention be held in Brussels. With September 20 fixed as the date for its opening, little more than a fortnight remained to make preparations. The Belgian Minister of the Interior not only permitted the demonstration, but offered a government building and put Burritt and his associates in touch with Auguste Visschers, official, publicist, and philanthropist. This friend of peace organized a committee on arrangements which included some of Brussels' most distinguished public men. Their zeal led the American missionary of peace to note in his *Journal* that the Lord had at last "opened the hearts of all men to His work." In his delight at this unexpected success Burritt thought of the pleasure William Ladd would have taken in it.[4]

The Brussels Peace Congress opened its sessions on September 20, 1848, the English delegation, numbering one hundred and fifty, having arrived the night before. All in all, its personnel was such as to command attention, including as it did scholars, philanthropists, jurists, public men. Visschers was elected president, and at the second session the Congress began its con-

---

[4] Burritt, Ms. *Journal*, August, 1848, *passim;* letter of Burritt, dated Birmingham, September 29, in *Christian Citizen*, October 21, 1848, Burritt, Ms. *Journal*, September 1 to September 12, 1848.

sideration of the resolutions prepared by the committee on arrangements. Burritt held his breath while the first resolution, which had seemed too sweeping to most of the Belgians, was presented. But with a single exception, the whole assembly rose, and after a moment's silence, burst into applause, thus unanimously declaring that the appeal to arms for regulating international disputes was a custom opposed to religion, reason, justice, and the interest of the people, and that it was the consequent duty of the civilized world to "adopt suitable measures in order to effect the entire abolishment of war." The discussions were made the more lively by the chauvinistic arguments of the single contrary spirit at the Congress, Don Ramon de la Sagra, Spanish traveler and publicist. The following day the Congress adopted a resolution recommending the incorporation of an arbitration clause in all international treaties.

The next subject for discussion was that of a Congress of Nations. M. Bourson, general secretary of the Congress, read Burritt's essay, and Professor Bertinatti, a jurist of Turin, presented a paper which made almost the same points. These essays were on the whole well received, and the Congress resolved that the project was both feasible and desirable.

With fervent eloquence Henry Vincent insisted that the nation which took the initiative in disarmament would be regarded by posterity as the first people who "understood the mission of humanity." The economic benefits of disarmament were described by M. Huet, a professor in the University of Ghent. Without a single opposing vote the resolution favoring general and simultaneous reduction of armaments throughout the civilized world was recorded on the balance sheet of the Congress.

The Congress also went on record as opposed to the practice of intervention in the internal affairs of a state; resolutions were adopted favoring international communication, postal reform, standard weights, measures, and coinage; and steps were taken to endorse the work of those engaged, through the edu-

cation of youth, in the eradication of political and national prejudices. Then the Congress framed an address to the civilized
governments of the world, which embodied the resolutions that
had been adopted.[5]

To give publicity to the Congress, Burritt and his friends
held huge meetings in London, Manchester, and Birmingham,
and a delegation presented its resolutions to Britain's Prime
Minister, Lord John Russell. In soft words that official deplored
the costly military establishments and admitted that such congresses as that at Brussels would doubtless tend to induce a spirit
of moderation and concession. Burritt referred to the arbitration
clause in the recent treaty by which peace had been concluded
between his own country and Mexico, and Lord Russell replied
that if the United States would suggest a similar clause to Great
Britain, "it would be taken into their most serious consideration."
This was regarded as an important admission, for if the United
States could be induced to act on the suggestion, it would mean
a general commitment to the principle of arbitration by two of
the leading nations of the world. Joseph Sturge felt that the
words from Lord Russell's lips were worth all the efforts and
expense required for the Brussels Congress.[6]

The press naturally divided on the demonstration in Belgium.
The note of alarm struck by such conservative journals as the
London *Times* and the *Spectator* suggested that the Peace Congress enjoyed support of a rather widespread character, and this
is borne out by the favorable notices in several influential newspapers both in England and on the Continent.[7] A more tangible
result was the fact that among others Richard Cobden was
brought actively into the peace movement and began his cam-

[5] Burritt, Ms. *Journal*, September 20 to 24, 1848; *Christian Citizen*, September
9, 1848.

[6] Burritt, Ms. *Journal*, October 30, 1848; London *Times*, November 1, 1848;
Christian Citizen, December 23, 1848.

[7] *Advocate of Peace*, vol. viii, January, 1849, pp. 7 ff., quoting London *Daily
News*, London *Express*, London *Wesleyan*, *Nonconformist*, Manchester *Times*,
Spectator, *La Presse*, *La Patrie*, *La Commerce*.

paign to commit the government to the negotiation of compulsory arbitration treaties. Across the Channel Francisque Bouvet, one of the delegates at Brussels, introduced into the French Chamber of Deputies a resolution for scaling down armaments. Though this resolution met defeat, it attracted wide attention in France and elsewhere.[8]

The American Peace Society had no hand in the Brussels Congress, but Beckwith reproduced from the *Herald of Peace* an account of its proceedings, with Burritt's part minimized. Charles Sumner, however, recognized him as the author and inspirer of the Congress, which, he added, marked an "epoch"; and in Whittier's stirring poem, "The Peace Convention at Brussels," we have a permanent tribute to the man who organized a peace congress in Europe in the year when his own country ended its war with Mexico.[9]

Plans were at once begun for another congress, and all eyes turned towards Paris. Burritt urged his American following, through the columns of the *Christian Citizen*, to spare no effort for organizing a large American delegation. If British pacifists outnumbered those from across the Atlantic, it would be hard to convince Europe that the congress was "international and catholic in composition and character." At this "turning point in the fever and excitement of Europe's revolution," it was the patriotic duty of Americans, continued Burritt, to exert their moral influence for peace.[10] He was thus interpreting the duty of his fellow countrymen towards revolutionary Europe in a way strikingly in contrast with the rhetorical appeals of Young America to intervene in Old World affairs.

The preparations for the Paris Peace Congress led, both in England and in the United States, to the coöperation of the League of Universal Brotherhood and the older peace societies.

[8] *Christian Citizen*, February 10, 1849.
[9] *Advocate of Peace*, vol. vii, December, 1848, p. 311; Sumner, *War System of the Commonwealth of Nations*, Boston, May 28, 1849, in *Works*, vol. ii, p. 251; Whittier, *Poetical Works*, New York, 1902, pp. 188-191.
[10] *Christian Citizen*, January 13, April 28, 1849, and *passim*.

In Great Britain a Peace Congress Committee was formed, and its secretaries, Burritt and Henry Richard, the reasonable and laborious secretary of the London Peace Society, worked harmoniously together. This broad-minded and practical Welsh clergyman, who possessed knowledge of the world and excellent organizing ability, sought the aid of men who supported peace for other than religious reasons, men whose interest in the cause was conditioned by economic and political rather than by moral considerations. Richard's active leadership in the London Peace Society is another indication of the fact that the movement was coming to have an increasingly economic and political character. Under the auspices of the Peace Congress Committee great demonstrations were held up and down the kingdom. These meetings secured delegates for the Paris Congress and won popular support for the resolution favoring arbitration treaties, which Cobden was to introduce, in June, 1849, in Parliament.[11] In America, the League of Universal Brotherhood united with the American Peace Society in forming a Peace Congress Committee, of which Charles Sumner was a member. This committee issued an appeal to the American people for delegates to Paris and held public meetings for the same purpose in Boston and other cities. Twenty-one American delegates thus enlisted made the voyage to Paris, including Amasa Walker, the Reverend Dr. Mahan of Oberlin College, and Charles Durkee, a Wisconsin member of the House of Representatives. Joshua Giddings abandoned his plan of attending for lack of promised financial support from Ohio friends of peace. More fortunate was the Reverend Cyrus Pierce, who had helped establish the normal school system in Massachusetts, for Horace Mann enabled him to make the journey.[12]

[11] Burritt, Ms. *Journal*, October 31, November 7, 1848, May 10, 1849; Charles S. Miall, *Henry Richard, a Biography*, London, 1889, *passim*.

[12] *Christian Citizen*, January 20, 27, April 7, May 5, 19, June 16, July 14, 1849; Burritt, Ms. *Journal*, January 2, 1849; *Advocate of Peace*, vol. viii, June, 1849, p. 52; Holland, Ms. *History of the American Peace Cause*, vol. ii, p. 66; *Herald of Peace*, vol. vi (n. s.), July, 1849, pp. 336-337; *Sumner Papers*, vol. 161, Giddings to Sumner, July 11, 1849.

April, 1849, found Burritt and Henry Richard in Paris making arrangements for the Congress. Émile de Girardin, editor of *La Presse,* and the Free Trade economists, Horace Say, Michel Chevalier, and F. Bastiat, no longer turned their backs on Burritt's entreaties for support, and even Lamartine, whom Burritt and Richard interviewed, permitted his name to be used as an adherent to the principles of the Congress. Though Burritt and Richard feared that the economists, who fêted them at dinner, might overemphasize the connection between Free Trade and peace in the agenda of the Congress, it was their assistance which insured the success of the undertaking. The Minister of Foreign Affairs, de Tocqueville, to whom George Sumner introduced Burritt and his English associate, received them graciously at breakfast and assured them that he felt certain that the government would authorize the Congress; and it did. On the score of ill health the Archbishop of Paris declined to accept the presidency of the Congress, but Victor Hugo agreed to accept this responsibility.[13]

After spending a fortnight in Germany to induce German scholars and philanthropists to attend the Paris demonstration, Burritt returned to that city a week before the date set for the opening of the Congress, August 22. The program had already been completed by the Committee on Arrangements, a committee including some of the officers of the Society of Christian Morals—Francisque Bouvet, who early in 1849 sponsored the formation of the "Society for the Union of the Peoples," Joseph Garnier, editor of the *Journal des Économistes,* Deguerry, curé of the Madeleine, and Athanase Coquerel, leader of the French Protestants. The program was at once more restrained and more

[13] Burritt, Ms. *Journal,* April 20, 25, 27, May 30, July 5, 10, 13, 15; Miall, *Henry Richard,* pp. 38, 39, 52; *Christian Citizen,* March 3, 1849. There is preserved in the papers of George Bancroft a letter from Burritt, dated Paris, April 21, 1849, in which the American Minister to England is invited to participate in the Congress. Bancroft's reply is not to be found, although early in August, 1849, he was in Paris arranging for the collection of historical documents. Burritt's letter is printed by M. A. de Wolfe Howe in the *Outlook,* vol. 87, September 21, 1907, pp. 135-136.

extensive than that at Brussels. It guarded against participation in the discussions of "odious upholders of war," who might, indeed, at Paris, have absorbed a great part of the time of the Congress, and it also entered more widely into the study of the causes producing war. The influence of the French economists was shown in the added emphasis on the argument that war was opposed to the self-interest of nations, and in the lucid development of the idea that it was better to prevent war than to attempt to neutralize its effects after it had broken out. Cobden, who came in good season, rendered a great service to the English peace men and to Burritt by persuading the French committee to "uphold the high ground" of condemning all war, on religious as well as on utilitarian grounds. This was fortunate, since a large proportion of the four hundred British delegates were Friends.[14]

At the opening session, which was held in the Salle de Ste Cécile, Burritt was given an overwhelming tribute of applause. Following the election of officers came the dramatic speech of Victor Hugo. In sonorous words the great idealist prophesied that the day would come when cannon would be exhibited in public museums, just as instruments of torture were now marveled at, and that people would be astonished that such a thing as war could once have been an actuality. "A day will come," continued the speaker, "when those two immense groups, the United States of America and the United States of Europe, shall be seen placed in the presence of each other, extending the hand of fellowship across the ocean, exchanging their produce, their commerce, their industry, their arts, their genius, clearing the earth, peopling the deserts, improving creation under the eye of the Creator, and uniting, for the good of all, these two irresistible and infinite powers, the fraternity of men and the power

---

[14] Burritt, Ms. *Journal*, August, 1848; Joseph Garnier in *Journal des Économistes*, vol. xxii, August-November, 1849, pp. 101-102; Miall, *Henry Richard*, pp. 52-53; *Herald of Peace*, vol. vi (n. s.), April, 1849, pp. 269 ff.

SESSION OF THE PARIS PEACE CONGRESS
(London Illustrated News, Sept. 1, 1849)

of God."[15] The fifteen hundred persons who filled the hall, decorated with the flags of the nations, were deeply moved by these words of Victor Hugo. And what a striking thing—the fraternization between the Abbé Deguerry of the Madeleine and Pastor Cocquerel, sitting together there on the platform! The adherence of the Archbishop of Paris all the more emphasized the nonsectarian character of the Congress.[16]

As at Brussels, resolutions were introduced, then discussion and action on them followed. It was only Burritt's firmness, together with the help of Amasa Walker, which won the consent of the Committee for retaining the resolution favoring a Congress of Nations, for Auguste Visschers and Richard Cobden thought it altogether impracticable. Moreover, Cobden felt that such a Congress, far from inducing the representatives of different nations to agree, would be more apt to sow seeds of war. But Burritt had his way, and his paper, which traced the development of the idea from Penn to Ladd, compared the Congress of Nations to the American Supreme Court. Amasa Walker and the Abbé Deguerry also supported the resolution. Walker ably answered the leading objections to the plan.[17]

The chief difference between this congress and the previous one at Brussels was the greater prominence of economic arguments against war. A resolution was introduced condemning loans and imposts for conducting wars of aggression. The discussion clearly showed that the economists were bent on demonstrating that the chief causes of war were economic. Émile de Girardin attacked the evil consequences of the system of military preparedness as provocative of war and as a needless waste destructive of economic well-being. To bear out his point, he massed a formidable array of statistics on expenditures for such purposes, and Jules Avigdor, a banker of Nice, supported him.

[15] *Christian Citizen*, September 15, 1849.

[16] *Ibid.*, September 15, 1849.

[17] Burritt, Ms. *Journal*, June 22, August 20, 1849; *Christian Citizen*, September 15, 1849; *Herald of Peace* (n. s.), vol vi, June, 1849, pp. 332-3.

Frédéric Bastiat related the public debt of European countries to militarism, and Richard Cobden's eloquence on the same topic won him great applause. A letter from the prominent London banker, Samuel Gurney, expressed the conviction that, unless England altered her course in respect to military establishments and policy, bankruptcy would be the inevitable result.[18]

Little was added to what had been brought forward at Brussels in favor of international arbitration, though the discussions of President Mahan of Oberlin and Cobden on this subject suggested that the Americans in general preferred a perpetual congress for the arbitration of disputes, while the British upheld rather the appointment of special arbitrators for specific situations. For the most part the Congress followed its resolve to avoid controversial political questions, though two former slaves, William Brown and the Reverend J. W. C. Pennington, discussed the relation between slavery and war, and some of the French delegates made sympathetic references to the cause of Hungary.[19]

The Congress ended with a splendid entertainment for the delegates, which de Tocqueville arranged at the Hôtel des Affaires Étrangers. Here the leading orators of the Congress were received by ambassadors and members of the French Government with flattering attention. The fountains at Versailles were ordered to play on Monday, rather than on the usual day, Sunday, out of deference to the Sabbatarian prejudices of the delegates.

Although the Paris press at first seemed eager to turn the whole affair to ridicule, the personnel of the Congress, the earnestness and ability of the delegates, and the dignified character of the proceedings, modified the disposition of the most skeptical. Nearly all the journals showed remarkable graciousness. Proudhon, prince of Utopians, did, it is true, stigmatize

---

[18] *Journal des Économistes,* vol. xxiv, pp. 157, 160, 167 ff.; Miall, *Henry Richard,* p. 56.

[19] Miall, *op. cit.,* pp. 54-55; *Christian Citizen,* September 15, 1849.

the Congress in his paper as "jonglerie malthusienne," but even he inserted Victor Hugo's address in *La Voix du Peuple*. The European correspondent of the *National Era* reported favorable notices in the newspapers of Belgium, Italy, Berlin, Vienna, Hamburg, and Breslau. In England the *Quarterly Review* devoted twenty-four pages to a scathing attack on the peace men and wondered at the inconsistency of Cobden in crying peace when only a fortnight earlier he had actively taken the part of Hungary at a sympathy meeting in London Tavern. Did he not realize, the *Review* asked, that such conduct might involve England in war with Austria? The London *Times* sneered, although it no longer spoke of the peace party as "a small coterie of peace-loving ladies and gentlemen." The *Christian Examiner* testified that American journals made repeated mention of the Congress, passing both favorable and unfavorable judgments.[20]

A committee from the Congress presented its resolutions to the president of the French Republic, Louis Napoleon, who professed sympathy with the pacifist arguments. On November 24, 1849, Bouvet again struck at militarism by amending an appropriation bill in the Chamber of Deputies. At least he was enabled to present some of the arguments of the Paris Peace Congress to the official representatives of the French people.[21]

In England the precedent of holding great public meetings to advertise the Congress was followed, and French pacifists—Bastiat, Say, and Joseph Garnier—attended them. Five thousand came to Exeter Hall, seven thousand to the meeting in Birmingham, eight thousand to the one in Manchester. The chest of the

[20] *Journal des Économistes*, vol. xxiv, p. 173; *Christian Citizen*, October 13, 1849, February 16, 1850; *Quarterly Review*, June-September, 1849, vol. lxxxv, pp. 452 ff.; London *Times*, July 26, September 20, 1849; *Christian Examiner*, November, 1849, vol. xlvii (4 series, xii), pp. 467 ff.; *The Friend's Review*, March 2, 1850, vol. iii, p. 378; *American Quarterly Register and Magazine*, September, 1849, vol. ii, pp. 85 ff.; *Living Age*, vol. xxiii, December 29, 1849, pp. 612 ff.

[21] *Journal des Économistes*, vol. xxiv, p. 172; *Christian Citizen*, December 29, 1849.

Peace Congress Committee was reported to contain four thousand pounds.[22]

In the United States, a well attended meeting was held in Tremont Temple, Boston, with the Mayor, Josiah Quincy, as chairman, to welcome the returning delegates, Burritt among them. A like meeting at Worcester welcomed the Learned Blacksmith, who, eleven years earlier, had come as a humble artisan to enjoy his evenings at the Antiquarian Society. At Montreal a spirited meeting called to greet a returning delegate ended in the formation of a peace society. Burritt might well feel that the "grand campaign" had been "crowned with a great success" which he dared not anticipate.[23]

The chief importance of the congress the next year at Frankfort-on-Main lay in the educational effects of Burritt's campaign in the United States and in Germany—a peace campaign greater than perhaps any single effort for the cause that he made. Dissatisfied with the meager showing of delegates at Paris, Burritt arranged for peace conventions in as many as eighteen states for the purpose of explaining the nature of the peace congress movement and for stimulating interest in providing means for delegates. This series of conventions began in Augusta, Maine, February 13. At Montpelier a man drove in a sled forty miles to attend. On February 21, Burritt was addressing the legislature at Albany, and on March 24, two thousand were listening to him at Henry Ward Beecher's church in Brooklyn. And in the same way at Philadelphia, Washington, Pittsburgh, Wheeling, Cincinnati, Louisville, St. Louis, Cleveland, and Detroit, and more than a dozen other towns, he held conventions and tried to secure genuinely interested delegates for Frankfort.[24]

[22] *Herald of Peace*, no. 89, December, 1849, pp. 413-416; Richard, *Memoirs of Joseph Sturge*, p. 58; *Christian Citizen*, December 8, 1849, quoting London *Daily News*, November 24, 1850.

[23] *Christian Citizen*, September 29, December 1, 1849, January 19, 1850.

[24] Pierce, *Memoir of Charles Sumner*, vol. ii, p. 381; Burritt, Ms. *Journal*, February to April, 1850.

THE INTERNATIONAL PEACE CONGRESSES 179

Nor was this by any means the extent of Burritt's efforts. At Washington he interviewed Henry Clay and tried to enlist his support for obtaining a national ship to carry the peace crusaders to Europe. It was clear that while Clay approved all "judicious measures" for abolishing war, he doubted whether men would, in the present state of society, acquiesce in an award of arbitration. Vice-President Fillmore, however, entered cordially into Burritt's plans for a peace ship and took him to the Department of State to introduce him to Clayton. Joshua Giddings, Charles Durkee, Amos Tuck, Preston King, and David Wilmot and other members of Congress promised to advance the cause which Burritt had at heart and circulated petitions for a national ship to carry the olive leaf to Frankfort.[25] Though the discussions at most of the peace conventions, save in New England and Philadelphia, showed how weak the cause really was, Burritt rejoiced in the success which attended his efforts to enlist delegates. Even Beckwith admitted that the task of securing them was largely Burritt's work, for the American Peace Society appointed only two representatives. Forty Americans turned up at the opening session of the Frankfort Congress.[26]

On June 21, 1850, Burritt, with Henry Richard, made sure of a Paris delegation, and in Brussels he found that the anti-war group had grown in numbers and had kept informed of the movement in England and America through the *Christian Citizen*. But in Frankfort it was found that to bring men of different political opinions and religious creeds into a committee of organization to prepare a peace congress, in the midst of a military nation, was a matter of "great delicacy and difficulty." But Dr. Caroise of Heidelberg and Dr. Varrentrapp, a Frankfort physician, smoothed over many difficult situations resulting from the unpopularity of liberals at Frankfort. Burritt and

[25] Burritt, Ms. *Journal*, April 1, 2, 1850; *Christian Citizen*, April 20, 1850; Richard Rathbone to Charles Sumner, July 27, 1850, *Sumner Papers*.
[26] *Advocate of Peace*, vol. viii, May and June, 1850, p. 219.

Richard were joined by Visschers, and the three traveled all over Germany campaigning for delegates. In Berlin the Connecticut Yankee observed in his *Journal* that "to see this great city given entirely over to the idolatry of this military system, seemed like throwing the seeds among the worst order of thorns." Most of the distinguished German scholars and public men that were interviewed seemed "to have no faith in anything except brute force." It was, indeed, at the height of the reaction against the liberal failure to unite Germany and at a time when Germans were renewing faith in military means for accomplishing national unity, that an American and an English peace missionary were trying to organize a peace congress, with their coöperation and on their military soil. Baron von Humboldt, Dr. Friedrich Tholuck of Halle, Professor Wachmuth, the historian at Leipzig, and Dr. Haenel of the same city were sympathetic, but scarcely enthusiastic. Professor Liebig at Giessen, whose work had shown the relation between war and economic interests, promised to attend. At Nuremberg the hotel keeper would not allow a meeting in his house, fearing the police. The few burghers that met in the bedroom of Burritt and Richard told them that all Germany was convinced that consolidation could be obtained only by fighting for it. At Munich, Dr. Johann Joseph Döllinger, the famous Catholic scholar, defended the necessity of standing armies to suppress political disaffection, and at Stuttgart none of the gentlemen canvassed could be moved because of their "unbelief." Herr Jaup, former prime minister of Hesse-Darmstadt, did consent to act as president of the Congress. As at Paris, it was clear that the Continental group, which had been making arrangements at Frankfort, seemed likely, in drawing up the program and resolutions, to compromise Quaker peace principles. The Germans insisted that armies were necessary to preserve internal order, but the conciliatory spirit of Cobden helped smooth over critical issues. Richard was "unspeakably

SESSION OF THE CHAMBER NEAR M. MOLIÈRE

relieved and thankful" at having avoided some of the formidable difficulties that lay in the path of the Congress.[27]

On August 21, all things being thus arranged, at least five hundred persons, "not a few of them ladies," started from London to attend the Congress. One of the delegates describes the high spirits of the party, cheering Burritt and Richard as they boarded the specially chartered Rhine steamers with the requisite exemptions of passports the Prussian Government had granted. The sessions of the Congress were held in St. Paul's church, the scene of the famous Frankfort Parliament in 1848. Visitors crowded the galleries; the two thousand tickets that were issued were far from sufficient. General Haynau, "the Austrian butcher," sat among the visitors. Was Cobden serious in believing that his presence might be taken as proof that peace principles were arresting attention?

Although eighty German delegates came, there seems to have been a scarcity of German speakers. Several letters from prominent Germans were read, letters expressing sympathy for the cause, among them one from Baron von Humboldt. Order and good temper marked the proceedings; the atmosphere was less formal and interest more sustained than at Paris. Economic arguments were again in the ascendency. Cobden, Joseph Garnier, and Émile de Girardin attacked the wastefulness of standing armies. It was felt that the condemnation of war loans by M. Drucker, a banker of Amsterdam, was significant. Were those whose chests financed war at last learning the lesson that their course was financially unwise?[28]

The American delegates by no means took a back place at the Congress. For one thing there was Copway, the converted Indian chief from Canada, whose native costume and broken, picturesque English and plaintive pleas for the self-determina-

[27] Burritt, Ms. *Journal,* June 21 to August 10, 1850; Miall, *Henry Richard,* pp. 63 ff., and 74-76.

[28] *Christian Citizen,* September 2, from the *Nonconformist; Advocate of Peace,* vol. viii, November and December, p. 310; Burritt, Ms. *Journal,* August 22, 1850.

tion of peoples brought volleys of cheers. According to an English delegate, the Reverend E. E. Chapin's speech—he had come from New York—"fairly carried the audience away." Besides, Henry Garnett, an American colored preacher, could not but attract attention. It is true that Burritt was so depressed by the "weak, hobbling speech" of President Hitchcock of Amherst, and by the "bombastic laudation of America" that came from the lips of Dr. Bullard, of St. Louis, to say nothing of the long, prosy speech of the Reverend E. B. Hall, of Providence, that he almost decided to refrain from talking on the Congress of Nations, a subject unpopular with the European and especially the German delegates. None the less the Learned Blacksmith ascended the tribune. An applause, again and again renewed, burst from every part of the building. "With eyes fixed aloft, and in clear, measured tones, he developed and endeavored to show the feasibility of the plan" which had absorbed so much of his thought and energy. It seemed to Miall, an English witness, that Burritt was insensible to all outside influence as he spoke, and that he hastened away from the present to the grand future which his poetic mind had already grasped.[29] Two years before, another audience, the Frankfort Parliament, had listened to Arnold Ruge expound the same subject from the same tribune. Much water since then had flowed under the bridge, but Burritt had not lost faith. The twelve thousand miles that he had traveled and the six months of severe work he had spent to make the Frankfort Congress possible seemed to him small tribute for its success; it was in every way worthy of its great antecedent at Paris. It had completely surpassed his expectation.[30]

And, indeed, the Congress certainly made the cause of peace better known and better regarded in the Germanies. Within six days after the assembly broke up eight pamphlets on peace had appeared, and as late as December, 1850, Burritt said that

[29] *Christian Citizen*, September 2, 1850 (quoting Miall).
[30] Burritt, Ms. *Journal*, August 23, 1850.

almost daily one could find in some German journal allusions to the Frankfort Congress. There is other and independent evidence on this point. In the summer of 1850 the first peace society in Prussia was organized at Königsberg, where Immanuel Kant had written his essay "On Eternal Peace." This promising organization, which was a direct result of the Frankfort Congress, was suppressed by the Government because at one of the meetings an extract from the *Herald of Peace* was read, and the police regarded this as unlawful correspondence with the London Peace Society.[31]

In France, only the *Journal des Débats,* the *Constitutionnel,* and the *Pays* tried to turn the Congress to ridicule. The London *Times* took pains to send a special correspondent to Frankfort, and if its sneers were not less marked than in 1849, it was clear that the English press was noticing the peace movement with increasing respect. If the Congress met with ridicule in important places, friends of peace recalled that perhaps a dozen years before such a congress could not have assembled in Europe.[32] It was in part the adherence of these mid-century congresses to the rule excluding from their agenda all discussion of contemporary politics that kept them "above the battle."

It was this rule which prevented the Frankfort Congress from lending ears to a tempting request which came to it on the last day of its sitting. That request was from a representative of the Constitutionalists of Schleswig-Holstein, who begged the Congress to appoint a commission to inquire into their controversy with Denmark. For the moment there was a truce between the two belligerents. All Germany, and especially

[31] *Advocate of Peace,* vol. ix, January and February, 1851, p. 14; *Christian Citizen,* January 25, 1851; *Friend's Review,* vol. v, November 15, 1851, pp. 131-133; *Herald of Peace,* vol. i (n. s.), October, 1850, pp. 41-42, April, 1851, pp. 110-112, July, pp. 152-153.

[32] *Christian Citizen,* August 31, October 5, 1850; *Advocate of Peace,* vol. ix, January and February, 1851, pp. 16-17;*Littell's Living Age,* vol. xxviii, pp. 362 ff.; Hirst, *The Quakers in Peace and War,* p. 258, note; Holland, Ms. *History of the American Peace Cause,* vol. iii, p. 74.

Prussia, was involved in this thorny dispute between Denmark and the duchies. Would organized pacifism help? Since the Congress could not take official action, it was thought that three members might go in a voluntary and individual capacity for the purpose of trying to induce the belligerent parties to refer the dispute to arbitration. The ambassador of the duchies in Frankfort assured Sturge, Burritt, and Richard that his government would welcome their disinterested efforts for the restoration of peace. Hence Sturge, Burritt, and Frederick Wheeler, of Rochester, England, set out on such a mission.[33]

At Kiel the provisional government of the duchies received the peace messengers courteously, and they were told that they might indicate to Denmark willingness on the part of the duchies to negotiate, were Denmark similarly minded. At Copenhagen the American minister, Walter Forward, facilitated the object of the peace mission, and de Reedtz, Danish Minister of Foreign Affairs, agreed to make use of the services of the mission as a medium of communication, and, further, to consider any official and practical proposition, involving the principle of arbitration, which the Schleswig-Holstein authorities might present. Distinguished civilians were appointed by both governments, at the suggestion of the peace mission, to correspond in regard to the possible arbitration. For three months Burritt stayed in Hamburg, conducting the necessary correspondence for bringing the belligerents together for negotiation.[34]

Then the authorities at Copenhagen about-faced and refused to negotiate with the duchies, on the basis that to do so would mean the recognition of their independence. Burritt felt that his mission was at an end, but he determined to try one more straw. He obtained from the provisional government of the duchies official authority for the arbitration proposal and informed the Danish Government that the world would know of its defection from its pacific commitment. Henry Richard, in his life of Joseph Sturge, and Charles Northend, Burritt's biographer, later asserted that Burritt's negotiations would have proved successful in inducing the belligerents to negotiate had not Austria closed the affair by marching forcibly into Schleswig-Holstein. Burritt's *Journal,* which contains the complete correspondence between the mission and the two governments, shows that this claim is quite unjustified.[35] Reedtz, on October 29, 1850, thanked Burritt for his communications "as evidence of the pacific disposition prevailing among the adverse party," but practical results, he went on to say, could be obtained only by negotiations carried on "by proper authorities and responsible men of business." The letter testified as to the value of Burritt's labors and stated that his suggestions, sanctioned by the provisional government of the duchies, were being considered. But the authorities and expert advisers of the duchies regarded Reedtz's letter as full of evasions and "double entendre." They regarded the reference to negotiations by proper authorities as meaning, not those of the duchies, but other powers, like the German Diet, Russia, or France. Burritt, on the other hand, reasoned that Reedtz meant that negotiations must merely pass out of private hands, like his own, into official channels.

But if this were the meaning, the Danish Government took no steps in such a direction. The Chevalier Bunsen, Prussian minister at London, who had previously told Sturge that the informal mission had had more effect than official diplomacy, regarded Reedtz's meaning as "evasive, civil, and unmeaning." Cobden thought the letter of the Danish foreign minister was intended civilly to tell the peace men to mind their own business in the future. The London *Times* insisted that Burritt had not contributed "one jot to the peace which is about to be established

[35] The correspondence between Burritt and the authorities and civilians of Denmark and the duchies is in his *Journal,* especially from October 10-14. Richard, *Memoirs of Joseph Sturge,* p. 454; Charles Northend, *Life and Labors of Elihu Burritt,* p. 105.

by the intervention of Austrian bayonets." The London *Daily News,* though of like mind, none the less believed that the peace party was the gainer by having made actual endeavors to put into effect their ideals. Although it is questionable whether Denmark and the duchies would have come to terms had the Powers not intervened, it is significant that the peace men believed they would have done so, that Sturge could write to Burritt, when it was all over, that "there has never been a circumstance more calculated to advance our peace cause more than the result of this mission."[36]

The following year—1851—saw the last of the mid-century peace congresses, that at London. It was the largest of the series, partly because many of its two thousand delegates were attracted by the Crystal Palace Exhibition. Before the Congress actually met, there had been the usual problems, and some new ones. Should there be a resolution favoring a Congress of Nations? Cobden thought no, and most of the English friends of peace would gladly have thrown out the whole proposition, but Burritt had his way. Should a Mrs. Bateham, of Ohio, one of the sixty American delegates, be admitted? The idea of a woman taking an active part and speaking in such an assembly, according to Burritt, was "repugnant to the English mind." Should the committee plan another congress? Beckwith read a letter from William Jay, president of the American Peace Society, discouraging the idea of holding annual peace congresses, and it appeared that most of the members of the London Peace Society felt very much the same way. To Burritt this was indeed an ill omen, and he stoutly contended for the value of an annual congress.[37]

[36] Burritt, Ms. *Journal,* October 5, 31, 1850; November 10, 11, 24, 1850; London *Daily News,* October 7, 1850, in *Littell's Living Age,* November 30, 1850, vol. xxvii, pp. 414-415.

[37] Burritt, Ms. *Journal,* May 23, June 28, July 8, 11, 21, 1851; *Christian Citizen,* February 8, 22, May 8, 1851; *Bond of Brotherhood,* new series, no. 13, August, 1851, p. 5.

But the three thousand persons who kept an impressive silence for a moment before Sir David Brewster opened the Congress knew little about these things. They listened intently to Thomas Carlyle's letter, which wished the peace workers "all possible speed" in ending the disastrous "cutting of throats," and to a very sympathetic greeting from the president of the Chamber of Deputies at Turin. They heard Beckwith discourse on his labors for peace and his interviews with members of Congress. They received Burritt more kindly than he had ever been received before. They applauded fifteen French working-men, representing as many different French trades, whose chief business in London was to attend the Crystal Palace Exhibition, but whom Henry Vincent brought to the Congress, and they listened to one of their number deliver himself of a short speech.[38]

The chief new note was the resolution which condemned the aggression of civilized nations on barbarian peoples. The Reverend Frederic Crowe of Guatemala gave his personal experiences of the demoralization European imperialism had wrought in Central America, and Émile de Girardin, seconded by Cobden, moved that nations making war on weak tribes should be called "strong, but not civilized, nations." Despite this anti-imperialistic talk, Horace Greeley found the atmosphere of the Congress unendurable. How could peace be realized, he wondered, until the dynastic tyrannies of Europe had been replaced by the freedom of the struggling nationalities. Here was another example of conflict between two kinds of loyalties, one to the self-determination of peoples and a map of Europe that squared somewhat with justice and another to the cause of peace.[39]

[38] *Herald of Peace*, August, 1851; Northend, *Life and Labors of Elihu Burritt*, pp. 122-123.
[39] Burritt, Ms. *Journal*, July 22-23, 1851; *Journal des Économistes*, May to August, 1851, vol. xxix, pp. 177-180; Horace Greeley, *A Glance at Europe*, New York, 1851, p. 281.

The London *Times* forbore its customary invective and allowed the last great Peace Congress to depart in peace. According to the editor of the *Nonconformist,* a large section of the weekly press in town and country heartily supported the demonstration.[40]

None the less, enthusiasm for such meetings was dwindling. English peace men were occupied with their work against the British militia bill, while Burritt and his American friends were becoming increasingly interested in pre-Civil-War problems at home.[41] Besides, this series of international meetings had accomplished the chief purposes for which it had been inaugurated. It had served vigorously to register pacifist protest against the militarism of mid-century Europe. It had strengthened the peace movement in the eyes of the world. It had clarified, elaborated, and given publicity to the chief peace arguments and plans. The congresses enlisted new men and new agencies in the peace movement, especially men of public affairs. Cobden's active work in the peace movement dates from the Brussels Conference. The congresses and demonstrations following them further appealed to a large part of the laboring population, to whom the cause had never before made an effective appeal. In all probability but few friends of peace had ever hoped for more than this.

The history of peace activities following the Congresses proves that the estimates which were made of their importance by the peace men were far too optimistic,[42] but they probably represented the greatest single accomplishment of the early movement.

[40] Holland Ms. *History of the American Peace Cause,* vol. iii, p. 74; Miall, *Henry Richard*, pp. 85-86.

[41] Holland, *op. cit.,* vol. iii, p. 80.

[42] Holland, *ibid.,* pp. 83-84; Emerson Davis, *The Half Century,* Boston, 1851, p. 183.

IX

STIPULATED ARBITRATION, 1842-1854

EACH OF THE international peace congresses, not excepting
the London Convention of 1843, recommended that there be
included in all international agreements clauses requiring the
arbitration of disputes. It was hoped and expected that the increase of such arbitration clauses in international treaties would
in the end result in a Court and Congress of Nations. Both
ideas—stipulated arbitration and the Congress and Court of
Nations—had their jealous champions. Until the death of William Ladd in 1841 the American peace movement favored the
project of a Court and Congress of Nations, and thereafter
Elihu Burritt, Joshua P. Blanchard, and Amasa Walker kept
the idea alive. But the scheme of stipulated arbitration enjoyed
greater popularity during the period from 1842 to 1854, partly
because it was championed by the President of the American
Peace Society, William Jay, and by leading men in the London
organization, such as Henry Richard and Cobden, and partly
because arbitration seemed a more immediately practicable plan
than a Congress of Nations. Burritt, however, having little faith
in the efficacy of stipulated arbitration, kept his eye steadfast
on what seemed to him the better, if the more remote, goal.

The idea of writing compulsory arbitration clauses into
treaties, though it found congenial soil in England, came from
America. It was William Jay, lawyer, judge, and reformer, whose
little book, *War and Peace, the Evils of the First, and a Plan for
Preserving the Last* (1842) especially developed this idea of arbitration, in which, indeed, his father had been interested. As a
mode for "preserving peace" calculated to "shock no prejudice"
and "to excite no alarm," he proposed the insertion of an article
in our next treaty with France, interestingly enough, which
would bind the two powers to submit to the arbitration of one
or more friendly powers *all* disputes that might come up and to

abide by the award. Jay felt that the strength of the plan lay in the fact that the parties bound themselves in advance of the controversy to arbitrate, thus eliminating the obstacles to such a decision when passions were inflamed after the dispute arose. In other words, this plan which he advanced differed from that of the later Peaceful Settlement Convention of the Hague Conference in going beyond a mere recommendation for arbitration. It was nothing less than a definite pledge to arbitrate without exception all future disputes.[1]

When Joseph Sturge visited the United States in 1841 he was much impressed by the idea of such arbitration treaties as instruments for keeping the peace. Stating that the plan was Jay's, Sturge presented it on July 29, 1841, to a peace meeting in Boston, which took to the idea with decided favor and recommended measures for its adoption in America and Europe. As a result of this meeting, petitions were sent to the President and to the Senate asking for the insertion of a stipulated arbitration clause in all future treaties.[2] Through Sturge's influence the subject of such arbitration provisions became the chief concern of the London Peace Convention in 1843. Three years later Dr. John Bowring, political economist and parliamentary reformer, presented to the House of Commons a petition for the insertion of arbitration clauses in treaties, and during the year 1847 at least thirty-four such petitions were presented to Parliament.[3]

Richard Cobden, then, was not an innovator when in 1848 he determined to sponsor the cause of compulsory arbitration in

[1] James Brown Scott, editor, William Jay, *War and Peace—the Evils of the First, and a Plan for Preserving the Last*, New York, 1919. For the life of William Jay, see Bernard Tuckerman, *William Jay and the Constitutional Movement for the Abolition of Slavery*, New York, 1893. Professor Upham of Bowdoin College advanced a plan very similar to that of Jay, and at almost the same time. *Advocate of Peace*, vol. iv, October to November, 1842, pp. 251 ff.

[2] *Advocate of Peace*, vol. iv, no. 3, October 1841, p. 66; vol. v, December 1843, p. 141; Ms. *Minutes of the Executive Committee of the American Peace Society*, June 7, August 27, 1842.

[3] The *Spectator*, reproduced in *Littell's Living Age*, vol. ix, May 23, 1846, pp. 366 ff., referred to this effort as the most practical one "yet put forth by our peace party"; Henry Richard, *Memoirs of Joseph Sturge*, pp. 351-352.

Parliament. Sturge certainly had a hand in bringing Cobden to this decision. Indeed, it was at the suggestion of the Birmingham Quaker that the great Free Trader received a delegation including Henry Richard and Elihu Burritt, and it was at this conference, November 13, 1848, that Cobden agreed to bring forward, in the next session of Parliament, a motion for arbitration treaties. None the less it needed courage to befriend such a scheme, for Cobden's colleagues in the House met the announcement of his intention by trying to laugh him out of court.[4]

Both the League of Universal Brotherhood and the London Peace Society strained every nerve to popularize the project and to win support for it. Burritt and Richard addressed as many as a hundred and fifty meetings and got up no less than a thousand petitions to Parliament containing, altogether, about two hundred thousand signatures. They sent out fifty thousand letters, and it was estimated that in addition hundreds of thousands of printed leaves were scattered far and wide. It is little wonder that Burritt was impressed by all this "mind-making machinery." Cobden himself was delighted with the showing that the peace movement made. The campaign ended with a huge meeting in Exeter Hall the night before Cobden was to introduce his resolution. Burritt, single-handed, had arranged this demonstration, as his colleagues on the Peace Congress Committee were reluctant to undertake the task. More than three thousand persons came out and listened to John Bright, Charles Hindley, William Ewart, and Joseph Brotherton, all members of Parliament, and to Edward Miall, George Thompson, the abolitionist, Henry Richard, and Elihu Burritt.[5] The afternoon before this great demonstration a delegation had visited the ex-Premier, Sir Robert Peel, who still exerted a good deal of

---

[4] Burritt, Ms. *Journal*, November 10, 13, 1848; Richard, *Memoirs of Joseph Sturge*, p. 424. Cobden as early as 1835 advocated peace, which he associated with Free Trade, and favored the holding of the London Peace Conference in 1843; he also sent a letter to the Brussels Peace Congress.

[5] Burritt, Ms. *Journal*, December 8, 1848, June 11, 1849; *Christian Citizen*, July 21, 1849; Richard, *Memoirs of Joseph Sturge*, pp. 423 ff.

influence on the government. Peel, though ready to assent to the value of arbitration in many situations, cited cases in which he felt it would not be practicable and others in which it would be surrounded with difficulties which could be met only as they occurred. Burritt assured Peel that friends of peace on both sides of the Atlantic looked to him, in view of what he had done in the Oregon crisis, for some kind of organized arrangement for superseding war by arbitration. This interview must have suggested to some peace men that they were riding for a fall.

The next day, June 12, 1849, Burritt was on hand in the strangers' gallery of the House of Commons and describes what took place. Some three hundred members heard Cobden introduce his resolution and anticipate in advance all possible opposition. Burritt regrets that the great Free Trader so specifically disapproved a Congress of Nations, but possibly such a disapproval may keep his critics from calling him a visionary! William Ewart seconded the motion, and Lord Grosvenor gave it cordial support. From the opposite side of the House Mr. Mackimmon expressed complete approval, while Colonel Thompson said that the proposal was so rational that it must ultimately succeed. Mr. Hobhouse, in supporting it, felt that the plan would supply a nation with a graceful means of retreating from an untenable position. Urquhart talked against it. Lord Palmerston, Minister of Foreign Affairs, opposed the adoption of the plan on the ground that it would involve "organizing a habit" or establishing a fixed procedure which might at times not be desirable. His Lordship went on to say that he would regret to meet the motion in such a way as to negative the principle, and he therefore moved the previous question. Milner Gibson tried to refute Palmerston by showing the advantage of a fixed system over a mere optional custom. Lord John Russell was next to speak in collateral opposition to the motion, dwelling on the practical difficulties of such a scheme, which failed to make exceptions of certain controversies not susceptible to arbitration. Cobden was on his feet showing that, in the last analysis, after the sword has been drawn, every controversy is really arbitrated.

When the division was called, seventy-nine notes were recorded in favor of the motion, and one hundred and seventy-six against. The House had occupied itself with the question for six hours. The friends of the motion were surprised and pleased by the strength of its support.[6] Later it appeared that votes against the motion represented less than three million people, while those favoring it represented 4,356,786. If the votes of placemen and officers of the army and navy had been deducted, there would have been, it was claimed, a clear majority of two million people favoring the motion.

While the idea involved in Cobden's resolution was not to win the sanction of Parliament until 1873,[7] this effort encouraged not only the English peace men but those in the United States as well. The Manchester *Examiner* interpreted the performance as a warning to the Government for an economical war budget.[8] Cobden's action may also have influenced Francisque Bouvet to introduce into the French National Assembly on January 9, 1849, a resolution of an even more sweeping nature. This was referred to the Committee on Foreign Affairs, which, although declining to recommend the project, seemed in its report to favor it in a left-handed way.[9]

Meantime, the American peace men were not letting the grass grow under their feet. Lame and hesitating as was article twenty-one of the Treaty of Guadalupe Hidalgo in recommending arbitration in future controversies between Mexico and its

[6] Burritt, Ms. *Journal*, June 11, 12, 1849; *Christian Citizen*, July 21, 1849; *Herald of Peace*, new series, no. 83, 1849, pp. 332 ff.; Edward Miall in the *Nonconformist* (reproduced in *Christian Citizen*, August 18, 1849); Hansard's *Parliamentary Debates*, cvi, 1849, 5th volume of session, pp. 54-122.

[7] J. A. Hobson, *Richard Cobden, the International Man*, New York, 1919, p. 58.

[8] *Littell's Living Age*, vol. xx, February, 1849, pp. 297 ff.

[9] *Herald of Peace*, new series, no. 79, February, 1849, pp. 277 ff.; August, 1849, p. 341.

northern neighbor,[10] it did, along with the relative success of the campaign for Cobden's resolution, encourage the American Peace Society to agitate the subject in Congress. On January 16, 1849, the House of Representatives refused leave to Amos Tuck, an anti-slavery Whig representative from New Hampshire, to introduce a resolution directing the Committee on Foreign Affairs to inquire into the expediency of authorizing the Secretary of State to correspond with foreign governments on the subject of procuring treaties for the arbitration of all future disputes. Not discouraged, Tuck on January 28, 1850, presented a memorial from the American Peace Society praying Congress to take action for securing arbitration treaties. Against Tuck's wishes, the memorial was referred, on the motion of David S. Kaufman of Texas, to the Committee on Foreign Affairs, rather than to a select committee. Southern opposition kept a similar Ohio petition from being referred to any committee at all, although the House, by a vote of 65 to 100, refused to lay it on the table. In opposing it one Southerner, Thompson of Alabama, said that the "whole foolery had gone far enough."[11]

Early in 1850 a number of Senators, I. P. Walker of Wisconsin, S. P. Chase, Lewis Cass, J. R. Underwood of Kentucky, William Seward, and John Hale of New Hampshire presented memorials from citizens in their states for the securing of arbitration treaties. These memorials went to the Committee on Foreign Relations, as did that of the American Peace Society which Robert Winthrop of Massachusetts presented on December 16, 1850. Winthrop referred to the fact that Cobden's motion had been respectfully received by the House of Commons and that Lord John Russell had expressed a readiness to entertain a

[10] Cf. *ante* p. 127.

[11] *Advocate of Peace*, vol. x, January, 1852, pp. 9, 14; *Congressional Globe*, 30 Cong., 2 sess., January 16, 1849, vol. xx, pp. 267, 448; 31 Cong., 1 sess., January 28, 1850, vol. xxi, Part 1, p. 228; January 28, February 11, 1850, pp. 230, 234.

proposition for general arbitration from the government of the United States.[12]

The peace men did not stop with this. President Taylor was interviewed in the spring of 1850, but all he had to say to Lord John Russell's proposal for a general arbitration treaty with the United States was that he, President Taylor, was the "greatest peace man in the country." The General added that, men's passions being what they had been for a thousand years, all the efforts for international peace were folly. To interview General Taylor was but to grasp a nettle.[13]

With lobbying Congress it might be different—at least Beckwith, corresponding secretary of the American Peace Society, hoped that it might be. To his surprise, the chairman of the Senate Committee on Foreign Affairs, Senator Foote, ex-general and a Southerner, was both courteous and sympathetic. After an introductory explanation, he interrupted Beckwith—"That's right, sir. I like the principle, it has much practical sense." He would see what he could do with his Committee.[14] Meantime senators had ample chance to read a specially prepared pamphlet, *Stipulated Arbitration: an Argument addressed to American Statesmen.*

On February 5, 1851, Foote reported a resolution from the Committee on Foreign Affairs indicating the desirability of government action in securing arbitration clauses in treaties with foreign powers. He urged the Senate to adopt the resolution at once and unanimously, as the Committee had done. Senator Clemens of Alabama had the resolution laid over. Although the failure of the measure has been largely attributed to southern and western opposition, it is interesting to note that the Committee on Foreign Affairs, which had reported favorably, was,

[12] *Congressional Globe, loc. cit.*, p. 119, p. 386, and 31 Cong., 2 sess., vol. xxiii, p. 55; *Christian Citizen,* February 2, March 9, March 23, 1850.

[13] *Christian Citizen,* March 9, 1850.

[14] *Advocate of Peace,* vol. x, June, 1853, Beckwith's address at the Twenty-fifth Anniversary of the American Peace Society, pp. 292 ff., 308 ff.

with one exception, made up of men who represented the South and West.[15]

Beckwith would not accept defeat. He took copies of the report to the President, members of the Cabinet, and some of the foreign ministers, not one of whom, he reported, objected to the principle—in fact, some even expressed themselves very strongly in its favor. Secretary Corwin of the Treasury Department said that if he were at the head of the State Department he would regard the resolution as making it imperative for him to negotiate for the insertion of a stipulated arbitration clause in all future treaties. Other members of the Cabinet, however, and President Fillmore were not so strong in their expressions of favor. The session was about to end, and arbitration had to wait a spell.[16]

On February 22, 1853, Senator J. R. Underwood, of Kentucky, submitted a report from the Committee on Foreign Affairs relative to another petition from the American Peace Society in support of the policy of stipulated arbitration. It is true that a minority of the Committee, for which J. M. Mason of Virginia was spokesman, dissented from the majority report. The text of the resolution simply recommended to the President that, whenever practicable, clauses be secured in treaties for the reference of disputes to mutually chosen arbiters. It is interesting, in view of the unfriendly attitude of Mason and Douglas towards this report, that the *Advocate of Peace* should report the action of the Committee on Foreign Affairs as "unanimous and cordial." Perhaps it is an example of wishful thinking on the part of peace men. Still, it is significant that such a report should have been made at all, considering that the years 1852-1853 marked the height of the Young American movement and that jingoism and filibustering were so popular. Whether it was for lack of

---

[15] *Congressional Globe,* 31 Cong., 2 sess., vol. xxiii, p. 437; *Advocate of Peace,* vol. x, March to April, 1851, pp. 52-53.

[16] Beckwith, in the *Advocate of Peace,* vol. x, June, 1853, p. 309.

time—the peace men professed to believe it was—or for other reasons, the Senate took no action on this report.[17]

Very likely the attitude of the Senate may have been due to a feeling that, since the Free Soil Party had adopted stipulated arbitration in their Pittsburgh platform of 1852, the project smacked of antislavery. This inference seems the more natural, since the sectional character of the peace movement was suggested when the legislatures of Vermont, Massachusetts, Maine, Rhode Island, and Connecticut adopted during the years 1852 and 1853, practically unanimously, resolutions recommending that the federal government secure treaty provisions for the arbitration of future disputes.[18] Since immediate success was the goal, it was probably unfortunate that the movement for arbitration, in both England and the United States, was sponsored in legislative bodies by men who had made many political enemies by their advocacy of Free Trade and reforms on the one hand and antislavery measures on the other.

In America there were no great public demonstrations comparable to the spectacular ones carried out in England before Cobden's resolution met its Waterloo in Parliament. So far as one may judge from references in the *Advocate of Peace* and the *Christian Citizen,* the American press bothered itself very little about the campaign for stipulated arbitration. The *North American Review* characteristically printed an article which held that in many disputes the circumstances were too complicated for any umpire to grasp.[19]

---

[17] *Congressional Globe,* 32 Cong., 2 sess., vol. xxvi, p. 761. The report in its entirety is printed in the *Advocate of Peace,* vol. x, April, 1853, pp. 257 ff., September, 1852, p. 158, June, 1853, p. 312.

[18] *Vermont Legislative Journals,* 1852: *Journal of the House,* October 16, 1852, pp. 17, 181, 245, 261, 367; *Journal of the Senate,* October 10, 1852, pp. 39, 209; *Advocate of Peace,* vol. x, July, 1853, p. 318, August, pp. 329-330, September, p. 158.

[19] For such press comment as caught the attention of the editor of the Society's periodical, see *Advocate of Peace,* vol. ix, January and February, 1851, pp. 29 ff., and also, *Christian Citizen,* February 24, 1849; *North American Review,* vol. lxviii, January, 1849, pp. 40 ff.

If the goal had not been achieved, none the less one more rung on the ladder had been reached. The peace men, after 1853, bent their energies towards securing the highly desired arbitration clause in the Claims and Fisheries treaties which were hanging fire between Great Britain and the United States. These negotiations concerned the serious misunderstandings resulting from the existing ambiguous treaties relating to the fisheries. To secure such a clause committing the two governments to future arbitration, Beckwith saw President Fillmore, Secretary of State Everett, and Crampton, the British minister. Fillmore and Everett at once assented to the correctness of the principle and favored its application in cases of difficulty as they arose, but they had not, apparently, thought of the importance of providing for arbitration by express treaty agreements. In a subsequent interview they indicated their readiness to insert such a provision if the British minister was willing. Crampton was reported as being ready to give his name to such a provision if his government so instructed him.[20]

In England a delegation from the Peace Conference Committee of London and Manchester waited on the Foreign Secretary, Lord Clarendon. This deputation included Richard Cobden, William Ewart, Joseph Hume, and Charles Hindley, members of Parliament, as well as Alexander Brockway and Henry Richard. Cobden came to the point at once by saying that they thought the time a suitable one for introducing into the treaties under negotiation a clause binding the contracting parties to refer their future disputes to arbitration. The Earl of Clarendon hedged. The question was a novel one; he would give it serious consideration. Cobden reminded him that the American Foreign Relations Committee had lately presented a report to the Senate advising the President to secure such clauses in treaties thereafter negotiated. Clarendon wanted to see the report, and Cobden promised to see that he got it.[21]

[20] *Advocate of Peace*, vol. x, June, 1853, p. 310; *Herald of Peace*, June, 1853, p. 227.

[21] *Herald of Peace*, new series, no. ii, June, 1853, pp. 233-234.

Meantime Beckwith was coming to the conclusion that seldom, if ever, had there been "an opportunity to accomplish so much for the cause of peace by a single vigorous effort." Hence he undertook a three-thousand-mile journey in the West, during which he circulated petitions asking the federal government to include a stipulated arbitration clause in the pending treaties. Besides the usual local agents, twenty friends of peace volunteered to get up similar petitions. Ecclesiastical bodies did what they could by passing resolutions, and new tracts aided the work. The circulation of the *Advocate* during this campaign was doubled, reaching four thousand copies.[22]

Although they produced no proof for their claim, the peace workers believed that their efforts were not altogether in vain. The Claims Convention of 1853, concluded a few days after Cobden's delegation interviewed Clarendon, and the Reciprocity Treaty as to Fisheries, Duties, and Navigation, concluded on June 5, 1854, provided for commissions to decide on disputed claims relevant to the questions at issue. An umpire was to settle disputes not otherwise adjustable. Thus, although the principle of arbitration was recognized, it was by no means to be applied to all future disputes between the two countries, as the peace party had visioned. Beckwith, although disappointed, made much of the fact that at least the principle of arbitration had been recognized and found further consolation in a provision in the treaty of 1853 with Mexico, though its terms lacked precision and though the parties were not bound to arbitrate against their will.[23] It would seem that even these conservative provisions for arbitration were not the direct result of the agitation of the peace crusaders.

Such were the accomplishments of the campaign prior to the Crimean War for the incorporation of stipulated arbitration

[22] *Advocate of Peace*, vol. x, August, 1853, pp. 324-329, November, 1853, p. 384.
[23] William M. Malloy, *Treaties, Conventions, International Acts, Protocols, and Agreements between the United States and other Powers, 1776-1909* (Washington, 1910), I, pp. 665, 669; *Advocate of Peace*, vol. xi, August, 1854, p. 126.

clauses into international agreements. As in the case of the peace congresses, the immediate value of the results was probably exaggerated by the peace group, who were, as ever, oversanguine. Perhaps this was necessary if they were to keep their courage. Their enthusiasm for their cause and the necessity of compensation for defeats made it easy for them to take the platitudes of politicians for more than they were worth. They were to suffer disillusionment in the trials that were before them.

X

THE WANING OF THE CRUSADE, 1853-1860

With the success of the international peace congresses of Paris, Frankfort, and London, and the optimism inspired by the work for arbitration, it seemed as if the peace movement were destined for an even more promising and significant development. As a matter of fact, an Iliad of woes befell the movement from 1853 to 1860, and its decline, though not entirely clear to men at the time, was both steady and fundamental.

On casual inspection the reports of the income of the American Peace Society might be taken to indicate growth rather than decline, and this interpretation was implied in the annual reports. In the fiscal year 1849 the Society's receipts were $3,698, "a sum greater than the average during the preceding years," and the next year the income jumped to $6,204. Although this was unusual, the next year saw an income of $5,345, and in 1860 it was still at a good figure. An inspection of the complete figures, however, shows a general downward trend, the high points being due to special bequests and legacies. The older members of the movement were rapidly dying, and, as the annual reports indicate, several left very generous legacies. However optimistically interpreted by the peace men, then, these data on financial income cannot be taken to indicate genuine growth in the movement. In fact, we can see in them some indication of a lessening in general support.[1]

Statistics as to membership are so incomplete that it is scarcely possible to interpret the strength of organized pacifism in America on that basis. After 1852 lists of life members were discontinued in the *Advocate of Peace,* and the archives of the American Peace Society throw no light on membership during this period. In 1852 there were 307 life members, of whom 31

[1] Annual Reports of the American Peace Society, 1849-1860, in the *Advocate of Peace,* vols. viii-xiii, *passim.* For legacies, see especially vol. x, June and July, 1852, p. 124, and vol. xi, June, 1855, p. 290 (p. 19).

were women and 93 were clergymen. Of the total number, 168 lived in Massachusetts.[2] Since the revenues of the Society did not increase during this period, apart from bequests, it may be inferred that membership remained about stationary. Naturally, the bequests made possible a good showing in the printing and circulating of peace literature.

Notwithstanding these outward appearances of vigor in the national organization, the American peace movement as a whole was less vital in 1860 than it was in 1853. By 1854 the League of Universal Brotherhood had given up even the semblance of an organization. Though the annual reports of the American Peace Society spoke with glowing pride of its relatively satisfactory funds and boasted of its agencies, its tracts, its periodical, the peace men were really dancing on a volcano. There were evident signs of the coming eruption long before the catastrophe of the Civil War, but it was not until May, 1861, that a peace leader frankly described what had been taking place. Elihu Burritt then pointed out that the past five years had been an ordeal for the friends of peace, filled with more troubling events than had ever before been concentrated in a like space of time. The darkness, he observed, had been deepest just after the break of day. In the five years beginning with 1848 permanent and universal peace had seemed to be "on the eve of its coronation." At each succeeding congress new and distinguished adherents were won for the cause. But, he continued, the terrible contest in the Crimea, the "murderous and malignant conflict" in India and in China, the war in Italy, marshaled such hosts and led to such carnage as Austerlitz and Waterloo had not known. "Never, since the first organization and associated efforts of the friends of peace, has such a deluge of antagonistic events overwhelmed their labors, hopes, and faith." Each of the wars, Burritt said, came with a peculiar temptation to many who felt themselves well grounded in the principles of peace, and those

[2] *Ibid.*, vol. x, June and July, 1852, pp. 125-128.

whom one war left unshaken, another swept into the current of popular sympathy and opinion. Thousands who had stood up against the conflict in the Crimea yielded to sympathy for Garibaldi's struggle in Italy.[3]

These disasters had their effect on the American peace workers. Even more significant than the apparent failure of the cause in the Old World were the signs in the United States of the coming storm. Although peace leaders for the most part ignored the gathering clouds, they occasionally confessed the danger. Burritt, however, was the only one who tried to meet it. The official attitude of the American Peace Society was that its work concerned only international war, and this remained its position during the whole period of the Civil War. It was such sidestepping that "chilled the heart and palsied the hands" of the more ardent and radical peace men, those who, in the main, represented the old reform group. This group had but little influence, and the peace movement in America was almost a shell. Even the determinedly optimistic Beckwith complained in issue after issue of the *Advocate of Peace* that there was an increasing lack of interest in the cause.[4]

In England the peace movement showed vitality until after the disillusioning Crimean War. From 1846 to 1853, there was widespread talk about the necessity of increasing armaments, especially of strengthening the militia. These arguments, thorns in the side of British peace men, goaded them to action. In their campaign against militarism and the aggressive foreign policy of Lord Palmerston, they were greatly aided by the co-operation of Richard Cobden. Cobden's antipathy to war and to preparation for it was neither sentimental nor religious. He disliked war because it was incompatible with social, political, and economic well-being. From 1849 onwards he was in con-

[3] Elihu Burritt, "Address before the American Peace Society," May, 1861, pp. 230 ff., in *Lectures and Speeches.*

[4] Holland, Ms. *History of the American Peace Cause,* vol. i, p. 4; *Advocate of Peace,* vol. xiii, September and October, 1858, p. 137; vol. xiv, January and February, 1859, pp. 201 ff.; November and December, 1859, pp. 361-362.

stant correspondence with Henry Richard and exerted a marked practical influence on the English peace movement. It was Cobden who directed the attention of the editor of the *Herald of Peace* to the "cowardly butchery" in Borneo in 1849 and urged upon him a public protest meeting. Again and again he brought to Richard's attention specific data which exposed the imperialistic policies of Lord Palmerston, and as a result there was wide publicity. In 1850 he urged on the peace movement the exposure of the Don Pacifico affair. In Parliament the great Free Trader constantly endeavored to secure the reduction of military and naval expenditures.

Although by no means in entire sympathy with the somewhat doctrinaire peace policy of the Quakers, the left wing of the Peace Society, and the League of Universal Brotherhood, he desired their support. At the same time he realized that if the anti-war propaganda was to be effective in practical politics, the agitation could not be based on the nonresistance principle. As Cobden understood it, his alliance with the peace men was to forward plans which, step by step, would condition men's minds to look upon the abolition of war as a possible, even if a remote, goal. The entente maintained between Cobden and the peace group was due largely to the tact and wisdom of Henry Richard. As Cobden said, the enemy took good care to turn everyone in the working alliance against militarism into Quakers, because their nonresistance principles put them "out of court as practical politicians."

With the *coup d'état* of Napoleon III the popular mind was stirred to fear invasion, and Cobden, Bright, Sturge, and Richard felt that the peace movement should bend every effort to counteract the hysteria. The military and naval men, the *Times*, the Government itself nourished the invasion panic. While Parliament in 1853 debated a new militia bill, the London Peace Society broadcasted bills urging resistance to militia service, held 160 public meetings of protest, and sent over 1300 petitions to

Parliament. It was at this time that Elihu Burritt again carried Friendly Addresses from English to French towns.[5] The Peace Congress Committee arranged a huge demonstration, which developed into the Manchester Peace Conference on January 27 and the following day. Joseph Sturge wrote to Lewis Tappan of New York that he hoped this conference, together with the widely circulated pamphlet of Richard Cobden, "1793 and 1853," would "check the continued abuse of the French by the London Press." Between five and six hundred delegates came to Manchester. They chose as presiding officer George Wilson, the well known chairman of the British Anti-Corn Law League. Within half an hour £4000 were contributed to the fund for fighting the war scare. The editor of the *Advocate of Peace* wondered when American friends of peace would be aroused to "like zeal and liberality."[6]

Burritt lay sick in bed from exhaustion, but other vigorous personalities made the Manchester Conference a success. Cobden's oratory and Bright's impassioned speaking made Henry Richard feel that the peace movement had never sponsored an assembly "so weighty and influential,—pervaded by a spirit so earnest and courageous."[7] A delegation from the conference interviewed Lord Aberdeen, recently come into power, and, according to Sir W. Molesworth, one of his colleagues, the Prime Minister was "uncommonly pleased" by the delegation. Not only Aberdeen himself, but some of his colleagues, made clear their pacific intentions, though it cannot be proved that their action was due to the peace agitation.[8] The incipient French peace

[5] Richard, *Memoirs of Joseph Sturge*, pp. 405-406; Hirst, *The Quakers in Peace and War*, p. 245; *Herald of Peace*, no. 67, February, 1848, *passim*; Miall, *Henry Richard*, p. 88; Thirty-Sixth Annual Report of the London Peace Society in *Advocate of Peace*, vol. x, August, 1852, pp. 132 ff.; John Morley, *The Life of Richard Cobden*, vol. ii, pp. 81-82; Hobson, *Richard Cobden, the International Man*, pp. 56 ff.

[6] J. A. Hobson, *Richard Cobden, the International Man*, pp. 93 ff.; *Advocate of Peace*, vol. xi, February, 1854, pp. 18 ff.; Richard, *Memoirs of Joseph Sturge*, pp. 406 ff.

[7] Burritt, Ms. *Journal*, January 27, 1853; Miall, *Henry Richard*, pp. 91-92.

[8] Miall, *op. cit.*, p. 94.

movement seems to have been quiescent during this invasion panic, although Frédéric Bastiat's letters in the Manchester *Times* advanced the economist's argument for peace. The panic petered out while the *Spectator* fumed because Lord Aberdeen seemed "half-inclined to accept the post of missionary in Mr. Cobden's Anti-War League."[9] Both British and American peace men believed that the lion's share of the credit in dissipating the hysteria aroused by fear of a French invasion belonged to the peace movement.

But if this fright was a storm in a teacup, it was quite clear that the war clouds looming up in the East threatened one in the open. Hence in October, 1853, the friends of peace staged another demonstration, the Edinburgh Peace Conference. Though war feeling ran high, the sessions were well attended. Cobden was on hand, and also Bright. Burritt noted in his *Journal* that Cobden made one of his "best efforts, which was irresistible," and that Bright spoke with "great power and eloquence."[10] But the tide was not stemmed. Sturge was insulted and refused a hearing in his beloved Birmingham, while Bright was burned in effigy by a Manchester mob. The *Times* and *Blackwood's Magazine* attacked the peace party fiercely.[11] The Peace Society and its political allies, the Manchester group of politicians, seemed to have reached the end of their resources. Certain Friends, however, determined to send a mission to St. Petersburg to try to restrain the Czar. Although Joseph Sturge, Henry Pease, and Robert Charleton were kindly received by Count Nesselrode and the Czar, their mission came to nothing. Both the London Peace Society and the American Peace Society

[9] *Spectator*, March 5, 1853, in *Littell's Living Age*, May 7, 1853, second series, vol. i, pp. 383-384. Charles Dickens's *Household Words* (vol. ii, February 1, 1851, p. 455; vol. iii, August 23, 1851, p. 506) gave valuable aid to the peace cause in its efforts to combat the invasion panic, as did *Punch*, vol. xxii, p. 96, and vol. xxiii, p. 137.

[10] *Advocate of Peace*, vol. xi, February, 1854, pp. 17 ff.; Miall, *Henry Richard*, p. 99; Burritt, Ms. *Journal*, October 3, 1853.

[11] Miall, *Henry Richard*, pp. 100, 124; *Blackwood's Magazine*, vol. 73, March, 1853, pp. 372 ff.; November, 1854, pp. 589 ff.

nevertheless took heart from this independent and courageous action of the British Friends.[12]

The English peace movement not only tried hard to prevent the Crimean War, but once hostilities began also did not flinch in opposing it. Bright published a "courageous and powerful letter denouncing the war," a letter which seemed to Burritt the "noblest act of moral courage" that he had ever known, issued as it was in the face of the bitterest attacks from the press.[13] Organized peace groups functioned openly and actively. The London Peace Society and an organization specially formed at this time, the End-the-War-League, held public meetings which averaged in attendance from 1000 to 4000 persons. They sent memorials to the Government—one bore 11,000 names—praying for an immediate cessation of hostilities. A flood of pamphlets, tracts, cards, and publications was issued to "instruct and influence the public mind." These included the "History and Origin of the War," based on government documents, parliamentary speeches denouncing the war, and descriptions of its horrors, waste and atrocities. It was estimated that during the year, 1853-1854, some 900,000 copies of such literature were circulated. The *Herald of Peace* urged friends of the cause not to support the movement for relief work. This could not be done, it maintained, without "directly contributing to feed and further the *system* by which those orphans and widows have been created, and which, the more it is encouraged, will only the more add to the number of such sufferers day by day and year by year."[14]

While undoubtedly many factors helped to explain the growing unpopularity of the war, peace men felt their efforts were

[12] Richard, *Memoirs of Joseph Sturge*, pp. 462 ff.; Hirst, *The Quakers in Peace and War*, p. 258, quotes an editorial from the London *Times* ridiculing the mission; *Herald of Peace*, new series, no. xlv, March, 1854, p. 25; *Advocate of Peace*, vol. xi, May, 1854, pp. 69-70.

[13] Burritt, Ms. *Journal*, November 15, 1854.

[14] Annual Report of London Peace Society in the *Advocate of Peace*, vol. xii, August and September, 1856, pp. 123-133; *Herald of Peace*, no. lv, new series, January, 1855, pp. 147 ff.; no. liv, new series, December, 1854, pp. 138-139.

largely responsible for the changed attitude of the public. It was a natural opinion, supported by the fact that their operations were sharply criticized on that ground by editorials or articles in *Frazer's Magazine,* the *Economist* (ministerial organ), the *North British Review,* the *Quarterly Review,* and *Blackwood's.*[15]

Individuals in both France[16] and America raised their voices in protest against the Crimean War. As early as July 9, 1853, Burritt went with Henry Richard to the American legation in London to persuade the minister, J. R. Ingersoll, to propose arbitration of the difficulties which seemed to threaten an Eastern war. What an opportunity, Burritt urged, to make good the recent report of the Senate Committee on Foreign Affairs, which had favored the principle of arbitration! After an interview lasting an hour and a half, Ingersoll thought he might ask for instructions and perhaps meanwhile undertake to offer conditional mediation. Though well disposed, in the end he shrank from the responsibility and returned to the United States.[17]

Burritt and Richard seem to have originated the idea of mediation on the part of the United States. On March 9, 1854, Richard wrote to Charles Sumner begging him to bring the question of an American offer of mediation before the Chief Executive. Sumner replied in such a way as to make the secretary of the London Peace Society feel under deep obligations to him.[18] Moreover, he acted in the spirit of this reply. On December 21, 1854, the Massachusetts Senator submitted a resolution directing the Committee on Foreign Affairs to consider the ex-

[15] Richard, *Memoirs of Joseph Sturge,* p. 489; Annual Report of London Peace Society, *Herald of Peace,* vol. iii, June, 1855, pp. 209 ff.; *Blackwood's Magazine,* vol. lxxvii, January, 1855, pp. 102 ff.; vol. lxxviii, July, 1855, pp. 116 ff.; vol. lxii, March, 1856, pp. 304 ff.; *North British Review,* vol. xcviii, March, 1856, p. 249; *Frazer's Magazine,* vol. x, July, 1854, p. 121.

[16] *Journal des Économistes,* 2 series, vol. iii, July and September, 1854, pp. 57-65 (Edouard Hervé, "La Paix, les échanges internationaux et l'Uniformité des mesures"); pp. 161-181; Molinari, "Des Progrès réalisés dans les coutumes de la Guerre"; Francisque Bouvet, *La Guerre,* Paris, 1855, especially pp. 265-266.

[17] Burritt, Ms. *Journal,* July 9, 14, 25, 1853.

[18] Richard to Sumner, London, May 6, 1854, *Sumner Papers, Foreign Letters,* 1852-1856.

pediency of tendering the mediation of the United States to the belligerents. He also called on President Pierce in an effort to persuade him to initiate such a policy. Neither Sumner's course nor that of Congressman Clingman of North Carolina, who introduced a similar resolution in the House, bore fruit. This defeat was in part due to the opposition of such men as E. M. Chamberlain, who opposed the Clingman resolution on the ground that such a policy would endanger our freedom from "entangling alliances."[19]

The Learned Blacksmith, who was now in Washington, kept in close touch with Sumner and of his own accord wrote to President Pierce urging the proffer of mediation. He emphasized the idea that such a course would increase our power and influence, and that it offered a great personal opportunity for the Chief Executive. Finally, at Sumner's suggestion, Burritt saw Pierce, who admitted that as a nation the United States had a great interest in the settlement of the controversy. He went on to say that he had considered mediation for some time, but that he had concluded we were not in a position to deal competently with the merits of the question. It was Sumner's conviction, after dining with President Pierce, that the real reason for not offering mediation was the fear that such tactics might provide the European powers with an opportunity to step in between the United States and Spain in the Cuban problem.[20] It is not clear whether this was really the circumstance which prevented the administration from taking action.[21]

It is noteworthy that the American Peace Society as such undertook no concerted efforts in behalf of the mediation move-

[19] *Congressional Globe,* vol. xxx, 33 Cong., 2 sess., December 11, 1854, p. 27, December 21, p. 105; January 24, 1855; Pierce, *Memoir of Charles Sumner,* vol. ii, p. 381.

[20] Burritt, Ms. *Journal,* March 29, April 2, 3, 7, 1854.

[21] Hülsemann, the Austrian Chargé, felt that the open opposition of Napoleon's minister in Washington, M. de Sartiges, was the chief reason why the administration did not offer mediation. Hülsemann to Buol-Schauenstein, December 31, 1854, no. 39, "Nord Amerika," Haus-Hof-und Statt Archiv, Vienna.

ment. It was the commercial interests in New York that sent petitions to Congress praying for favorable attention to the Sumner and Clingman resolutions. The Austrian Chargé d'Affaires, Hülsemann, agreed with the London *Economist* in the opinion that the chief support of the movement for mediation came from New York and Southern commercial interests, which suffered an interruption of trade as a result of the war.[22] Though American peace men were not the only or the most influential supporters of the movement for mediation, the *Herald of Peace* rejoiced that such an effort had been made.[23]

This organ of the London Peace Society also continually cited American criticisms of the war. This, it said, was "to show our countrymen how things look from a distance." American peace champions freely admired their British brethren's stand. William Jay, President of the American Peace Society, wrote to Joseph Sturge that the British Quakers and those that acted with them, were the real heroes of the war. Such moral support proved a great satisfaction to the English opponents of the war.[24]

If the American Peace Society did not follow the example of the London Peace Society, which during the Mexican War had sought to further mediation, it nevertheless drew abundant lessons from the Crimean War. Jay and Beckwith moralized, now describing in lurid detail the atrocities of the war, now citing evidence to show its interference with Christian missions. They scorned the idea that the war was a religious struggle: Russian archbishops justified the struggle as a holy crusade on the one hand, while the Pope and British bishops on the other hand claimed God's help in sending Christian brethren to hell.

[22] *The Economist,* January 13, 1855, in *Littell's Living Age,* vol. viii, p. 559. Like this British government organ, the New York *Evening Post* (December 26, 1854) felt that the movement in Congress favoring the proffer of mediation was an example of American "intermeddling." Hülsemann to Buol-Schauenstein, *loc. cit.*

[23] *Herald of Peace,* vol. lvi, new series, February, 1855, p. 163.

[24] *Ibid.,* no. lxi, new series, July, 1855, pp. 228 ff.; Richard, *Memoirs of Joseph Sturge,* pp. 494-495; Amasa Walker to the secretary of the London Peace Society, in *Herald of Peace,* no. lxiii, new series, September, 1855, p. 247.

In general American pacifists felt that the War resulted rather from "that infamous figment of European diplomacy, the Balance of Power." How significant that each party tried to prove the other the aggressor! This clearly brought to light, it was said, the nature of those war delusions which were part and parcel of every appeal to the sword. The economic waste and destruction due to the Crimean struggle were capitalized in great arrays of statistics, and the loss of life and limb was melodramatically itemized.[25]

One of the most searching American indictments of the European war was that of W. R. Alger, whose *An American Voice on the Lessons of the War* made the point that the war sprang from jealousy, national rivalry, and wicked pride and not, as was claimed, from generous sympathy with the oppressed. Another American, William H. Allen, President of Girard College, wrote of England and France that, "under the pretence of preserving the Balance of Power, they are illustrating the fable of the dog in the manger; if they cannot get possession of Old Byzantium themselves, they are determined that the hungry beast who stands over it, shall not." Allen concluded by wondering when nations would learn that they cannot thrive on the misfortunes of their neighbors.[26]

In his denunciation of "this most outrageous war," Elihu Burritt felt that the leading journals of England were in a peculiar sense responsible for the calamity. They had also, he believed, "impregnated the American mind with British prejudices." In his *Citizen of the World*, founded in 1855, and in the *Bond of Brotherhood*, this shrewd Yankee demonstrated the inadequacy of the Balance of Power, and at the same time hammered away on the dangers of "secret and uncontrolled

[25] *Advocate of Peace*, vol. xi, June, 1855, pp. 5 ff.; May, 1854, p. 73; August and September, 1855, p. 336; April, 1854, p. 50; February, 1855, p. 217; April, 1854, pp. 49-52; May, 1854, pp. 79 ff.; August and September, 1855, p. 334.

[26] W. E. Alger, *An American Voice on the Late War in the East*, Boston, 1856, pp. 42-43; Allen, Address Before American Peace Society, May, 1854, in *Advocate of Peace*, vol. xi, July, 1854, pp. 114 ff.

editorship." This latter evil, he insisted, was "graver than secret diplomacy; it may set a continent on fire." Burritt seldom thought more sanely than when he was condemning the press, "which victimizes and deludes the people." Though he feared his stand would lose him many British as well as American friends, he hoped in some small way to impress his fellow men, and draw some little good out of the wretched experience of the war.[27]

As soon as peace negotiations were talked of, a large delegation, including eighteen members of Parliament, together with the leading officials of the London Peace Society, presented a memorial to Lord Palmerston, asking to have inserted in the treaty a clause binding the contracting powers to refer to arbitration any subsequent causes of differences. When the Prime Minister made objections, Cobden called his attention to the precedent in the recent treaty between the United States and Great Britain, which provided for the arbitration of disputes arising from the fisheries question. Cobden went on to say that his Majesty's Government had just proposed arbitration with respect to the Anglo-American disputes in Central America. Palmerston, though polite, was unconvinced. Arbitration of minor matters was one thing; arbitration of great questions involving national rights and advantages was quite another.[28]

This interview did not, however, darken the hopes of Henry Richard. He determined to go to Paris and take the wolves by the ear. Joseph Sturge and Charles Hindley went with him. They placed before the plenipotentiaries at the Congress of Paris a memorial in behalf of the cause of mediation and arbitration, with the request that it be sent to their sovereigns. As a result, communications were received from Cavour, Count Walewski (the French delegate), and the Prussian representatives. The

<hr />

[27] Burritt, Ms. *Journal*, February 2, 1856: *Bond of Brotherhood*, no. 3, new series, June, 1856; *Journal*, January 24, February 1, 5, March 6, 1855.

[28] *Herald of Peace*, vol. iii (n. s.), April, 1856, pp. 38-39; Report of the Delegation in the *Advocate of Peace*, vol. xii, May, 1856, pp. 72-75; Richard, *Memoirs of Joseph Sturge*, pp. 496-497.

latter informed Sturge and Richard that their King, after receiving the memorial, instructed them to support the proposition if it came before the Congress. The chief problem was precisely that of getting the project before the Congress. Lord Clarendon, the British delegate, after an interview with the peace men at the Hôtel du Louvre, promised to do what he could. The petitioners, after three weeks of anxiety, left Paris with no very high hopes, for Clarendon assured them that it would be very difficult to persuade governments to bind themselves to arbitration.[29]

When the Protocols of the Congress of Paris were published, however, they found that Clarendon had kept his promise. It is true that he found no support for the principle of compulsory arbitration or mediation, but the plenipotentiaries finally passed a resolution expressing the wish that nations, before resorting to arms, would have recourse to the good offices of a friendly power. This indeed was a far cry from the binding arbitration that the memorialists had requested. Still it was something for a Congress of the Powers to endorse the general principle of mediation, and Henry Richard and George C. Beckwith made the most of the crumbs offered them. Actually the Protocol (number 23) was in itself hollow and almost worthless. Yet it did represent a small gain. In 1869, recourse to the Protocol was taken in one of the almost innumerable conflicts between Greece and Turkey, and in the following year Great Britain invoked it, without success, in the Franco-Prussian conflict. At the First Hague Congress the Protocol was cited as a precedent for the international recognition of the principle of arbitration.[30] Thus the peace men made a positive, if indirect, contribution to the development of international arbitration.

Friends of peace in America and Britain rejoiced also in other

[29] *Herald of Peace*, vol. iii (n. s.), May, 1856, p. 57; Richard, *Memoirs of Joseph Sturge*, pp. 449-500.

[30] *Ibid.*; Sir Francis Biggott, *The Declaration of Paris of 1856*, London, 1919, pp. 60 ff.; J. B. Scott, *Proceedings of the Hague Peace Conferences*, Carnegie Endowment for International Peace, New York, 1920, Part iv, Annex i,c, pp. 804-808; Lange, *Histoire de la Doctrine Pacifique*, p. 217.

provisions of the Treaty and especially in the Declaration of Paris. Free ships were declared to make free goods; a neutral flag was to protect whatever it covered; and commerce of a neutral was to be unmolested in war as in peace, while nothing but articles "strictly contraband of war" were to be placed under the ban. "Such ameliorations of war," wrote Beckwith in the *Advocate of Peace,* "are a long stride towards the final abolition of war itself."[31] Burritt also took pleasure in noticing these "gains for peace," while the American Peace Society at its annual meeting in 1856 adopted a laudatory resolution. If nothing except the abolition of privateering had resulted from forty years of peace agitation, this one accomplishment, said the Annual Report, would have been worth the effort. Whether because of determined optimism or by a process of rationalization, the peace men at any rate elected to believe that organized pacifism was responsible for these advances.[32]

Since American peace men so generally believed that these gains were an important victory for peace, they might well have agitated for the official recognition of the same principles by the American Government. The fact that they remained passive, content merely with commending the Declaration of Paris, is perhaps an evidence that the peace movement lacked vitality. Although the principles adopted in the Declaration, with the exception of that abolishing privateering, accorded with our long-maintained doctrines of neutral rights, the United States refused to adhere to it. Burritt wrote to Marcy, Secretary of State, commending his proposal to extend the provision regarding the abolition of privateering so as to guarantee all private commerce against search and seizure by national warships of belligerents, except when such vessels violated the laws of contraband and trade. But the American peace movement made no concerted effort to popularize Marcy's proposals, and his successor, Cass, backed water.[33]

The American peace men, though they had not worked to influence the government, confessed their disappointment in its failure to act. Their buoyant enthusiasm for the Declaration of Paris waned when it appeared that their own country—the scene of their own labors—ignored those principles, the sole good outcome of the catastrophe. In the final outcome, therefore, the gains for peace which they had thought resulted from the Crimean War seemed bare. The London Peace Society confessed in its annual report that "the sinister legacy of the Eastern war has for the present taken possession of many of our countrymen."[34]

There followed closely upon the Crimean War the Indian Mutiny, the Anglo-Persian War, and the second Anglo-Chinese War. Month after month the *Herald of Peace* exposed the British atrocities in India, while in America the *Advocate* drew abundant illustration of the suicidal folly of resorting to the sword. In interfering with missionary work the Mutiny, in Beckwith's eyes, proved clearly how opposed the sword was to Christ's Gospel. In England all the old pacifist methods—placards, lectures, demonstrations, memorials—were brought to play, though the showing was not so good as in the preceding crisis. The situation seemed so hopeless that at last Joseph Sturge volunteered to lead a deputation to India to study the causes of the revolt and to suggest remedies. His friends, however, discouraged him from undertaking such a venture because of his advanced age and ill health.[35]

At the same time the London Peace Society investigated the

[33] C. R. Fish, *American Diplomacy*, p. 288; Burritt, Ms. *Journal*, September 4, 5, 1856; *Advocate of Peace*, vol. xii, March and April, 1857, p. 253.

[34] *Advocate of Peace*, vol. xiii, November and December, 1857, p. 355; Holland, Ms. *History of the American Peace Cause*, vol. iii, p. 104; *Advocate of Peace*, vol. xiii, September and October, 1857, pp. 342 ff.

[35] *Advocate of Peace*, vol. xiii, June, 1858, p. 71; January and February, 1858, pp. 10-13, pp. 24-25; September and October, 1858, pp. 147 ff.; *Herald of Peace*, no. 91, February, 1851, *passim*; Richard, *Memoirs of Joseph Sturge*, pp. 522-523.

facts in the war that had broken out with China and laid the blame at Britain's door. The Government's measures were held to be violent, extreme, and wholly "unnecessary and unjustified." A copy of the report of this investigation was forwarded to each member of Parliament and to many persons of influence. Cobden and Bright were not returned to Parliament, but they labored as well as they could against the Government's policies.[36] It is noteworthy that little was claimed for all this peace activity. War was piling up on war, and protests and investigations, valuable as they were, did not obscure the fact that little had been accomplished by the peace movement in the way of actually checking military conflicts.

There was also much feeling that the conflicts between British and Americans in Central America endangered the peaceful relations of the two countries. In both the press took on a threatening tone. Hence the London Peace Society urged religious bodies to send addresses on peace to kindred groups in America, and the Congregationalists and Baptists responded to the summons. The League of Universal Brotherhood, as a kind of swan song, got up twenty addresses to American cities from corresponding British towns. Newspapers in London and throughout the kingdom, as well as on the Continent, printed an Address bearing 31,000 names which a demonstration at Manchester sent to America. This document, intrusted to Beckwith, was said to have been printed in more than a hundred American papers.[37] It is significant that the initiative was taken by the Britishers. Although this may have been partly due to the fact that Americans felt the war danger less acutely, still the sluggishness of their response indicates a less active policy.

[36] Advocate of Peace, vol. xiv, March and April, 1860, pp. 66-67.

[37] Citations from British press in Littell's Living Age, vol. l, pp. 116 ff., 241 ff., 443 ff.; J. P. Blanchard in Advocate of Peace, vol. xii, March, 1856, p. 35; Burritt, Ms. Journal, March 15, and May 30, November 16, 1856; 43rd Annual Report of the London Peace Society, in Advocate of Peace, vol. xii, July, August, September, 1856, pp. 123 ff.; 44th Annual Report of the London Peace Society, Advocate of Peace, September and October, 1857, p. 345; Bond of Brotherhood, no. 75, October, 1856.

Still another evidence of the weakness of the American peace movement in this period was its failure to carry its activities into the South and West. By 1850 New England and New York had been well cultivated, and those who were susceptible to peace arguments, the workers felt, had been for the most part reached. Mild friends of peace were tired of incessant pleas for support. It seemed clear that if the American peace movement was to be a really living force, it must make itself felt in the West. This need had been realized ever since the Oregon and Mexican crises, but little had been done. Until 1854 only a few copies of the Society's periodical had circulated in the South.[38] In that year the Reverend William Potter, as agent of the Society, toured Tennessee and Alabama and met with what he described as "a kind reception." While many seemed open to appeals, they were practically all unacquainted with the subject of peace.[39]

If slightly better success attended the efforts to win the West for peace, it was largely because of the presence of eastern and especially New England men. In Chicago Zachary Eastman edited a short-lived periodical designed, among other things, to promote the cause, and he occasionally lectured in the surrounding country. The new peace society formed in Ohio in 1850 seems to have been stillborn, as was that formed in Wisconsin, of which Charles Durkee was president.[40]

In 1852 the Executive Committee of the American Peace Society appointed an agent for the West. This man, the Reverend E. E. Seward, could find in Wisconsin only one minister and two laymen willing to undertake the sale of the *Review of the Mexican War*. Two years later the Reverend A. C. Hand and the Reverend Henry Snyder were able to influence the Methodist conferences of Wisconsin and Michigan to adopt

---

[38] *Advocate of Peace*, vol. xiii, April, 1855, p. 77; June, 1855, pp. 19 ff.; vol. vi, October, 1845, p. 117; vol. x, March, 1852, pp. 47-48; October, 1853, p. 366; *Christian Citizen*, July 19, 1845.

[39] *Advocate of Peace*, vol. xi, April, 1854, p. 63.

[40] *Ibid.*, vol. ix, January and February, 1851, p. 31; vol. x, February, 1852, p. 31; vol. xiii, September and October, 1858, p. 143.

resolutions recognizing the Christian character of the aims of the American Peace Society and advising ministers to support it. In 1858 Snyder reported that while he found some Christians "warm peace men," few except New England ministers domiciled in the West would do anything for the movement. An Illinois pastor who sent his own little annual donation apologized for the fact that his church sent nothing at all and urged that its indifference proved that the officers of the Peace Society should bear in mind that "the Western field was crying aloud, O how loud, for help." The church at Beloit, Wisconsin, considered for two years the question of whether or not to allow an agent of the Peace Society to occupy the pulpit. The trustees of many a congregation in Michigan refused the Reverend W. W. Crane, an agent of the Society, permission to ask for financial aid, while most ministers received him coldly.[41]

One reason for this western indifference was the question of slavery in Kansas. At two lectures in a Michigan town a peace agent was able to raise a total of but three and a half dollars, while an anti-slavery speaker, whose eloquence was said not to have surpassed that of the pacifist, got one hundred and thirty dollars from one lecture. Another reason ascribed for western apathy was the militant anti-British feeling, while prejudices against the Mormons and enthusiasm for the Mormon war of 1858 also proved obstacles in certain communities.[42]

The failure to win the South and West meant that the American peace movement was still essentially sectional and its influence, therefore, limited. In 1853 the secretary of the Society pointed out in his annual report that if permanent peace were to be insured, "the Great Valley of the West, with its teeming myriads," must be won, since it was certain "alike to control

[41] *Ibid.*, vol. x, May, 1852, p. 77; vol. xi, October, 1854, p. 160; May, 1855, pp. 77, 80; vol. xiii, September and October, 1858, p. 143; March and April, 1859, pp. 254-255.
[42] *Ibid.*, vol. xi, June and July, 1857, pp. 313-314; vol. xi, June, 1856, p. 100; vol. xiii, March and April, 1858, p. 43; January and February, 1859, pp. 218-219. The *Advocate* strenuously opposed the Mormon war.

the domestic and foreign policy of the Republic."[43] The realization that the West was not being converted helps to explain the discouragement creeping into the ranks of the faithful.

But this failure to win the West was only one reason for the lean character of the peace work during the years preceding the Civil War. In this very period, during which the movement failed to ward off a great European war and to spread its influence in America, its ranks both in England and in the United States were being thinned by death. Year after year, in the 'fifties, the annual reports catalogued the death of liberal benefactors and ardent workers. To make matters worse, Beckwith was struck with severe illness in 1856, and for several years had to relinquish a large part of his work.[44] The only man who could have compensated in some measure for these losses was Elihu Burritt, and he was now devoting his energies to another work. The peace movement had relied too much on the earlier momentum it gained and failed to train up younger men to carry on its work.

Another factor contributing to the discouragement, which was not always veiled, was the more frank acknowledgment during this period of the indifference of the churches. In 1858 the *American Presbyterian* accused the American Peace Society of "an impracticable ultraism, false philanthropy, pitiful sentimentality."[45] The *Advocate of Peace* at last admitted that such strictures were "pretty fair indications of the general mind." Only here and there, confessed the *Advocate,* was a minister habitually faithful to the cause. An Hawaiian missionary, the Reverend Titus Coan, had sent a hundred dollars almost every year during the decade to the American Peace Society; and this contribution, it was admitted, exceeded that from all the Amer-

[43] *Ibid.*, vol. x, June, 1853, p. 294.

[44] *Ibid.*, vol. x, June and July, 1852, p. 114; vol. xi, June, 1854, p. 78; June, 1855, p. 19; vol. xii, June and July, 1856, p. 90; vol. xi, June and July, 1857, p. 311; November, 1857, p. 382; vol. xiii, July and August, 1858, p. 121; November and December, 1858, p. 189.

[45] *Ibid.*, vol. xiii, March and April, 1858, pp. 33-34.

ican churches sent in as church contributions.[46] This frankly pessimistic tone regarding the failure to enlist the active support of the churches added its weight to the lowering of enthusiasm and activity in the American peace movement.

Growing signs of militarism also aroused the alarm of American peace workers during this period. President Buchanan's inaugural address urged a larger navy, and in 1858 the editor of the *Advocate* was shocked to record that the militia throughout New England was being "galvanized into the show of strength and respectability." Yet even in admitting the triumph of "energetic military spirits," the unquenchable editor of the *Advocate of Peace* refused to face the facts squarely.[47]

If the periodical of the American Peace Society half-heartedly recognized the failure of the peace movement to prevent the revival of the militia, it took an even more equivocal position towards the danger of civil war. Elihu Burritt alone seemed to realize the dangers to peace involved in the slavery question. From 1856 on Burritt turned his attention towards the work of trying to solve peaceably the slavery problem. Although overburdened with debt, he put his whole soul into a campaign for compensated emancipation.

Beckwith and the American Peace Society, on the other hand, consistently dodged the issue of slavery. It is true that in an editorial in the *Advocate* in 1856 Beckwith admitted the paramount importance of the Kansas civil strife. "The present is a time of sore trial to the friends of peace in our country. The antagonistic forces of Freedom and Slavery now stand before the nation and the world face to face in a sort of internecine contest; God only knows how or where it will end."[48] Yet he

[46] *Ibid.*, vol. xiii, May and June, 1859, p. 267; vol. x, March, 1853, p. 251; vol. xi, May, 1854, p. 73; vol. xiii, September, 1859, p. 141.

[47] *Ibid.*, vol. viii, September and October, 1850, p. 266; vol. ix, May and June, 1851, p. 73; vol. xiii, March and April, 1858, pp. 54 ff.; vol. xiii, January and February, 1859, p. 213; *Christian Citizen*, August 2, 1845, October 23, 1847, May 13, 1848, April 14, and September 1, 1849, February 16, and April 20, 1850, January 18, 1851.

[48] *Advocate of Peace*, vol. xi, October and November, 1856, p. 147.

went on to admit that nothing had been said publicly by the peace men, because the question of civil war, provoked by the slavery question in Kansas, was not within the sphere of the peace movement. The sole purpose of the American Peace Society, Beckwith continued, was to oppose the custom of international war.[49] True, an unsigned article in the *Advocate* implied that war was preferable to slavery and that, if worst came to worst, peace men would want to fight in the interests of freedom. Editorially, however, Beckwith followed a policy of studied silence on the slavery issue. "It is no part of our policy, as laborers in the cause of peace, to discuss this great national issue."[50] Whether or not the *Advocate* took a stand on slavery, it might well have pointed out that war was a useless, foolish, and immoral way of settling disputes, even such a dispute as slavery. It missed the opportunity, and yet it was aware of the danger, for it had confessed the fear that slavery "will soon be found to lie directly across the path of our cause."[51] The danger to peace was admitted, but the issue was dodged.

Beckwith's policy apparently had the sanction of the American Peace Society. In 1858 Gerrit Smith, the well-known abolitionist, in giving the annual address before the Society, maintained that an armed force was necessary to prevent the fugitive from being returned to his former master. "If the Government has become too corrupt to summon such a force," he went on to say, "then the brave and just must extemporize government for this purpose. The Jerrys and the Burnes must be delivered."[52] Thus was the use of the sword advocated, openly and without

[49] *Ibid.*, p. 148.

[50] *Ibid.*, vol. xiii, May and June, 1858, pp. 68-69.

[51] *Ibid.*, vol. xi, December, 1856, editorial footnote comment, p. 189. The Executive Committee on November 24, 1857, decided that it was inexpedient to renew the mild program of petitioning Congress for the insertion of arbitration clauses in treaties "in view of the present political condition of our country." Ms. *Records of American Peace Society, 1856-1860*, p. 21, in the archives of the American Peace Society, Washington, D. C.

[52] *Advocate of Peace*, vol. xiii, July and August, 1858, p. 107.

recorded opposition, at an annual meeting of the American Peace Society.

It was only when the John Brown raid brought the whole question of force and slavery to a focus that the *Advocate of Peace* took a forthright stand. It was then maintained that violence and force were not Christian methods for obtaining God's end, that civil government was the only means by which social evils could be met.[53] This opinion was not unlikely that of Joshua P. Blanchard, who during Beckwith's illness gave much aid in conducting the periodical.

If the publication of the American Peace Society had earlier taken this position, the peace cause might have been more respected. What with the inconsistently noncommittal policy of Beckwith and the great attention the slavery issue was exciting, there is little reason to doubt that some of the weakness of the peace movement in the United States was closely associated with the slavery agitation. As early as 1853 Blanchard wrote to Burritt that the public could not be made to listen to the claims of peace, so much more engrossing and exciting was the antislavery agitation. "We might as well urge a man whose house is on fire and who is exerting himself to extinguish it, to enter into a discussion on the best mode of building, as to bring our intelligent citizens to examine the merits of peace and war, which they consider a remote, if not a settled question."[54] It was perhaps such a conviction that led Burritt to take the course he did. His young friend, J. B. Syme, wrote from Worcester that since 1850 the demands on the antislavery people, who were the friends of peace at the same time, had been so incessant that the cause of peace had suffered. "No other question can be generally or heartily entertained until this great volcanic question is settled."[55]

[53] *Ibid.*, vol. xiv, March and April, 1860, pp. 64-65.
[54] J. P. Blanchard to Burritt, *Bond of Brotherhood,* new series, no. 33, April, 1853.
[55] J. B. Syme to Burritt, *Bond of Brotherhood,* new series, no. 30, January, 1853.

The friends of peace, then, were at last forced openly to admit the fact of "the backward swing of the pendulum" as Beckwith termed the decline of the American peace movement. The Crimean War, the Far Eastern catastrophes and the wars of Italian liberation took much wind from the sails of peace men everywhere. When old and tried peace veterans died, the ranks were thinned, and new recruits were hard to find when so much reform energy went into antislavery agitation. The "do-nothing" policy of the American Peace Society in the face of admitted danger of civil war was both a proof and a cause of its incompetency. Annual meetings were held as before, addresses were made, the *Advocate of Peace* printed and circulated, but there was nevertheless a fundamental decline of the movement. Neither the South nor the West was won, nor was the coöperation with peace men abroad, as it had been developed in the great peace congresses, maintained. In May, 1860, for the first time since the organization of the American Peace Society in 1828, an anniversary passed without the necessary quorum for the business meeting. There were thus none to hear the Annual Report which went so far as to admit that the "entire, permanent cure of war may prove the work of all future time, a reform to end only with the end of the world itself."[56]

What happened to the peace movement in the Civil War is another story. Horace Greeley preferred to let the erring sisters depart in peace rather than to face civil conflict; and others, like Elihu Burritt, remained true to their ideals throughout the War. The peace movement, even if it seemed impotent in the face of domestic upheaval, was not dead.[57]

[56] *Advocate of Peace*, vol. xiv, July and August, 1860, p. 90.
[57] For antiwar opinion see Mary Scrughàm, *The Peaceable Americans, 1860-1861, Columbia University Studies in History, Economics, and Public Law*, XCVI, no. 3; Edward Chase Kirkland, *The Peacemakers of 1864*, New York, 1927; Elbert J. Benton, *The Movement for Peace without a Victory during the Civil War, Collections of the Western Reserve Historical Society*, Publication no. 99, Cleveland, 1918; A. Sellew Roberts, "The Peace Movement in North Carolina," *Miss. Valley Hist. Rev.*, vol. xi, pp. 190-199.

CONCLUSION

THE WORD "reformer" seems of late years to have become, in many circles, a term of reproach. The general derogatory use of the word "uplift" reveals the attitude of many intellectuals toward reform movements. Is this attitude justified? Is consciously directed, organized reform worth while, judged by results accomplished?

In the case of the peace agitation, the historian can give an answer to these questions. This particular reform movement has to its credit in the first thirty-five years of its existence a definite showing in positive accomplishments. In the first place, it solved the difficult problems of organization and finance, so that by 1860 there were in the United States and England organizations for peace the permanence of which was assured through legacies and a well-planned financial policy, organizations maintaining permanent secretaries and keeping closely in touch not only with branch societies, but with societies abroad. The establishment of an organization which friends of peace knew would last, no matter what the opposition or how serious a war was raging, was an important achievement of the agitation.

A second positive contribution was the establishment of machinery for publicity. In the first few years of their existence the peace societies were hardly noticed by the press, and their members were ridiculed as impractical and unimportant radicals. By 1850, however, the societies were widely noticed throughout Europe and America. Through the formation of branch societies and the holding of public meetings and peace congresses many persons were drawn into the work. The holding of public lectures, the institution of peace sermons, the employment of field agents, and the sending in of memorials and petitions to legislative bodies—all these devices served as important means of publicity. By the middle of the century the activities of the peace societies had acquired such news value that they were widely noticed and discussed in the press. Meanwhile, through the establishment of peace periodicals, the members of the various societies were kept informed of important developments. From 1816 to the present day an official peace magazine has been published regularly in the United States, no issue being omitted during any war. The net effect of all this publicity was to make the peace agitation fairly well known. The early societies pointed with special pride to the number of "respectable clergymen" and prominent men on their membership list. By 1860, however, this was no longer necessary; everyone knew that among the members of peace societies were not only clergymen and professional men, but also business men and politicians. The movement for peace had at last become respectable.

Perhaps the most striking contribution of early organized pacifism was the development of a body of brilliant arguments against war. By 1860 practically every argument against war now familiar had been suggested, and almost every current plan for securing peace had been at least anticipated. While the arguments against war in the earlier years were chiefly religious, moral, and philanthropic, they tended to become less and less an expression of the general spirit of liberalism and romanticism. They tended to become increasingly realistic and to make greater use of economic and political considerations. This was in part due to the working alliance of the free traders and peace men in England and to the influence of French socialist thought on the opponents of war. Increasing attention was given, for example, to the wastefulness of war and to the burdens it inflicted on the working classes. Much emphasis was put on the desirability of developing closer economic ties, bankers' agreements for the refusal of war loans, workingmen's international associations, and other types of economic federations. By 1850 Elihu Burritt had urged that an organized general strike of the workers of the world against war was the only possible alternative to a court and congress of nations. Nor were there lacking acute minds to point out the relations between competitive economic imperialism and war. In the political sphere, it was well understood that war threatened political democracy.

A fourth important contribution of the early crusade for peace was the working out of definite practical plans looking toward the ultimate establishment of world peace. The plan for the inclusion in international treaties of stipulated arbitration clauses was first advanced by an American, William Jay, and was vigorously supported both here and abroad. The most important practical plan, however, was William Ladd's scheme for a court and congress of nations, a plan the main features of which are now embodied in the League of Nations and the Hague Tribunal. Plans were also made for the codification of international law, for disarmament, and for the development of internationalism through educational and other projects.

A fifth contribution of the peace agitation in the period of its foundation was the fact that it sought and secured international coöperation in its activities. From the first, British peace men worked hand in hand with those in America, and after a time not only French and Germans, but also men of other countries on the Continent, were enlisted. Thus American reformers were made to think and act in international terms, and a good beginning was made in developing that practical and personal association between internationalists of different countries which is vitally important in furthering work for peace.

Finally, we cannot properly estimate the contribution of this half-forgotten peace crusade without considering the fact that it nourished and developed leaders who were to play important rôles in the later years of the agitation. In England Henry Richard gave up his work for peace only when death took him in 1888. Sir Randal Cremer, the founder of the International Arbitration League and the Workmen's Peace Society, and one of the originators of the Interparliamentary Union, heard, as a youth, one of the lecturers of the Peace Society, who "sowed the seed of International Arbitration" in his mind. In France the revival of the peace movement in the latter part of the century seems to have been due in part to Edmond Potonié-Pierre, who as a boy attended the Paris Peace Congress in 1849 and who heard his father discuss the problem with his neighbor, Victor Hugo.[1] Joseph Garnier, Michel Chevalier, and Frédéric Passy,[2] who were pioneers of peace in France, continued their activities into the period succeeding that of this study. In America, Burritt, Sumner, and Beckwith served as connecting links between the earlier agitation and the one following it.

While these positive accomplishments of the early peace crusade testify to its potential strength and promise, it is still probably true that the organized work against war failed to exert any marked influence on governments, that it had little if any influence either in modifying treaties or in averting conflicts. Such a failure to achieve immediate practical ends is not hard to understand. In the first place, such agitation meets the tremendous inertia of human nature, the persistence of social and political habits of long standing in the face even of the most logical arguments against them. In the second place, the peace sentiment has always been fraught with dissensions over the fundamental problem of how far the principles of pacifism should be carried. These quandaries have dissipated the strength of the agitation by leading to secessions as well as quarrels. In the third place, pacifism did not in the period under consideration appeal to any special economic interests. Though friends of peace were early begining to dwell on economic arguments against war, they in general relied rather on idealistic propaganda and emotional appeal; and no very influential groups of men became so convinced that their pocketbooks were concerned that they joined the peace movement. In the fourth place, the peace crusade often suffered because its ideal came into conflict with other liberal ideals that at times proved stronger. Particularly was this

---

[1] Edmond Potonié-Pierre, *Historique du Mouvement Pacifique.* Berne, 1889, pp. 82-93. For this reference I am indebted to Mr. Earl Lee Cruickshank.

[2] Frédéric Passy, *Pour la Paix, notes et documents,* Paris, 1909, p. 3.

true during the period of the mid-century revolutions, when nationalistic ideals were dominant. The peace crusade perhaps prospered less than other reform movements launched at the same time, such as antislavery and temperance, because it was in more direct conflict with the prevailing political temper of the century. One would hardly expect a doctrine of internationalism to gain great headway during the very decades when the ideals of nationalism were so firing the imagination, not only of the masses, but of their intellectual leaders. The wonder is that peace men themselves stood by their colors as well as they did.

The story of pacifist sentiment up to the Civil War is, we have seen, a story of hard work with little to show for it. But it is in many ways a stirring story. The enthusiasm of the founders, leading them to every sort of sacrifice, is reflected in reports of their adventures—tales of difficult travels into distant regions, of strategies in outwitting hostile townsmen who sought to prevent their appearance, of battles against illness and poverty, discouragement and active opposition. Its meetings were not always dull gatherings of up-in-the-air idealists who merely talked vague and agreeable platitudes. Who could ask for a livelier meeting than the annual one of 1851, when the radicals packed the house and tried by strategy to gain their points; when the old guard led by the faithful Beckwith tried to outwit them by an unannounced meeting; and when finally such pandemonium reigned that the gathering had to be dispersed? The secession of the nonresistance group and its activities show how high the feeling ran. Another time when excitement reigned was in 1848, when an International Peace Congress met at Brussels in the midst of revolution.[3]

The story of the peace crusade is thus, rightly understood, a moving story, a story of pioneers who were willing to toil their lives long for the sake of rewards that would come to

<hr />

[3] M. E. Curti, "The Peace Movement and the Mid-Century Revolutions," *Advocate of Peace*, vol. 90, no. 5, May, 1928, pp. 305-310.

others after they were dead. Among the leaders in the early days were hard-headed business men like Dodge, who neglected their work to follow a vision. There were capable executives like Henry Richard. There were sages like Noah Worcester, whose *Solemn Review* still stirs the hearts of men. The agitation had its martyrs like William Ladd, who literally gave up his life for the cause of peace. It had its prophets like Elihu Burritt, the wise and gentle blacksmith, whose eyes saw so much further than those of other peace men of his time. Above all, the peace movement had its heroes.

Whatever one may think about the merits of the pacifist position, it must be admitted that even to-day it takes courage to be a thoroughgoing pacifist, especially in time of war. But in the very early years of the crusade, it must have required even more courage to be a peace crusader. The founders of the movement, both in America and in England, were in a sense all heroic men. And the leaders who in later years faced apathy, derision, and hate, who carried on the work even while wars were waging—certainly these leaders were heroes. Some day they may be mentioned in the school textbooks along with the heroes of war.

Although the dream of peace for which Ladd died and Sturge and Burritt risked the hatred of their countrymen is still far from realization, it cannot be said that the work of these men and their fellows was in vain. It is impossible to guess what may have been the influence of one of their lectures, of a single tract, or even a chance conversation about war. Nor can we know what emotions and hopes may thus have been aroused, or how these emotions and hopes advanced the conviction that nations must learn war no more. However much or little these men accomplished in their day, the fact of their labor, of their courage, remains a legacy to other generations. When world peace comes, if it comes, the story of those who began the peace movement, who labored weary nights and days to make it live, will find recognition in the annals of the human race.

BIBLIOGRAPHY

Manuscript Material

Minutes of the New York Peace Society, 1826-1828 (Archives of the American Peace Society, Washington).

Records of the American Peace Society. Two volumes, the first covering the period July 7, 1835 to October 13, 1854, and the second the period from January 17, 1855 to May 13, 1896, are of great value. These volumes contain the minutes of the Executive Committee, of the Board of Directors, and of the Society.

Ladd Manuscripts (American Peace Society). These manuscripts consist of a *Letter Book* containing twenty-one letters written by Ladd to distinguished peace workers in this country and in England, and to members of his family. The letters cover the period 1827 to 1837, and abound with details of Ladd's prodigious activities in behalf of peace. These letters were not wisely used by John Hemmenway in his *Memoir of William Ladd, Apostle of Peace* (Boston, 1877), since his excerpts are often unrepresentative. The second item in the *Ladd Manuscripts* is entitled *A Memoir of William Ladd, Apostle of Peace. Second Edition, revised and enlarged. By John Hemmenway* (November 10, 1890). Between 1877 and 1890, the date of this manuscript, Hemmenway collected additional letters written by Ladd, and fortunately, instead of making excerpts from them, seems to have incorporated many of them, in their entirety, together with many from which he had merely taken selections in the first and printed collection. Thus the manuscript is of far greater importance than the published *Memoir*. The picture of Ladd that one gets from it is not only richer in detail but actually different. Ladd appears not only as a great idealist, but as a practical man who saw actual problems and who tried to meet them in a practical way. The revised manuscript has not heretofore been used. It is not unlikely that many of Ladd's letters might still be found in England.

Elihu Burritt Papers. The larger portion of these papers is in the Library of the Institute of New Britain, New Britain, Connecticut. There are about thirty unmounted letters which Burritt received during the active period of his life. Much more valuable are the Diaries, in twenty-two volumes, each numbering from four hundred to six hundred closely written pages. Often Burritt copied in the Diary letters which he sent and which he received. The Diaries are the most important single manuscript source for a history of the early peace movement. The Library of the American Antiquarian Society in Worcester contains a manuscript lecture on "The League of Universal Brotherhood," which lecture Burritt gave many times in England and in America, and which was not printed. It is the most valuable source for the aims and purposes of the League of Universal Brotherhood. There is also in this library a *Letter Book of Elihu Burritt for the years 1837 to 1838.*

Journal and Commonplace Book of Henry Clarke Wright, 29 volumes, 1832 to 1842, in the Harvard College Library. Wright, as agent of the American Peace Society and as one of the Non-Resistants, played a leading part in the history of the American peace cause, and his *Journals* are of great value.

Diaries of William Watson, 12 volumes, 1819-1836, describing in detail Watson's activities in the peace movement, and including copies of important correspondence between Watson and other peace leaders. These diaries are in the possession of Miss Elizabeth Dana, a granddaughter of William Watson.

Samuel E. Coues, *Peace Album,* Harvard College Library. In 1844 the newly-elected president of the American Peace Society, Samuel E. Coues, of Portsmouth, New Hampshire, circulated an album among the early advocates of peace, who described their contributions to the cause and in many cases told how they happened to become pacifists. These records are of rare value and interest. The American Peace Society also possesses the manuscripts of some of Samuel E. Coues's peace lectures.

Charles Sumner Papers, Harvard College Library. This collection is of especial value by reason of the fact that it includes much correspondence between Sumner and British and American friends of peace.

Frederic W. Holland, a Boston Unitarian minister, wrote a three-volume *History of the American Peace Cause,* which is in the Boston Public Library. Holland realized that the manuscript would probably never be published, and its bitterness towards "the conservatives" is therefore unrestrained. His picture of Beckwith is unjust, though as a contemporary history of the peace movement, this manuscript is rich in detail otherwise inaccessible. The fact that it represents "the reform group" enhances its usefulness, since the conservatives controlled the official publications of the American Peace Society.

The papers of Thomas Jefferson (especially volumes 205-208) in the Library of Congress contain correspondence between Noah Worcester and Jefferson in reference to the organized peace movement. The papers of Nicholas Trist, in the same library, throw much light on the origin of the famous Article XXI in the Treaty of Guadalupe Hidalgo, and damage the claims of the pacifists as to their share in the matter.

OFFICIAL PEACE PUBLICATIONS

The official peace publications were in the form of annual reports of the peace societies, addresses delivered to peace societies, reports of the international peace congresses, and periodicals of peace organizations. The periodicals themselves are the most important printed materials, as they contain the annual reports and many of the sermons and addresses which also were circulated in tract form.

Friend of Peace, Boston, 1816-1828. Noah Worcester, editor. This appeared as a quarterly.

Herald of Peace, London. The first number appeared in January, 1819, and during the first two years, this organ of the Society for the Promotion of Permanent and Universal Peace was a monthly publication. It then became and remained a quarterly magazine.

Harbinger of Peace, 3 volumes, May 1828 to April, 1831, a monthly duodecimo of twenty-four pages, and printed wherever the editor, William Ladd, happened to be at the time.

Calumet, a bimonthly octavo of thirty-two pages, New York. While Ladd was nominally its editor, the Reverend L. D. Dewey of New York, D. E. Wheeler, R. M. Chapman and the Reverend George Bush were successively associated with Ladd in its management. The American Peace Society relinquished the *Calumet* in 1835 for the *American Advocate of Peace,* a quarterly begun in June, 1834, by William Watson, and ably edited by Francis Fellows and the Reverend C. S. Henry at Hartford, as the organ of the Connecticut Peace Society. Its last number appeared in November, 1836.

Advocate of Peace, begun under the editorship of the Reverend George C. Beckwith, in Boston, in 1836, was edited by him throughout the period, with the exception of the calendar year 1846, when Burritt edited the periodical under the title *Advocate of Peace and Universal Brotherhood.* The *Advocate of Peace* was published monthly from 1837 to 1839, and bimonthly from 1839 to 1845. Burritt made it a monthly, but from 1847 on the periodical was again a bimonthly.

The Non-Resistant, the official organ of the New England Non-Resistance Society, begun in 1839, and edited in Boston by William Lloyd Garrison and a committee of the Society. This periodical is invaluable for the left wing of the peace movement. The only file that the writer could find is that in the library of the World Peace Foundation, Boston.

Bond of Universal Brotherhood, the organ of the League of Universal Brotherhood, was begun at Worcester on April 8, 1846. From 1846 until 1856 it was edited and printed in England by Burritt and Edmund Fry. The largest number of copies of this lively, popular monthly is to be found in the American Antiquarian Society.

NEWSPAPERS AND PERIODICALS

Christian Citizen. A weekly newspaper published at Worcester, the first number being that of January 6, 1844, and the last being that of May 3, 1851. The only complete file the writer has discovered is that belonging to the American Antiquarian Society. No other printed source rivals the *Christian Citizen* for the history of the international peace movement from 1844 to 1851.

Christian Mirror, 1825-1827, Portland, Maine (weekly).

A study of the indexes of the great collection of periodicals in the American Antiquarian Society resulted in finding that sixty-three periodicals, in the volumes between 1815 and 1860, contained material on the peace movement. Most of the periodicals were of a religious character, and use has been made of a large number of them, as well as of the secular periodicals. Those most valuable are referred to in the footnotes. British periodicals, especially *Blackwood's Edinburgh Magazine, North British Review, Douglas Jerrold's Shilling Magazine,* Charles Dickens's *Household Words, Chambers's Edinburgh Journal,* and the *Spectator* were used. The most useful Continental periodical was the *Journal des Économistes,* edited by Michel Chevalier, Paris.

GOVERNMENT DOCUMENTS

Adelaide R. Hasse's *Index to United States Documents Relating to Foreign Affairs, 1828-1861, in three parts* (Washington, 1914, 1918, 1921) was an invaluable guide to the great body of petitions and memorials presented to Congress on subjects of interest to pacifists.

The *Congressional Globe,* especially for the 25th, 26th, 30th, 31st, 32d, and 33d Congresses, contains debates on these memorials and petitions.

Reports of Committees include reports of the Committees on Foreign Relations on peace memorials.

The *Massachusetts State Documents, Massachusetts Resolves,* 1835-1838, and the *Vermont Legislative Journals,* 1852, were the most fruitful of a large number of state documents consulted. These volumes record the action taken by the two respective legislatures on petitions favoring legislative commitment on the projects of a Congress of Nations and treaties of permanent arbitration.

PEACE TREATISES

Ballou, Adin, *Christian Non-Resistance, in all its Important Bearings, illustrated and defended.* Philadelphia, 1846.

Bazan, Patrice, *D'une paix universelle et permanente. Discours couronné par la Société de la Morale Chrétienne.* Paris, 1842.

Beckwith, George C., *The Book of Peace.* Philadelphia, 1845.

————, *The Peace Manual: or War and its Remedies.* Boston, 1847.

Berry, Phillip, *A Review of the Mexican War on Christian Principles.* Columbia, South Carolina, 1849.

Burritt, Elihu, *Lectures and Speeches*. London, 1869.

————, *Thoughts of Things at Home and Abroad*. Boston, 1854.

————, *The Works of Elihu Burritt*. London. No date.

————, *Year Book of the Nations*. New York, 1856. A statistical abstract of war expenditures by different nations.

Clarkson, Thomas, *An Essay on the Doctrines and Practises of the early Christians as they relate to war*. London, 1817, 2d edition.

Dresser, Amos, *The Bible Against War*. Oberlin, 1849.

Duncan, Philip Berry, *The Motives of War*. London, 1844.

Durand, Ferdinand, *Des Tendances pacifiques de la société Européenne, et du rôle des armées dans l'avenir*. Paris, 1841.

Dymond, Jonathan, *An Inquiry into the Accordancy of War with the Principles of Christianity*. 4th edition, London, 1843.

Girardin, Émile de, *La Politique Universelle*. Paris, 1854.

Hancock, Thomas, *Principles of Peace, exemplified in the conduct of the Society of Friends in Ireland, during the rebellion of 1798*. Philadelphia, 1829.

Holcombe, Henry, *The First Fruits, in a series of Letters*. Philadelphia, 1812.

————, *The Martial Christian's Manual*. Philadelphia, 1823.

Jay, William, *War and Peace, the Evils of the first and a Plan for securing the last*. New York, London, 1842.

Ladd, William, *Essay on a Congress of Nations, for the Adjustment of international Disputes, and for the promotion of universal peace without resort to arms*. Boston, 1840. The same was reprinted, with an excellent introduction by James Brown Scott, for the Carnegie Endowment for International Peace, New York, 1916.

————, ed., *Prize Essays on a Congress of Nations for the adjustment of international disputes, together with a sixth essay comprising the substance of rejected Essays*. Boston, 1840.

————, *The Hero of Macedon, or History of Alexander the Great, viewed in the light of the Gospel*. Boston, 1832.

Livermore, Abiel Abbott, *The War with Mexico Reviewed*. Boston, 1850.

Macnamara, Henry T. J., *Peace, Permanent and Universal.* London, 1841.

Marchand, P., *Nouveau Project de traité de paix perpétuelle.* Paris, 1842.

Paoli-Chagny, François Étienne Auguste, comte de, *Projet d'une organisation politique pour l'Europe.* Hamburg, 1818.

Peace and War: an Essay in Two Parts. London, 1823 (no author given).

Pecqueur, Constantin, *Des armées dans leurs rapports avec l'industrie, la morale, et la liberté, ou, des devoirs civiques des militaires.* Paris, 1842.

Sellon, Comte de, *Nouveaux mélanges, politiques, moraux et littéraires.* Geneva, 1838.

Thrush, Thomas, *The Apology of an Officer for withdrawing from the profession of arms.* 2d edition, London, 1833.

Upham, Thomas, *The Manual of Peace.* New York, 1836.

Whelpley, Samuel, *Letters Addressed to Caleb Strong.* Providence, 1818.

Worcester, Noah, *Friend of Youth.* 2d edition, Boston, 1833.

Wright, Henry C., *Defensive War Proved to be a Denial of Christianity and of the Government of God.* London, 1846.

SELECTIVE LIST OF PAMPHLETS, TRACTS, AND ADDRESSES

(No effort is made to give a complete list of the pamphlets, tracts and addresses used.)

A Plea with Ministers for Cause of Peace. Boston, 185—?

Beckwith, George C., *A Universal Peace Society, with the basis of coöperation in the cause of Peace.* Boston, 1844.

——————, *Eulogy on William Ladd, late President of the American Peace Society.* Boston, 1841.

Blanchard, J. P., *Communications on Peace.* Boston, 1848.

——————, *To the Members of the American Peace Society.* Boston, 1851.

Bogue, David, *On Universal Peace—extracts from a Discourse delivered in October, 1813.* New Vienna, Ohio, 1869.

Bouvet, Francisque, *La Guerre et la Civilisation.* Paris, 1855.

Brooks, Charles, *An Address delivered before the Hingham Peace Society,* December 6, 1821. Boston, 1821.

Burritt, Elihu, *People-Diplomacy: or the mission of friendly International Addresses between England and France.* London, 1852.

————, *The Olive Leaf Movement.* London, 1852.

Chalmers, Thomas, *Thoughts on Universal Peace.* New York, 1813.

Channing, William Ellery, *Sermon on War.* Boston, 1816.

Coues, Samuel E., *War and Christianity.* Boston, 1842.

Dodge, David Low, *The Mediator's Kingdom not of this World.* New York, 1809.

————, *War Inconsistent with the Religion of Jesus Christ.* New York, 1815.

Flournoy, John J., *An Earnest Appeal for Peace, to All Christians.* Athens, Georgia, 1838.

Furness, William Henry, *Put Up Thy Sword. A Discourse delivered before Theodore Parker's Society, March 11, 1860.* Boston, 1860.

Garnier, Joseph, *Congrès des aims de la paix universelle réunis à Paris.* Paris, 1849.

Gibbes, George M., *A Letter to the American Peace Society from a member of the committee in Paris.* Paris, 1849.

Grimké, Thomas, *A Letter to the People of South Carolina.* Charleston, 1832.

————, *An Address on the truth, dignity, power and beauty of the Principles of peace, and on the unchristian character and influence of war and the warrior.* Hartford, 1832.

Hugo, Victor Marie, *The United States of Europe, Presidential Address at the International Peace Congress, Paris, August 22, 1849.* World Peace Foundation, 1914.

Jay, William, *The Eastern War, an argument for the Cause of Peace.* Boston, 1855.

————, *The Kossuth Excitement: a letter from the Hon. William Jay.* Boston, 1852.

Judd, Reverend Sylvester, *A Moral Review of the Revolutionary War, or some of the evils of that event considered.* Hallowell, Maine, 1842.

Ladd, William, *A Brief Illustration of the Principles of War and Peace, by Philanthropos.* Albany, 1831.

————, *The Duty of Females to Promote the Cause of Peace.* Boston, 1836.

————, *The History of the Peace Societies.* In *Scientific Tracts for the Diffusion of Useful Knowledge.* Boston, 1836.

Lessore, J. B. L., *Appeal des Français à toutes les nations, pour l'entier désarmement, la paix; ou, projet de pacte social entre les nations.* Paris, 1831.

Lord, John, *An Address delivered before the Peace Society of Amherst College,* July 4, 1839. Amherst, 1839.

Parker, Theodore, *A Sermon on War, preached at the Melodeon, on June 7, 1846.* Boston, 1846.

Parsons, Thomas, *Christianity, a System of Peace.* Burlington, New Jersey, 1813.

Peace Principles Safe and Right. Tract of American Peace Society. Boston, n.d.

Principles of the Non-Resistance Society. Boston, 1839.

Rees, Evan, *Sketches of the Horrors of War.* London, 1818.

Roberts, Mary, *Peace Societies, and the scenes which have occurred within the last Sixty Years.* London, 1833.

Sigourney, Mrs. L. H. *Olive Buds.* Hartford, Connecticut, 1836.

Sumner, Charles, *The True Grandeur of Nations.* Address before the municipal authorities of Boston, July 4, 1845, and the *Abolition of War in the Commonwealth of Nations.* Address before the American Peace Society, on May 28, 1849, in the *Works of Charles Sumner,* 12 vols., vol. ii, pp. 171-278, and vol. i, pp. 5-133. Boston, 1875-1877.

Walker, Amasa, *Le Monde: or, in Time of Peace Prepare for War.* Boston, n.d.

Whipple, Charles King, *Dialogues between Frank and William illustrating the Principles of Peace.* Boston, 1838.

Worcester, Noah, *A Solemn Review of the Custom of War.* Greenfield, Massachusetts, 1817.

————, *Abraham and Lot, a sermon on the Way of Peace and the Evils of War, August 20, 1812.* Concord, New Hampshire, 1812.

————, *The Peace Catechism on Christian Principles.* Boston, 1816.

OTHER CONTEMPORARY WRITINGS

Adams, John Quincy, *Memoirs of John Quincy Adams, comprising portions of his Diary from 1795-1848.* Charles Francis *Adams,* ed., 13 vols., Philadelphia, 1874-1877.

Ballou, Adin, *Autobiography of Adin Ballou, 1803-1890.* William S. Heywood, ed., Lowell, 1896.

Bartlett, David W., *Modern Agitators: or Pen Portraits of Living American Reformers.* New York, 1855.

Davis, Emerson, *The Half-Century,* with introduction by Mark Hopkins. Boston, 1851.

Emerson, Ralph Waldo, *Emerson's Complete Works.* Riverside Edition, with preface by J. E. Cabot, 12 vols., Boston, 1891-1893.

Greeley, Horace, *A Glance at Europe.* New York, 1851. This contains an interesting description of the peace congress at London, 1850.

Gurney, Joseph J., *A Journey to North America.* Norwich, England, 1841.

Jerrold, Douglas, *Writings.* 8 vols., London, 1851-1854.

Norton, Charles E., *The Letters of James Russell Lowell.* 2 vols., London, 1894.

Smith, Gerrit, *Speeches of Gerrit Smith.* New York, 1855.

Thoreau, H. D., *The Writings of Henry David Thoreau.* 20 vols., Boston and New York, 1906.

Watson, William, *Extracts from the Diary of William Watson, New England Historical and Genealogical Register,* vol. lxxx, no. 318, January, 1926, pp. 54-72.

Wilder, S. V. S., *Records from the Life of Sampson Vryling Stoddard Wilder.* American Tract Society, New York, 1867.

Wright, Henry Clark, *Human Life: illustrated in my individual Experience as a child, youth and a man.* Boston, 1849.

SECONDARY MATERIALS: ARTICLES

Call, Arthur Deerin, "The Will to End War," in *Advocate of Peace,* vol. lxxxvi, no. 4 and no. 5 (April and May, 1924) pp. 228-238 and 297-309.

Curti, M. E., "Young America," *American Historical Review*, vol. xxxii, no. 1, November, 1926, pp. 34-55.

Moore, John Bassett, "The United States and International Arbitration," American Historical Association, *Annual Report for 1891*, pp. 65-85.

SECONDARY MATERIALS: BOOKS

Arbitration and the United States. A Summary of the Development of Pacific Settlement of International Disputes with Special Reference to American Policy. World Peace Foundation, Pamphlets, vol. ix, nos. 6-7, Boston, 1926.

Biggott, Sir Francis, *The Declaration of Paris of 1856*. London, 1919.

Bosanquet, Mrs. Helen Dendy, *Free Trade and Peace in the Nineteenth Century*. Kristiania, 1924.

Channing, William Henry, *Memoir of William Ellery Channing, with extracts from his correspondence and manuscripts*. 3 vols., Boston, 1848.

Dodge, David L., *Memorial of David Low Dodge*. Boston, 1854.

Emerson, George B., May, Samuel, Mumford, Thomas J., *Memoir of Samuel Joseph May*. Boston, 1876.

Frothingham, Octavius Brooks, *Theodore Parker: A Biography*. Boston, 1874.

Garrison, F. J. and W. P., *William Lloyd Garrison, The Story of His Life Told by His Children*. 4 vols., New York, 1885.

Hemmenway, John, *Memoir of William Ladd, Apostle of Peace*. Boston, 1877.

Hirst, Margaret E., *The Quakers in Peace and War*. London, 1923.

Hobson, J. A., *Richard Cobden, The International Man*. New York, 1919.

Lange, Christian L., *Histoire de la Doctrine Pacifique et de son Influence sur le Développement du Droit International*. Paris, 1927. This valuable survey of the history of pacifist ideas and of the peace movement, with special reference to international law, is the work of a scholar and prominent advocate of peace.

La Fontaine, Henri, *Bibliographie de la Paix et de l'arbitrage International.* A systematic bibliography of the peace movement to 1903. Monaco.

Miall, Charles S., *Henry Richard, a Biography.* London, 1889.

Moritzen, Julius, *The Peace Movement in America.* New York, 1912. This book is not a history of the peace movement, but an account of some of its aspects in the years preceding 1912.

Morley, John, *The Life of Richard Cobden.* 2 vols., London, 1908.

Northend, Charles, *Elihu Burritt: a memorial volume containing a Sketch of His Life and Labors with Selections from his Writings and Lectures, and extracts from his private journals in Europe and America.* New York, 1879.

Puech, J. L., *La Tradition Socialiste en France et la Société des Nations.* Paris, 1921.

Pierce, Edward L., *Memoir and Letters of Charles Sumner.* 4 vols., Boston, 1876.

Richard, Henry, *Memoir of Joseph Sturge.* London, 1862.

Thomas, Wilbur K., *The Quakers and Social Reform.* Unpublished doctoral dissertation in the library of Boston University. It throws but little light on the relations of the Friends to the Peace Movement.

Ware, Henry, *Memoirs of the Reverend Noah Worcester, with a Preface, Notes and a concluding chapter by Samuel Worcester.* Boston, 1844.

Whitney, Elwin L., *The American Peace Society, A Centennial History.* Washington, D. C., 1928. A conventional account, which does not adequately correlate the activities of the American Peace Society with those of the peace movement as a whole.

Winthrop, Robert C., Jr., *A Memoir of Robert C. Winthrop prepared for the Massachusetts Historical Society.* Boston, 1897.

INDEX

INDEX